ST ANDREWS STUDIES
IN PHILOSOPHY AND PUBLIC AFFAIRS
Founding and General Editor:
John Haldane, University of St Andrews

Values, Education and the Human World
edited by John Haldane

Philosophy and its Public Role
edited by William Aiken and John Haldane

Relativism and the Foundations of Liberalism
by Graham Long

Human Life, Action and Ethics: Essays by G.E.M. Anscombe
edited by Mary Geach and Luke Gormally

The Institution of Intellectual Values:
Realism and Idealism in Higher Education
by Gordon Graham

Life, Liberty and the Pursuit of Utility
by Anthony Kenny and Charles Kenny

Distributing Healthcare: Principles, Practices and Politics
edited by Niall Maclean

Liberalism, Education and Schooling: Essays by T.M. Mclaughlin
edited by David Carr, Mark Halstead and Richard Pring

The Landscape of Humanity: Art, Culture & Society
by Anthony O'Hear

Faith in a Hard Ground:
Essays on Religion, Philosophy and Ethics by G.E.M. Anscombe
edited by Mary Geach and Luke Gormally

Subjectivity and Being Somebody
by Grant Gillett

Understanding Faith: Religious Belief and Its Place in Society
by Stephen R.L. Clark

Profit, Prudence and Virtue:
Essays in Ethics, Business & Management
edited by Samuel Gregg and James Stoner

The Philosophy of Punishment

By Anthony Ellis

St Andrews
Studies in
Philosophy and
Public Affairs

ia

imprint-academic.com

Published in the UK by Imprint Academic
PO Box 200, Exeter EX5 5YX, UK

Published in the USA by Imprint Academic
Philosophy Documentation Center
PO Box 7147, Charlottesville, VA 22906-7147, USA

ISBN 9781845402532 paperback
ISBN 9781845402525 cloth

A CIP catalogue record for this book is available from the
British Library and US Library of Congress

Cover Photograph:
St Salvator's Quadrangle, St Andrews by Peter Adamson
from the University of St Andrews collection

Contents

Acknowledgments

Substantial parts of this book were written with the help of two Grants-in-Aid awarded by Virginia Commonwealth University; I am very grateful for the assistance.

Versions of all of this material have been read and commented on by Eugene Mills, Peter Vallentyne, Michael Davis, and Mikhail Valdman; most of it has been read and commented on by Brad Hooker, and Trenton Merricks; I am extremely grateful for their help. I have also received comments on parts of the book from Antony Duff, Andrew Cross, Robert Berman, and David Dolinko, and I should like to thank them too. I am, of course, responsible for all of the errors that remain. I should also like to thank John Haldane for encouraging me to write this book.

An earlier version of Chapter 9 appeared in *Philosophical Quarterly*, vol. 53 (2003), pp. 338–351, and vol. 55 (2005), pp. 98–101. I have also used a few paragraphs from 'War Crimes, Punishment and the Burden of Proof', *Res Publica*, vol. 16 (2010), pp. 181–196. I am grateful to the editors for permission to use that material here.

Introduction

'The death penalty is said to serve two principal social purposes: retribution and deterrence of capital crimes by prospective offenders.'[1]

I

When we punish someone, we do to them what, in most other circumstances, it would be wrong to do. And though most punishments, which, in our own systems are commonly fines, seem relatively trivial, even so, they stand in need of justification. Some think that there is no justification.[2] In this book, I try to show what, given a commonly accepted moral and political framework, that justification must be.

In the quotation above, the United States Supreme Court was speaking of capital punishment. But I imagine that most people, if asked what the main point of punishment is, would also refer to retribution and deterrence.[3] Other things too might perhaps be mentioned. Some punishments, for instance, incapacitate offenders, at least in the sense that they confine criminal behaviour within prison walls. Punishment can also satisfy the victim's desire for revenge, and the desire for vicarious revenge on the part of citizens generally. It can foster a sense of security in the citizenry, both a sense that they are less likely to be victimized and a sense that they live in a society in which justice is done. It can perhaps contribute to the education of citizens in the ways of right and wrong. It can, occasionally, rehabilitate offenders. It can be, and is, used to promote politicians' campaigns for office. The list could go on, but I think that most people would say that retribution and deterrence are the dominant aims. At any rate, those are the main focuses of this book. I shall try to suggest that there is no satisfactory way of justifying punishment by appeal to the idea of retribution; and that the notion of deterrence, suitably understood, will give us all that we could reasonably ask from a theory of punishment.

There was a time when the philosophical issues about punishment seemed more or less settled; it seemed that there could be a synthesis of all that one might want from both deterrent and retributive theories. On the one hand, the goals of punishment were to be thought of in a broadly utilitarian fashion: the end was to prevent crime, and the means consisted largely in deterrence. On the other hand, the *bête noire* of straightforwardly utilitarian theories of punishment — deliberate punishment of the innocent for the public good — seemed to have been slain by the simple expedient of introducing side-constraints on how the goals may be accomplished; however much it may conduce to the general good, one was not to punish the innocent, or punish the guilty more than they deserved. Variants of the idea were around in many writers[4] but the *locus classicus* for the view was H.L.A. Hart's *Punishment and Responsibility*.[5] Hart saw that many writers had moved from the thought that punishment must be constrained by broadly retributive considerations to the thought that the exaction of retribution must be its 'general justifying aim'; or, conversely, from the thought that since the general justifying aim of the law is utilitarian so must be all of the considerations brought to bear upon punishment; he saw that both moves were a mistake, and he argued that we could respect the requirements of 'retribution in Distribution' without abandoning the idea that punishment's general justifying aim is broadly utilitarian. He accepted that the retributive side-constraints could not be motivated by purely utilitarian considerations; they must stem from independent moral values, such as justice or fairness.

This general approach had other defenders.[6] But the most notable development of the past twenty-five years or so has been the resurgence of theories generally, though not, as I shall suggest, very helpfully, referred to as 'retributive'. Sometimes these theories have retained a broadly Hartian structure; they accept that the aims of punishment are forward-looking — mainly crime prevention — but take much more seriously than Hart seemed to the claim that sentences must, and can, be proportioned to the moral guilt of the offender.[7] Some, however, have rejected the Hartian scheme altogether, holding that the justifying aim of punishment is not to be found at all in some independently specifiable end which it is hoped that it will promote, but in some irreducibly moral aim to which punishment has a much tighter connection—giving offenders what they deserve,[8] for instance, or making them 'pay for their offences', or 'paying them back' for them.

The renewed enthusiasm for this general direction of thought has not been characteristic only of philosophers. Moved in part by the failure to find evidence that punishment has any significant rehabilitative effect, or even the sort of deterrent effect that was widely canvassed by some writers, and by the abuses of indeterminate and mandatory sentencing, even the more practically oriented branches of penology, have fallen under its sway, leading to the demand that offenders be given their 'just deserts'.[9] Whether this has been for good or for ill is another matter. It is now clear that 'just deserts' has been, on many lips, little more than a code for 'harsher sentences'. In the United States, it was translated into 'truth in sentencing' and used to justify the widespread abolition of parole, leading to effective prison sentences yet more draconian than those already in effect. The United Kingdom has, to some extent, followed suit. But such developments are not our present concern.

One part of the explanation for this change no doubt lies in very general social and political developments that have taken place in the United States and the United Kingdom (and in other places too) over the past quarter of a century. Those social and political changes produced a minor renaissance of conservative thought, and in the past twenty-five years conservative attitudes have had a sort of intellectual respectability which they have often lacked. And that has included attitudes to punishment, in particular to the idea that offenders are morally to blame and that they deserve to suffer. But if there is a connection here—and no doubt there is[10]—it is a complicated one. The idea that punishment is justified by the moral fault of the offender is an idea not generally found in the writings of the great, classical conservatives; and the most recent, notable versions of theories that have this idea at their centre are not generally very congenial to popular conservative attitudes to punishment.

In any case, from our point of view the more important part of the explanation lies in changes that have taken place in the discipline of philosophy, in particular the renaissance of ethical theory that has taken place since the 1960s.

Students of philosophy in the 1960s typically had courses in modern ethics; and they usually encountered in them the issue of punishment. They were taken through what were popularly referred to as the 'isms': intuitionism, emotivism, prescriptivism, naturalism, and utilitarianism. In so far as utilitarianism fitted this scheme at all, it was because it can be interpreted as a naturalistic doctrine (though implausibly, given the philosophical machinery then available), and students had their attentions focused largely on Moore's contemptuous dismissal of Mill.[11] But utilitarianism was also supposed to fall prey to another strategy: it was counter-intuitive. And it was here that the student was most likely to encounter the issue of punishment. It seemed that act-utilitarianism at least was committed to the view that it would be right to punish an innocent person if this were to maximize happiness; and it was generally assumed that this told strongly against the theory. It would not be quite accurate to say that this was the full extent of the student's encounter with the topic of punishment. Almost, but not quite, for students might also encounter punishment in another context: there was some discussion of 'the concept of punishment', and how this might bear upon the question of its justification. But serious discussions of that justification for its own sake, such as there were, were completely outside of the mainstream.[12]

All this has now changed, of course. Normative ethical and political philosophy now flourish—perhaps as never before. And this has involved a different attitude to moral sentiments from that which was current in the 1960s. At that time, moral sentiments were, in one sense, respected, for they were used as data to test moral theories. But, in part because of the broadly expressivist approach that was widely adop-ted towards ethics, and which was somehow thought to imply that moral judgments are not susceptible of justification in any interesting way, there was little serious attempt to explore the content of those sentiments to see whether they might have any rational hold on us, or even any less compelling claim to our respect. Now, of course, the philosophical world is full of ethical theories — systematic accounts of the content of our morality, accounts which hope to reveal, at the least, rational connections between its various parts.

And viewed from a perspective in which theory is a central goal, the whole structure of the Hartian account may seem to have a somewhat unsatisfying, *ad hoc* quality; the values that determine the constraints upon the means of punishment are quite different from those that determine its aims, and the constraints are motivated wholly by the desire to bring the theory into line with antecedent moral intuitions.[13] Perhaps ultimately we shall simply have to accept this; perhaps morality consists of a plurality of irreducible values,[14] and our understanding of punishment may have to reflect that.[15] But the hope for a more unified theory is an understandable one.[16] It is also, I believe, not a forlorn one.

II

The book is divided into two parts, the first mainly negative, the second more positive. In the first chapter, I deal with theories of punishment in general, by which I mean theories as to why punishment is (or is not) justified. I divide such theories into two types, externalist and internalist. Externalist theories justify punishment by reference to an aim the specification of which does not require that it should be, or even that it can successfully be, promoted by punishment. The deterrence theory is presumably the most obvious of such theories; the point of punishment, according to the deterrence theory, is the prevention of crime, and that is a goal that can be specified without requiring that it be promoted by punishment. The most common reform theories are also externalist. According to them, the aim of punishment is to reform offenders (usually with the more ultimate goal of crime prevention), and the reform envisaged is typically of a sort that could, in principle, be achieved by means other than punishment; indeed, many of those who have been attracted to reform theories have eventually rejected punishment as an effective means. Internalist theories, by contrast, justify punishment by reference to an aim whose very specification requires either that it must be, or that it can successfully be, achieved by punishment. Theories which hold that the aim of punishment is simply to inflict on offenders the suffering they deserve are naturally of this type; it is an obvious conceptual truth there is no way of achieving this aim without inflicting suffering on offenders; and inflicting suitably constrained suffering on offenders just is punishment. But other types of theory can be internalist too, including, as we shall see, some reform theories. All plausible theories will be either internalist or externalist.

Discussions of punishment are often cast in terms of a distinction between consequentialist theories and 'retributive' theories. This, I suggest, is not helpful. The word 'retributivism' has no tight and generally accepted definition, and can probably be discarded without loss. The more revealing contrast is between internalist and externalist theories, and it is internalist theories that I shall be attacking in the first part of the book.

A justification of punishment, I suggest, must do three things. First, it must explain satisfactorily why the fact that someone has committed an offence should make it justifiable to cause him suffering. Second, it must explain why it is legitimate for *the state* to punish, for the fact that an action is justifiable does not by itself entail that it is justifiable for the state to perform it. Third, the justification it offers must be consistent with at least most of the settled intuitions we have about the *moral* constraints that punishment labours under.

The detailed work starts in Chapter 2, where I discuss what I call the Simple Desert Theory. That theory holds that offenders, simply in virtue of their offences, deserve to suffer, and to suffer in proportion to their moral guilt. The emphasis is wholly on moral desert, and it is crucial to this theory that there is no further reason to be given as to *why* offenders deserve to suffer. The appropriateness is, as it is sometimes put, 'foundational': one just has to see it. Many people claim that they do indeed see it, so the theory is worth refuting in detail. It raises a number of questions. We may wonder, first, whether there is any good reason to accept the claim that offenders simply *deserve* to suffer, with no further reason available as to why this should be so; many people have suspected that this thought is really just the desire for vengeance in disguise. And if we could allay that suspicion, we should still be left with the problem of explaining why it is justifiable for *the state* to inflict punishment on offenders. But the most pressing question is whether the theory is even coherent. The thought that it is not has often been voiced, though less often pursued in any detail: many have thought that there is no suitable sense to be made of the idea of a proportion between the severity of a punishment and the moral gravity of an offence, that they are incommensurable, as it is often put, and I try to show that, as far as this theory is concerned, the thought is correct.

Chapter 3 deals with a theory that can perhaps surmount this central objection to the Simple Desert Theory, the theory I call the Just Distribution Theory. Briefly, this theory claims that the legal order generates a system of burdens and benefits: in return for restraining our lawless impulses we are, to some extent, protected against the lawless impulses of others. An offender, however, takes an unfair advantage, by receiving the benefits but not carrying his share of the burdens. The aim of punishment is to rectify that injustice by imposing upon him a proportionate burden.

Because it does not hold that the offender's deserving to suffer is simply a foundational claim, with no further explication possible, the problem of incommensurability may be less pressing for this theory than for the Simple Desert Theory; whether it can avoid that problem depends upon just how we are to interpret the idea that the offender has derived from his offence a benefit to which he is not entitled, for that idea is open to a number of different interpretations. On some interpretations, it can indeed probably avoid it. However, now a different problem arises; none of the available interpretations will leave a theory which is consistent with our deepest convictions about the constraints upon punishment. The Just Distribution Theory, then, fails to answer the third of the questions that a theory of punishment must answer.

And even if it avoids the problem of incommensurability, it still fails to give a satisfactory answer to the first two questions. It may seem otherwise on the surface: the rectification of injustice may sound like precisely the sort of thing that would justify the state in causing suffering to those who have put themselves in the wrong. But the appearance is illusory. The theoretical base of the theory is what is known as the Principle of Fair Play; the idea, roughly, that anyone who accepts the benefits of a cooperative venture has a duty to bear some part of the burdens. Interpreted vaguely, the principle has some appeal. But there is, I argue, no interpretation of it which is both plausible and able to generate an acceptable theory of punishment.

In Chapter 4 we turn to the idea of reform. Perhaps the most natural version of this idea is an externalist one, but internalist versions have in recent years commanded some attention. Both versions face a number of questions. One of these is why reform should be the central focus of punishment in the first place. The most attractive, and plausible, reform theories are motivated by an amiable respect for the humanity of the offender. But if punishment is to have a forward-looking aim, as any reform theory does, then the deterrence theory is a natural competitor for pride of place. That theory has as its central aim the protection of potential victims, and their good seems at least as demanding of respect as that of offenders. Of course, a version of the reform theory could have that focus too; but then we should wonder why, if the point of punishment is to protect potential victims, we should wait until there is an actual victim before acting.

A second question is why we should think that causing offenders to suffer is in any case likely to reform them. To the modern mind, at least, the most plausible explanation of the reformative effect of punishment will be that it somehow has an educative effect. But the empirical evidence hardly bears this out. One response is to hold that it is not merely an empirical claim, and to cast the theory in an internalist mould; but this too will fail.

Chapters 5 and 6 deal with various so-called 'expressive', 'denunciatory', or 'communicative' theories. The most familiar such theories have been externalist theories; they are therefore not part of our purview though, like internalist versions, they must grapple with two questions. The first is why we should bother to denounce crime—as opposed to, for instance, simply trying to prevent it. The second is why, if we wish to denounce crime, causing suffering to the criminal is the appropriate method of doing so. Externalist theories typically claim that, in various ways, denouncing crime will itself help to prevent it; this involves a set of empirical claims that have little support, but that is not our central concern. The answer to the second question will presumably be that punishing offenders is a particularly effective way of denouncing crime; if this is an empirical claim — as it ought to be — it too has little support.

Internalist theories must give different answers, and in Chapter 5 I examine three such theories. The first holds that it is morally appropriate, simply for its own sake, to give active expression to the condemnation of wrongdoing. We may reasonably question this, I suggest. And if we did not, we should still be left wondering why the condemnation must involve the infliction of suffering. A second approach is that an offender, in his offence, has become 'disconnected' from true values, and punishment will necessarily reconnect him. If we could attach a suitable sense to the idea of being 'connected to values', a sense which would reveal what merit there is in merely being 'connected' to true values, then this might be the beginnings of an acceptable response to the questions. Unfortunately, as I argue, we cannot. A third, quite different, approach holds that an offence sends a message to the effect that the offender is superior to his victim, and that punishment is necessary to counter this message. But this theory is fragile along the whole of its structure. It is by no means clear that an offence 'sends a message' in the appropriate sense; nor that, if it did, it would be the message in question; nor that, if it were, there would be any point in going to great pains to counter it. All of these theories, then, fall at the first hurdle: they are unable even to answer the question why it is legitimate to inflict suffering on offenders.

In Chapter 6 we turn to a theory that marries denunciation and reform, that of Antony Duff. Duff holds that the demands of a broadly liberal communitarian political theory, and a broadly Kantian conception of autonomy lead to the conclusion that, though the proper aim of the law is to prevent wrongdoing, it must do so only through repentance and reform on the part of offenders, and reconciliation between offenders and victims. And these three things, the three Rs as Duff calls them, can be accomplished only by punishment. The sentiment that largely drives Duff's argument is for the most part laudable; the argument itself, however, fails, or so I argue. We cannot justify punishment merely by showing that it leads to the three Rs unless we can show also that it does so in a way more satisfactory than other methods; that is what Duff tries, and fails, to show.

We have looked at the most powerful internalist theories, and, I argue, they all fail. They do so in different and largely unconnected ways, but they share a common failing that we have not yet touched on. In common with many others, I believe that a justification of coercion must have as a bedrock something like Mill's famous principle that 'the sole end for which mankind are warranted... in interfering with the liberty of action of any of their number, is self-protection'.[17] And since punishment is at least a form of coercion (even when voluntarily accepted) the theory of punishment must have that bedrock too. And, as I argue in Chapter 7, this brings punishment under the category of self-defence: roughly, we must see the institution of punishment as a way in which society protects itself, and its members, from conduct which violates constraints that we are justified in upholding to promote individual welfare.

If we think of punishment in this way, it will be natural to see it as mainly a system of deterrent threats, because, for reasons that are not difficult to see, deterrence is the only way in which a penal system can have any significant effect on the level of crime. Imprisonment and execution can, of course, prevent offenders from committing further offences; but in a system such as our own, most punishments are simply fines, and they do not prevent offenders from committing further offences. Other preventive effects of punishment have been put forward but, as I shall suggest, there is little empirical evidence to suggest that these effects — independently of the contribution they make to deterrence — have any significant effect.

The traditional deterrence theory has been attacked on a number of grounds, and examining these attacks will enable us to see what an acceptable deterrence theory of punishment will look like. The traditional theory holds that punishment is inflicted on the actual offender in order to deter potential offenders; in other words, the offender is made to suffer in order to modify the behaviour of others. And this may seem to contravene the generally accepted prohibition on using someone merely as a means. The deterrence theory, however, need not hold that punishment is inflicted on the offender in order to deter others; we should think rather of the institution of punishment as one in which a threat is issued to potential offenders, and the justification for actually carrying out this threat makes no reference to its tendency to deter others. How that is to be done is the subject of Chapter 8. Some of the consequences of this way of thinking for current penal practice occupy Chapter 9.

To what extent, if any, the institution of punishment deters potential offenders from offending is a matter of dispute; that is an empirical dispute and so, in one way, it is outside the purview of this book. However, if it could be shown that, in the circumstances in which we live, penal institutions had no deterrent effect, or insufficient deterrent effect to justify the immense costs that they impose, this would leave punishment with very little justification on the theory I propose. Incarceration might be still be justified in some cases, though since its aim would be directly preventive some would question whether it would properly be called 'punishment'. But I think that much of the scepticism about the deterrent effect of punishment stems from a misunderstanding of what deterrence is, and how it works. When it is properly understood, I think that there is a very heavy burden of proof on those who are sceptical about whether penal institutions have a significant deterrent effect, and a burden that they do not seem to me to have carried. There still remains, of course, the question whether its deterrent benefits outweigh its costs. That is a much more difficult question, and one to which I do not venture an answer in this book. However, like many people, I am sceptical about whether the theory I propose can justify the scale of the penal institutions with which we are familiar in the US and the UK, and in particular the severity of punishment that many offences incur (especially in the US). But I doubt whether any sensible theory of punishment could justify that.

---

1   *Gregg v. Georgia* (1976), 428 U.S. 153, at 183.

2   Cf., e.g. David Boonin, *The Problem of Punishment* (Cambridge University Press, 2008); Michael Zimmerman, *The Immorality of Punishment* (Broadview Press, 2011).

3   But cf. a UK White Paper: 'The first objective for all sentences is denunciation of and retribution for the crime' (*Crime, Justice and Protecting the Public: The Government's Proposals for Legislation* (H.M.S.O, 1991), p. 6). However, the 2003 Criminal Justice Act gives the following as the 'purposes of sentencing': '(a) the punishment of offenders, (b) the reduction of crime (including its reduction by deterrence), (c) the reform and rehabilitation of offenders, (d) the protection of the public, and (e) the making of reparation by offenders to persons affected by their offences.' Presumably, by 'punishment' is meant 'retribution'.

4   See, for instance, J.D. Mabbott's 'Punishment', *Mind*, vol. xlviii (1939), pp. 152–167; and John Rawls' 'Two Concepts of Rules', *Philosophical Review*, vol. lxiv (1955), pp. 3–13.

5   Clarendon Press, 1968; see especially, Ch. I.

6   See, for instance, C.L. Ten, *Crime, Guilt and Punishment* (Clarendon Press, 1987); Nigel Walker, *Why Punish?* (Oxford University Press, 1991); and Andrew von Hirsch, *Censure and Sanctions* (Oxford University Press, 1993).

7   Cp., e.g. Douglas Husak, *Overcriminalization: The Limits of the Criminal Law* (Oxford University Press, 2008).

8   Cp., e.g. Michael Moore, *Placing Blame: A General Theory of the Criminal Law* (Clarendon Press, 1997); and 'A Tale of Two Theories', *Criminal Justice Ethics*, vol. xxviii (2009), pp. 27–48.

9   The most influential text was probably Andrew von Hirsch's *Doing Justice* (Hill and Wang, 1976). For a brief account of the movement in penal systems towards a desert rationale for punishment, see Andrew Ashworth, *Sentencing and Criminal Justice* (Butterworths, 2nd ed. 1995), Ch. 13, § 2; William J. Stuntz, *The Collapse of American Criminal Justice* (Harvard University Press, 2011), pp. 55f.

10 It is a commonplace to connect vaguely retributive attitudes with a conservative political stance. See, for instance, Dworkin's passing remark in *Law's Empire* (Harvard University Press, 1986), p. 358.

11 For G.E. Moore on Mill, see his *Principia Ethica* (Cambridge University Press, 1903); for a standard textbook, see, for instance, Geoffrey Warnock's *Contemporary Moral Philosophy* (Macmillan, 1967).

12 A useful collection of articles is H.B. Acton (ed.), *The Philosophy of Punishment: A Collection of Papers* (Macmillan, 1969).

13 Cf. Moore, 'A Tale of Two Theories'; Phillip Montague, *Punishment as Societal-Defense* (Rowman and Littlefield, 1995), p. 91; and John Tasioulas, 'Punishment and Repentance', *Philosophy*, vol. lxxxi (2006), pp. 279–322, at pp. 281f.

14 Cf. Isaiah Berlin, *Concepts and Categories* (Penguin, 1981).

15 Tasioulas in fact thinks this (*op. cit.*), but undertakes to avoid the opportunism of accounts like Hart's.

16 It is shared by, for instance, Nicola Lacey in *State Punishment: Political Principles and Community Values* (Routledge, 1988), p. 70.; Antony Duff in *Punishment, Communication, and Community*, p. 89; and J. Angelo Corlett, 'Making Sense of Retributivism', *Philosophy*, vol. lxxvi (2001), pp. 77–110.

17 J.S. Mill, *On Liberty and Other Writings*, ed. Stefan Collini (Cambridge University Press, 1989), p. 13.
    'Self-protection' includes, of course, the protection of others too.

Chapter One

Theories of Punishment

Let us start by a distinguishing two senses of 'a theory of punishment'. A theory of punishment could be an account of *the concept* of punishment; it could also refer to a *justification* of punishment. This book will focus primarily on the latter, but first a few remarks about the concept.

It is doubtful whether we can give a set of generally accepted, necessary and sufficient conditions for some act being an act of punishment;[1] the concept of punishment is no different in that respect from many other concepts. But here are a few salient points.

At the centre of the concept is the idea of *the infliction of suffering for an offence*.[2] Some prefer to add further elements, as, for instance, the infliction of suffering *on an offender* for *her* offence.[3] However, if this were correct, it would make no sense to ask whether it is permissible to punish those who are not guilty of an offence; but whether it is ever permissible to punish the innocent is surely a substantive question, and it may be an error to claim that those who are punished for what they did not do are justly punished, but it is not a conceptual error.[4] In the more minimal definition, the word 'for' does no more than to indicate that there should be some suitable relation between the suffering and the offence; it tells us little about what that relation should be. The mere fact that, for instance, the punishment administered is specified by statute for a particular offence would be enough to make it proper to say that someone has been punished 'for' that offence (even if he did not commit it). If, by contrast, we were talking about the *justification* of punishment then things would be different: we would require that the suffering be inflicted for an offence in a much fuller sense of 'for'; but that is a different matter, and one to which we shall return.

It has also been held, as a conceptual claim, that the *aim* of punishment is to inflict suffering.[5] I think that is wrong. As I shall later try to show, the actual infliction of punishment need have no aim, though *threatening* punishment certainly has; that punishing itself has no aim could be wrong, but it is not ruled out merely by the content of the concept. It is more plausible to hold the weaker view that the infliction of suffering is *intended*, not as an ultimate aim, but as a means to some further end.[6] I shall later suggest this is not quite right either, though a system of punishment must involve *conditional* intentions about suffering.

The reference to suffering is accepted by nearly all writers. Feinberg nicely glosses 'suffering' as 'hard treatment'.[7]

This account says nothing about *who* may inflict punishment, and in fact there is little to say. Some writers regard punishment by the state as the central case and think of other cases as secondary, or analogous or sub-standard.[8] But I see little to recommend this. My own concern is with punishment by the state, and I shall have virtually nothing to say about other forms of punishment. But punishment of a recalcitrant child is, as far as the concept is concerned, just as much punishment as is punishment of a legal offender by the state, though we might demand quite different kinds of *justification* for the two. We could go even further, and hold that punishment does not have to be inflicted by *anyone*, at least not in the normal sense: accidental harm befalling an offender might be regarded as a punishment. We might prefer to think of this as a metaphor. But there would be no need to insist on the point. Punishment is certainly an *intentional* notion, but perhaps intentionality will be present so long as someone sees a certain sort of appropriateness in the harm befalling the offender. I do not wish to defend such a thought,[9] but it seems wrong to rule it out by definition.

It is sometimes said that it is part of the concept of punishment that it be an expression of disapproval.[10] Maybe so, but it is a thin notion of disapproval. There would be no conceptual impropriety in saying that someone was punished for an act that *nobody* in fact disapproved of, so long as the act was against the law. To say that the punishment expresses disapproval, then, seems to say little more than that the behaviour for which it was inflicted was prohibited. Perhaps the prohibition itself expresses disapproval in a fuller sense, though there are surely actions the performance of which is to be disapproved of only because they are prohibited; but that is anyway another matter.

Theories

By 'a theory of punishment', then, I shall mean a theory as to the *justification* of punishment. But here there are different questions.

There is, first, the question of whether a theory of punishment offers a justification for actually inflicting punishment on a particular person at a particular time, or a justification for the penal system in general, a system that has properties in excess of the sum of the properties possessed by individual acts of punishment considered in isolation. Some theories take the particular punishment to be the primary bearer of justification, deriving the justification for the penal system from that. For instance, a theory that focuses simply on what offenders *deserve* may hold that it is the particular punishment that carries all of the justificatory weight. Others may take the reverse approach: a deterrent theorist, for instance, may hold that it is the penal system that carries the justificatory weight, individual acts of punishment being justified simply by what they contribute to promoting the penal system's effectiveness. These are not, of course, the only alternatives, and the deterrence theory I shall put forward here is different from the one just characterized.

Second, when I speak of justification, I mean only what might be called a *prima facie* justification.[11] Theories of punishment typically hold that even when punishment is justified according to the considerations specific to punishment, it can be right to waive it if there are sufficiently strong countervailing considerations, such as the various costs that punishment might impose in the particular case. But this hardly seems worth stating explicitly since it states a condition binding upon any moral judgment whatever, and a condition whose precise terms it may be impossible to spell out and which may be quite open-ended. I shall express this, then, by saying that a full theory of punishment gives only a *prima facie* justification.

Third, a theory of punishment might justify an *obligation* on the part of the state to punish offenders, or merely a *permission* to do so.

With theories that ground the justification of punishment in the notion of what the offender *deserves*, the more demanding requirement may seem too strong to some; no one, perhaps, is obligated to give people what they deserve (as opposed to what they are entitled to from them). But if one thought that, say, threatening offenders with punishment would be likely to prevent significant harm to the innocent, it would seem more plausible to think that this generated at least a *prima facie* obligation to do something.

Internalism and Externalism

As Aristotle famously remarked,[12] all action can be said to aim at some good. And specifying, under a suitable description, the good at which an action aims will normally contribute to making the action intelligible. But an action can be related to what it aims at in different ways. Presumably, the most obvious way is that an action can aim to secure, or generally promote, some *independently specifiable* good — specifiable, that is to say, independently of the fact that it is to be secured by that sort of action, or of the fact that that sort of action necessarily secures it. For instance, I may put on a coat with the end of keeping warm. But 'keeping warm', in itself, contains no reference to putting on a coat; and nor does putting on a coat imply anything about keeping warm. When an aim is related to an action in this way, I shall say that they are related externally.

But an action may also have an aim which is not specifiable independently of the fact that it is to be achieved by that sort of action. For instance, someone may say that he refrains from killing innocent people in order not to be a murderer. Assuming for the moment that killing an innocent person just is murder, the specification of the agent's end here which makes intelligible his action must covertly make reference to the means. That need not make it trivial; if it does no more, it makes intelligible his refraining by endorsing a moral condemnation of a certain sort of person. When an aim is related to an action in this way, I shall say that they are related internally.

I have spoken so far of making actions *intelligible*, and have said that this can be achieved by referring to two different types of aim, those that have a merely external connection with the action and those that have an internal connection. *Justifications* of action may, in turn, refer to either type of aim. I shall call a justification of a type of action which refers only to the first sort of aim 'externalist'; justifications which refer to the second sort of aim I shall refer to as 'internalist'.

We may thus distinguish theories of punishment according to whether they are externalist or internalist.

Externalist theories hold that punishment is justified on the grounds that it promotes some good specifiable independently of the fact that it is to be secured by punishment. Crime prevention is the most commonly assumed aim, though there are other candidates (not necessarily mutually exclusive), such as the promotion of social cohesion or the reform of the offender (thought of not merely as ways of reducing crime, but as good in themselves). If such theories are to justify punishment, then they require a contingent claim about the likelihood of punishment achieving its goal.

By contrast, some theories of punishment make no mention of an independently specifiable goal. That will be so for a theory of punishment that takes as a moral principle that offenders deserve to suffer for their offences. Given the contingent fact that someone has committed an offence, along with the moral principle that offenders deserve to be punished and the claim that punishment just is being made to suffer for an offence, nothing more is required for the conclusion that the offender deserves to be punished. Perhaps further moral principles, or conceptual claims, connecting desert with moral obligations (or permissions) are required; but no further contingent input is required. In that sense, end and means conceptually imply each other: given an offender, punishment cannot but succeed in its aim, and nothing but punishment could succeed. But there are also cases where the implication goes in only one direction. Most obvious are cases in which the end implies the means but the means does not imply the end. A theory, for instance, which holds that the point of punishment is to give victims the satisfaction of seeing offenders suffer for their offences would be of this kind. There is no possibility of achieving that end without inflicting suffering on offenders for their offences; but doing so is not guaranteed to achieve the end desired (for, in the event, some victims may not receive any satisfaction). There is also logical space for a sort of explanation in which the implication goes only in the opposite direction, where the means is sufficient for the end, but not vice versa; perhaps some sorts of expressive theory of punishment are like this. Theories of these types I shall also refer to as internalist.[13]

Externalist theories may differ not only about what the aim of punishment is, but also about how that aim is to be achieved. But punishment is typically, though inaccurately, said to promote the goals most commonly assigned to it in one, or more, of fours ways: by deterring potential offenders, reforming actual offenders, incapacitating offenders, and by expressing some sort of message. We thus have four broad types of externalist theory:

The Reform Theory is a family of views holding, roughly, that punishment is justified to the extent that it makes offenders less likely to commit further offences, usually by reducing their desire to do so.[14] This may be thought of primarily as a benefit to the offender in particular or to society more generally. And the benefit may be thought of as either moral or material. (None of these alternatives are exclusive, of course.)

Reformation has long been thought one of the aims of punishment. The most famous philosophical exposition of the idea is presumably that of Plato. But Aristotle also speaks of punishment as a cure,[15] as do St Augustine,[16] St Thomas Aquinas,[17] and Grotius.[18] The heyday of the reform theory, however, began in the eighteenth century, and was associated with the prison reform movement. John Howard's *The State of the Prisons in England and Wales*[19] had great influence on penal thought, though less on its actual practice. One of those influenced by Howard was Jeremy Bentham, who thought that reformation was one of the two central justifications of punishment, though less important than deterrence, the other central justification in his view.[20] The ideal of reform remained central in penal thought until about the middle of the twentieth century, when the apparent failure of punishment to reform on any significant scale, and what was widely seen as the abuse of the indeterminate sentences to which it seemed to point, led to its virtual demise.

The Incapacitation Theory holds that punishment is justified to the extent that it actually prevents offenders from re-offending.

Only capital punishment serves as a wholly effective preventive measure, and no doubt this has always been a reason for carrying it out (though it, and its methods, have been motivated by other considerations too). Some punishments, such as fines, have hardly any preventive effect.

Incarceration is the form of punishment which most commonly has this effect. However, the use of imprisonment as a form of *punishment* was sporadic until the early modern period. The sixth-century *Corpus Juris Civilis* made it, in principle, illegal in Civil Law countries to use imprisonment as a form of punishment; but Roman law had little effective authority even in Civil Law countries through the mediaeval and early modern periods and the infrequency in the use of imprisonment may have had more to do with practical considerations. Transportation of offenders began in the reign of Elizabeth I; it was officially thought of as an extension of hard labour, but it is surely certain that one of the reasons the system stayed alive for two hundred years was the thought of getting rid of offenders. But incarceration and transportation do not typically prevent offenders from re-offending, though they may confine their offences to what are thought to be more desirable locations. (As is well known, lawbreaking in American and British prisons is endemic.) And imprisonment was often simply coercive, as with the debtors' prisons the Fleet and Marshalsea.

We do not encounter the clearly articulated thought that it is part of the justification of punishment that it directly prevents offenders from re-offending until quite late. One may think of Locke: '*Reparation* and *Restraint*... the only reasons why man may lawfully do harm to another.'[21] But

Locke is thinking of deterrence when he uses the word 'restraint'. Grotius, however, speaks clearly of punishment as a form of incapacitation.[22] And Bentham thinks of 'disablement' as one of the functions of punishment.[23] In recent years, the idea has gained considerable popular support.[24]

The Deterrence Theory holds that punishment is justified because it deters potential offenders from offending.

Deterrence in punishment is often divided into special deterrence (the effect of punishment on the actual offender) and general deterrence (the effect on the general population). But making the distinction in these terms is misleading: so-called 'particular deterrence' is not really a form of deterrence at all, because, by definition, all that can *deter* is the threat of future punishment and actual punishment is not a threat of future punishment. If actual punishment makes the offender less likely to commit future crimes, it can do so only by making him more *deterrable*, and this is really a matter of *reform*. Only threats of *more* punishment can *deter* him, but that is just *'general* deterrence' again because his future self is now subsumed in the general population. And in the way that actual punishment may make *actual* offenders more deterrable, it can, given suitable publicity, make *potential* offenders more deterrable too — though leaving it to threats of future punishment to *deter* them. Punishment, and the threat of punishment, then, work in exactly the same way for both actual offenders and potential offenders, and so there is little work for the distinction to do.

Still, this points us towards a fourfold distinction, unclarified in the rough account of the deterrence theory just given. First, there is the actual infliction of punishment on a particular occasion. Second, there is the general institution of punishing people. Third, there is the individual threat of punishment. And, fourth, there is the general institution of threatening people with punishment. The traditional deterrence theory claims that each of these is justified by its contribution to deterrence. But a deterrence theory might also hold that only the third and fourth are susceptible of this sort of justification; or so I shall later suggest.

It seems likely that the need for deterrence has played a role in legal institutions from the earliest times.[25] Certainly, many, perhaps most, of those who have thought about punishment have held that deterrence is at least one legitimate aim of punishment. So, for instance, Plato,[26] Aristotle,[27] Aquinas,[28]   Grotius,[29]   Hobbes,[30]   Locke,[31]   Beccaria,[32] Bentham,[33] and T.H. Green.[34]

Expressive Theories hold that punishment is justified — both the institution and actual punishments — because it achieves some suitable goal through the message it expresses. The theories that are typically thought of as expressive focus on the *denunciatory* aspect of punishment.[35] Punishment is normally taken to express denunciation or condemnation, and this condemnation may be thought to promote social commitment to the immorality of the offence, or to educate society about its illegality; either of these may be thought to be a good in itself,[36] or may be regarded simply as a way of reducing crime; again, actual punishment may be thought to reform the offender by inducing repentance through the communication of the wrongness of the offence,[37] or through the experience of shame;[38] and this too might be thought to be good in itself, or it may be regarded merely as just another way of reducing crime; again, in a variation on the traditional deterrence theory, the threat of punishment may be thought to deter potential offenders through the fear of being shamed;[39] or it may be thought to siphon off the society's feelings of outrage, feelings which would otherwise express themselves in Lynch law; or penal systems may be thought to promote social cohesion generally, which is often taken to have numerous social benefits, including a reduction in the rate of crime.

Probably Emile Durkheim is the most famous exponent of such a theory, but James Fitzjames Stephen's view is better known to philosophers and jurisprudents.[40]

We should perhaps mention one last family of externalist theories.

The Assurance Theory holds that punishment is justified — and again this applies to both the institution and to actual instances of punishment — because of the assurance that it offers to law-abiding citizens that others will obey the law too.[41] Without that assurance, they may suspect that the system is steeped in unfairness, and they will not respect it and will be correspondingly less likely to conform to its demands. Or the thought may simply be that unless enough others conform with its demands to ensure that everyone has a reasonable probability of benefiting, it would be foolish to conform to it oneself; punishment may be thought to offer some assurance that enough others will indeed do so. Yet more simply, the idea might be that the institution of punishment by the state is necessary to prevent private citizens from taking the law into their own hands.[42]

Theories of this sort, however, depend upon one or more of the theories already mentioned, because punishment can offer the sort of assurance canvassed only if it somehow reduces the level of offending, and it can presumably do so only by deterring potential offenders, or reforming or incapacitating actual offenders.

The most plausible types of internalist theories also — coincidentally — fall into four categories.

The Simple Desert Theory holds that punishment is justified for no further reason than that the offender deserves to suffer for his offence.

In ordinary thought, this is perhaps the most commonly held internalist theory, and the theory that most people think of when they think of retribution. The idea of desert is, however, frequently confused in this context with other notions, such as that of revenge, denunciation, or expiation.[43]

The Just Distribution Theory holds that punishment is justified because it restores the just distribution of burdens and benefits in society. The idea is, roughly, that the offender benefited unfairly from his offence — perhaps through the use of his ill-gotten gains, or perhaps merely in the sense that he did not restrain his lawless impulses when others did so — and his punishment restores the just balance of benefits and burdens. The restoration of that balance can be achieved, of course, only through the imposition on the offender of some burden or deprivation — through punishment, that is to say.

This seems to be a relatively modern doctrine, though it has been attributed to Aquinas[44] and Kant,[45] and Nietzsche seems to mention it as one possible 'meaning' of punishment.[46]

The Reform Theory, as before, holds that punishment is justified because it reforms the offender; however, reform theories will be internalist if they hold that, as a conceptual matter, the sort of reform that punishment aims at could not be achieved in any other way.

Plato may have held this view.[47] It is hard to find in other writers until quite recently, when marriage with the Expressive Theory has made it somewhat fashionable.[48]

The Expressive Theory holds that punishment is justified because of the conceptual connection it has to the expression of condemnation: it is a necessary truth that punishment expresses condemnation, and it is, so it is held, also a necessary truth that certain sorts of condemnation can be expressed only through punishment. Expressing condemnation of an offence may be thought to be good, or right, in itself,[49] or it may be thought to be justified as achieving some good: it may be thought to be required for repentance or reintegration into society, for instance, or for the reinstatement of the status of the victims of crime.

Compensation, Expiation, Annulment, Retribution

A number of possible theories have not been mentioned so far.

One is the increasingly influential view in popular thought that might be called a *Victim Compensation Theory*. This would be the idea that a justifying point of punishment is that it somehow does 'justice to the victim', presumably by affording victims some sort of compensatory satisfaction.[50] But it hardly seems likely that this could play a significant role in justifying punishment. This is not to deny that our institutions should focus more on compensation for the individual victims of crime than they currently do. But if we are really concerned with victim compensation, then making the offender suffer will not loom large in our thoughts; if it does so, we are probably thinking not of either justice or compensation but of revenge. This would generate a theory of punishment of course—punishment is justified because it enables victims to get revenge (vicariously, perhaps) — but, unless this aim were subservient to the further, and more laudable, aim of siphoning off the desire of victims for revenge in pursuit of a more orderly society, in which case the theory would simply be one of the expressive theories already mentioned, it would have little appeal. In any case, so-called victim compensation could not go far to justify punishment; how, for instance, would it justify punishment for homicides in which no one grieves for the victim?[51]

People have sometimes spoken of an *Expiation Theory* of punishment. The idea is that punishment somehow eradicates the guilt of the offender or 'washes away' his sin.[52] The thought has a long history — from its Judaic and Greek beginnings it found its way into some versions of the Christian doctrine of the atonement, and into some versions of the doctrine of purgatory — but I do not include it here because I think that, unless it is simply one of the other theories under a different name, it makes no sense. When an offender has committed an offence, he is guilty of it, and that at least cannot be changed. He may put right the wrong he did to the victim of his offence, and punishment may, adventitiously, bring this about. We may think of this, perhaps, as 'washing away' his sin, but this is wholly a matter of *reparation*, not of punishment. He may, through punishment, become a reformed character, repentant of his wrongdoing; again, we may think of his sin (though not his guilt) as being washed away, but this is just a version of the Reform Theory. Again, punishment may take back from him the gains that he made from his offence, but that is simply some version of the Just Distribution Theory. There is no distinctive expiation theory — at least, not one of which we can make any sense.

Again, people have sometimes spoken of an *Annulment Theory*, which holds that punishment annuls the offence. Here again, unless this is just another name for one of the theories already outlined, it fails to make sense.

Literally speaking, to annul something is to reduce it to nothing. Presumably, then, to annul an offence, or a past evil, would be to make it as if the offence, or the past evil, had never occurred (it could hardly be to make it the case that the offence never occurred). But this could mean only that we make it as if it had never occurred *in some respect or other*; and this in turn would mean that a number of the theories I have outlined could lay claim to being annulment theories. For instance, the Just Distribution Theory claims that punishment wipes out the advantage that an offender derived from his offence; it thus makes it, *as far as that advantage is concerned,* as if the offence had never occurred. And, as we shall see in more detail later, some versions of the Expressive Theory involve a notion that could be called annulment. There is, however, no distinctive annulment theory, or, at least, not an intelligible one.[53]

It is commonplace to present the issue of the justification of punishment as a debate between '*retributivism*' and '*consequentialism*'. It is also commonplace that if the notion of consequentialism is well-defined the notion of retributivism certainly is not:

> The range of such theories is very great. I have been astonished to find that Lady Wootton's theories... are spoken of by some as retributive.[54]

> The fact is that the word 'retributive' as used in philosophy has become so imprecise and multivocal that it is doubtful whether it any longer serves a useful purpose.[55]

> The word 'retribution' has come to have various senses in the writings of moral philosophers.[56]

> Non-consequentialist theories are often called 'retributivist', although this label has been applied to such different theories that its utility might now be doubted.[57]

Here, as an illustration, is a selection of accounts of the idea of retributivism taken from Christopher Bennett's book, *The Apology Ritual*:[58]

> Retributivism holds that 'punishment of a person who is responsible for some moral wrong is a good thing in itself';

> Retributivists 'see punishment as being justified in its own right: for instance, as being necessary to vindicate or avenge victims; or to restore justice; or to express the justified outrage of reasonable people';

> Retributivism 'finds the justification for punishment by looking *back* to the crime committed';

> 'The retributivist sees punishment as essentially charged with emotion and symbolism.'

There could perhaps be a theory of which all of these things are true, though, if there is, I doubt whether anyone has ever held it. But it is easy to see that each characterization is logically independent from each of the others:[59] there is, in fact, no significant, unifying idea to the theories regarded as retributive (other than their rejection of a certain type of consequentialism). One could perhaps say that any theory that accepted any of these characterizations would be retributive. But, if we are to classify theories of punishment at all, then, given the great logical diversity between the theories so classified, this would seem an unhelpful way to do so.

On the other hand, the internalist/externalist distinction marks a clear and useful demarcation of theories. Internalist theories are of course a wide variety too; but what they have in common is significant. In rejecting the most standard sort of means–end justification for punishment, they give punishment a certain sort of moral significance. Externalist theories (including the one that I shall later defend) think of punishment as a means to an independently specifiable goal. The most typical of an indefinite number of possible goals is the prevention of crime, and punishment is one means of achieving this. On such theories, there is nothing special about punishment, save contingently; if there were other means of preventing crime, means which imposed fewer costs (moral costs included), then those means would be preferable, and punishment could satisfactorily wither away. Punishment is thus, in principle, no more than one, contingently appropriate, response to crime; we stick with it simply because we have not yet discovered any more economical way of dealing with the problem. Internalist theories, on the other hand, all set themselves against this way of thinking. If, for instance, one's aim were to give the victims of an offence the satisfaction of seeing the offender suffer, there would be, conceptually, no way of doing this without punishing him. One might reject the aim, of course, though theories of punishment usually claim to be based ultimately on a fundamental moral principle that cannot reasonably be rejected; but if one accepted the aim then there would be only one way of achieving it. So punishment would not be merely one appropriate response to crime, adopted simply because we have not been able to find a more effective one; given the aim, the idea that there could be a more 'effective' response to crime would make no sense. Internalist theories differ over just why punishment is such a uniquely appropriate response. Some hold that it is because it is what is owed to the offender, though they differ over the basis of that debt; others hold that it is what is owed to the victim; yet others do not think of it in terms of something owed to anyone, but merely as a response that is uniquely fitting. But those who justify punishment on internalist grounds share the thought that, perhaps given some more fundamental moral principle, an offence cries out for punishment, and that nothing else could adequately answer that call.[60] A theory which held not that the aim of punishment could not be achieved in any other way, but that punishment nonetheless cannot fail to achieve its aim, could not make this claim. Still, such theories claim to make punishment special in a way that externalist theories do not, for even on these theories what an offence cries out for is a response for which punishment is guaranteed to be appropriate.

This distinction is, I believe, a clear and useful one. And it may be, perhaps, that it captures something that underlies the theories that are most typically referred to as retributive. But it is needless to insist on the point. Given the distinction, we could refer to internalist theories as 'retributive', or we could simply retire the word. But this would be a matter of linguistic stipulation, a relatively trivial terminological matter.

What Must a Theory of Punishment Do?

I have spoken simply of the justification of punishment, but it is worth distinguishing three different, but related, elements that such a justification will involve.

The most obvious is this. Punishment involves, in one way or another, the infliction of suffering, or 'hard treatment'. This raises a question: why should the fact that someone has committed an offence justify the infliction of suffering on him? Sometimes it is justifiable to inflict suffering on people who in no way deserve it, simply for the common good; for instance, we quarantine those with infectious illnesses to prevent an epidemic, or we demand that, with reasonable compensation, landowners allow the government to take their land for public use. But only in the most exceptional circumstances (and not even then, according to many) can one justify *punishing* someone on no more complicated ground than that it is for the common good. The explanation will typically have to be in other terms; it will have to show precisely why it is that it is the commission of an offence that makes the infliction of suffering justifiable. And this explanation can be expected to make clear why it is not, except in the most demanding circumstances, justifiable to punish the innocent.

The explanation will appeal to an aim, either internal or external, to be promoted by the infliction of suffering. But simply pointing to such an aim will not yet be a satisfactory answer to the question. For one thing, we shall need to be convinced that the aim is at least a permissible one; not all the aims that have been suggested as legitimating the infliction of suffering on offenders would command universal approval — vengeance, for instance.[61] Nor would that be enough; we should want to know that the aim is, typically, sufficiently worthwhile to offset the costs involved in punishment; one who thought, for instance, that some criminals deserve to die might yet think that giving such people what they deserve is not a sufficiently important aim that it justifies the enormous costs, moral costs amongst others perhaps, that the institution of capital punishment involves.

There is a second question that a theory of punishment must answer satisfactorily. Virtually everyone agrees that it is legitimate for the state to punish; for the most part, only those who deny the legitimacy of the state altogether will deny this. There is, of course, an abolitionist tradition which does not straightforwardly deny the legitimacy of the state; it is mostly concerned with the abolition of prisons, though some writers are more broadly concerned with the abolition of punishment generally.[62] But this is a view that appeals to few people; I shall not discuss it explicitly, though later I shall try to give reasons why penal institutions are indeed justified. We are left, then, with the question why it is legitimate for *the state* to pursue the aim in question, for not all desirable courses of action are within the legitimate ambit of state action: 'Vengeance is mine, saith the LORD; I will repay.'[63]

A third query is this. Everyone accepts that there are moral constraints upon the severity with which we may punish offenders (though how much agreement there is about the precise nature of these constraints is another matter). A theory of punishment, then, will need to satisfy us that it is consistent with these constraints. One aspect of this is often overlooked and so worth emphasising: there are deep differences about the moral constraints on the severity of punishment, and these differences resist consensus. Some moral views about punishment are not to be respected, for they might simply reflect thoughtlessness or depravity. But some conflicting views are to be respected; we simply do not have the philosophical resources to settle them and probably there are no such resources. In that case, a theory of punishment should aim to be acceptably modest: it should not try to foreclose serious and respectable difference of opinion about the acceptable level of punishment, and its doing so would arguably be a mark against it.

This structure of questions is easily illustrated if we think of the very simplest sort of deterrence theory. To the first question, it will reply that the infliction of suffering on actual offenders will deter potential offenders from offending. Is this a satisfactory aim? The hope is that deterring potential offenders will reduce crime sufficiently to offset the costs involved in punishment. Whether or not it does so is, of course, a question whose answer will require considerable empirical input. If the question is answered satisfactorily, the second question remains, but it too is plausibly answered; preventing crime is, in general, one of the most obviously legitimate actions of the state. In response to the third question, whether the theory is in line with our intuitions about the moral constraints on punishment, unless constrained by some further moral considerations it will presumably hold that it is justifiable to inflict whatever punishment is required in order to deter, no more and no less, and that this is consistent with the moral constraints in question.

Theories can, of course, fail to answer satisfactorily these three questions in different ways. Here are four. The answer to a question may involve some internal incoherence; or it may involve, or entail, some unacceptable moral judgment; or it may involve, or entail, some false empirical judgment;

or it may seem arbitrary, without satisfactory motivation. The simplest sort of deterrence theory is usually thought to fail, in the second of these ways, to deliver a satisfactory answer to the first question; punishing one person in order to deter others is commonly thought to be *using* the offender in a morally unacceptable way. It is also generally thought to fail, again in the second of these ways, on its answer to the third question. What levels of punishment will serve to deter potential offenders is a contingency by no means guaranteed to comport with our moral intuitions about what levels of punishment are morally justifiable.

I shall suggest later that a deterrence theory can do better than this. We shall not, however, be concerned immediately with deterrence theories. First, we shall enquire how internalist theories fare. For now, I shall observe, in anticipation, that they all fail, not all in one way, but each in one or more of the ways just mentioned. The justification of punishment must be an externalist one.

---

1   But see David Boonin, *The Problem of Punishment* (Cambridge University Press, 2008), pp. 3–6; Michael Zimmerman, *The Immorality of Punishment* (Broadview, 2011), p. 1.

2   Cf. 'cause (an offender) to suffer for an offence' (*The Concise Oxford Dictionary*, 9th ed.); 'to cause to undergo pain, loss or suffering for a crime or wrongdoing' (*Webster's New World Dictionary*).

3   Antony Duff, *Trials and Punishments* (Cambridge University Press, 1986), p. 262 [my emphases].

4   The point is recognized by Duff in *Punishment, Communication, and Community* (Oxford University Press, 2002), pp. xivf. Cf. also C.L. Ten, *Crime, Guilt, and Punishment* (Clarendon Press, 1987), p. 16.

5   Nathan Hanna, 'Say What? A Critique of Expressive Retributivism', *Law and Philosophy*, vol. xxvii (2007), pp. 123–150.

6   Cf. Boonin, pp. 12–17.

7   'The Expressive Function of Punishment', *The Monist*, 1965 (rp. in Feinberg's *Doing and Deserving: Essays in the Theory of Responsibility* (Princeton University Press, 1970), p. 95 in *Doing and Deserving*, to which edition my page references refer).

Jacob Adler denies that punishment involves suffering in *The Urgings of Conscience* (Temple University Press, 1991), Ch. 3. However, I think he runs together two different claims. One is that punishment must involve the infliction of what, under some other description, would be regarded as suffering. The other is that punishment may be welcomed as something valuable by the offender. As Adler emphasizes, the second of these claims is true. But so is the first, and its truth does not imply, as Adler seems to think, the falsity of the second.

8   Cf., for instance, H.L.A. Hart, *Punishment and Responsibility: Essays in the Philosophy of Law* (Clarendon Press, 1968), pp. 4ff.; Michael Davis, 'Punishment Theory's Golden Half-Century: A Survey of Developments from (about) 1957 to 2007', *The Journal of Ethics*, vol. xiii (2009), pp. 73–100. Leo Zaibert argues against this in *Punishment and Retribution* (Ashgate, 1966); however, his own definition of punishment seems to me to be hopelessly overbroad.

9   For a defence, see Peter Winch, 'Ethical Reward and Punishment', in *Ethics and Action* (Routledge and Kegan Paul, 1972).

10 'The Expressive Function of Punishment', *The Monist*, 1965 (rp. in Feinberg's *Doing and Deserving: Essays in the Theory of Responsibility* (Princeton University Press, 1970)). Feinberg espouses the same view in *The Moral Limits of the Criminal Law. Vol IV: Harmless Wrongdoing* (Oxford University Press, 1988), cf. pp. 149–150. See also Boonin, *The Problem of Punishment*, pp. 21f., and Michael Zimmerman, *The Immorality of Punishment* (Broadview, 2011), pp. 16f.

11 The interesting issue about *prima facie* duties concerns the status of overridden moral claims, but for our purposes we do not need to settle this general issue. For a discussion, see Jonathan Dancy, *Moral Reasons* (Blackwell, 1993), Ch. 6.

12 *Nicomachean Ethics*, 1094a1.

13 Michael Davis makes reference to what is probably intended to be the same distinction in 'Punishment Theory's Golden Half-Century'. However, he conflates this distinction with that between actions which are *empirically* connected to their ends and actions which are not. The distinction I have in mind is quite different: 'I do not eat meat on Fridays because God forbids it' is non-empirical but, at least on most theological views, externalist.

14 On the very broadest definition, of course, capital punishment would count as a reform theory.

15 *Nicomachean Ethics*, Bk. II, Ch. 1.

16 *Letter to Marcellinus*, in Ernest L. Fortin and Douglas Kries (eds.), *Augustine: Political Writings* (Hackett, 1994).

17 *Summa Theologica*, Quaestio LXXXVII, Art. 2.

18 *De Jure Belli ac Pacis*, translated by A.C. Campbell (Walter Dunne, 1901 (1st ed. 1625)), Bk. II, Ch. 20, §§ viii, ix, and x.

19 John Howard, *The State of the Prisons in England and Wales* (London, 1777).

20 See, for instance, *An Introduction to the Principles of Morals and Legislation* (Methuen, 1982), Ch. XIII, fn. a.

21 *Second Treatise of Government*, § 8.

22 *De Jure Belli ac Pacis*, Bk. II, Ch. 20, §§ viii, ix, and x.

23 *An Introduction to the Principles of Morals and Legislation*, Ch. XV, §§ 18–20; more fully: *Panopticon versus New South Wales* (Simpkin and Marshall, 1843). For an account of Bentham and his 'panopticon', see Janet Semple, *Bentham's Prison* (Clarendon Press, 1993).

24 For a classic, and balanced, discussion, see James Q. Wilson, *Thinking About Crime* (Vintage Books, revised ed. 1985 (1st ed. 1975)), Ch. 8. For a sceptical account, see Franklin E. Zimring and Gordon Hawkins, *Incapacitation* (Oxford University Press, 1995).

25 Richard Posner has argued that many of the central elements in primitive law — compensation, vengeance, retribution, pollution, for instance — are economically efficient modes of deterrence (*The Economics of Justice*, 2nd ed. (Harvard University Press, 1983), Chs. 7 and 8).

26 *Gorgias*, 525b. Deterrent punishment is reserved for those who are incurable. Protagoras, however, is portrayed as a deterrence theorist (*Protagoras*, 323c–324a).

27 Aristotle seems at least to countenance punishment as a deterrent in *Nicomachean Ethics*, Bk. III, Ch. 5 and Bk. X, Ch. 9.

28 *Summa Theologica*, Quaestio LXXXVII, Art. 2; Quaestio XCII, Art. 1.

29 *De Jure Belli ac Pacis*, Bk. II, Ch. 20, §§ ix and x.

30 *Leviathan*, Ch. 28. In Ch. 30, § 23, Hobbes also mentions 'correction… of the offender' as an acceptable aim of punishment.

31 *Second Treatise*, §§ 8, 12.

32 Cesare Beccaria, *On Crimes and Punishments*, Ch. 12.

33 *An Introduction to the Principles of Morals and Legislation*, Ch. XIII, fn. a.

34 T.H. Green, *Lectures on the Principles of Political Obligation, and other writings*, ed. Paul Harris and John Morrow (Cambridge University Press, 1986), pp. 144f.

35 The deterrence theory is, of course, an expressive theory in the wider sense.

36 This does not, of course, make the theory internalist: there is no conceptual guarantee that punishment is either necessary to achieve this aim or guaranteed to do so.

37 See Duff, *Trials and Punishments*, and *Punishment, Communication, and Community*.

38 See John Braithwaite, *Crime, Shame and Reintegration* (Cambridge University Press, 1999). Braithwaite is, however, sceptical about the general effectiveness of punishment, at least as it exists in most contemporary societies.

39 See, e.g. John Braithwaite, *Crime, Shame and Reintegration*, pp. 75, 179.

40 For a clear statement of Durkheim's view, see *Moral Education: A Study in the Theory and Application of the Sociology of Education* (The Free Press, 1961; French, 1925), Ch. 10. For Stephen's view, see *Liberty, Equality, Fraternity*, ed. R.J. White (Cambridge University Press,

1967), p. 152; and *A History of the Criminal Law of England, vol. 2* (Macmillan, 1883), pp. 79f.

[41]   See, for instance, Hyam Gross, *A Theory of Criminal Justice* (Oxford University Press, 1979). Nicola Lacey also seems to think of this as the 'principal' aim of punishment (*State Punishment: Political Principles and Community Values* (Routledge, 1988), pp. 182f.).

[42]   Oliver Wendell Holmes, for instance, saw the origins of the criminal law in a concern to prevent the victims of crime from seeking their own remedies. See Holmes, *The Common Law* (Boston, MA, Little, Brown, 1963 (first published 1881)).

[43]   So, perhaps, Plato's *Crito*, 49a–50a; *Gorgias*, 525b5.

[44]   See John Finnis, *Aquinas: Moral, Political, and Legal Theory* (Oxford University Press, 1998), pp. 210–215.

[45]   See Jeffrie Murphy, *Kant: The Philosophy of Right* (Macmillan, 1970), Ch. 4. For second thoughts, see Murphy's 'Does Kant Have a Theory of Punishment?', *Columbia Law Review*, vol. lxxxvii (1987), pp. 509–532.

[46]   See Friedrich Nietzsche, *On the Genealogy of Morals*, ed. Keith Ansell-Pearson (Cambridge University Press, 1994), p. 58.

[47]   See *Gorgias*, 525b. There is, I think, nothing other than the general tenor of Plato's style to suggest that he thought the connection was what we would call a conceptual one, and the question is probably anachronistic.

[48]   See, for instance, Duff's work cited in notes 3 and 4; Jean Hampton, 'The Moral Education Theory of Punishment', *Philosophy and Public Affairs*, vol. xiii (1984), pp. 208–238; and Christopher Bennett, *The Apology Ritual* (Cambridge University Press, 2008).

[49]   See, e.g. Andrew von Hirsch, *Censure and Sanctions* (Clarendon Press, 1993); Christopher Bennett, *The Apology Ritual* (Cambridge University Press, 2008).

[50]   Bentham thought of the suffering an offender undergoes in his punishment as affording some compensatory satisfaction to the victim: see *Introduction to the Principles of Moral and Legislation*, Ch. XIII, fn. a.

[51]   See Robert Nozick, *Anarchy, State and Utopia* (Basil Blackwell, 1974), Chs. 4–6, for quite different reasons to show that punishment cannot satisfactorily be reduced to compensation.
        This theory is to be distinguished from the sort of restitution theory put forward by, e.g. David Boonin in *The Problem of Punishment*; Boonin is quite explicit that this is not a theory of punishment, but a suggestion as to what could satisfactorily *replace* punishment.

[52]   'To do away or extinguish the guilt of (one's sin)' – sense 3 for 'expiate' in the *Oxford English Dictionary*.

[53]   The most famous 'annulment' theory of punishment is presumably that of Hegel (see his *Philosophy of Right*, translated by T.M. Knox (Clarendon Press, 1952), §§ 82–103). It would be pointless here, however, to try to disentangle the threads of Hegel's thoughts on this

matter, on which there is little agreement amongst Hegel scholars. For a variety of interpretations, see, for instance, David Cooper, 'Hegel's Theory of Punishment', in Z.A. Pelzcynski (ed.), *Hegel's Political Philosophy: Problems and Perspectives* (Cambridge University Press, 1971); Peter G. Steinberger, 'Hegel on Crime and Punishment', *American Political Science Review*, vol. lxxvii (1983), pp. 858–870; Igor Primoratz, *Justifying Legal Punishment* (Humanities Press, 1989), Ch. 4; Allen Wood, *Hegel's Ethical Thought* (Cambridge University Press, 1990); and Dudley Knowles, 'Hegel on the Justification of Punishment', in Robert R. Williams (ed.), *Beyond Liberalism and Communitarianism: Studies in Hegel's Philosophy of Right* (SUNY Press, 2001). Here is Knowles, a sympathetic commentator, on Hegel on annulment: 'Unfortunately, at this stage in the argument of the *Philosophy of Right*, Hegel's analysis looks as though it collapses into a string of metaphors that darken rather than clarify the position' (Williams (ed.), *Beyond Liberalism and Communitarianism*, p. 130). For a brief and balanced account of Hegel on punishment, see Michael Inwood, *A Hegel Dictionary* (Blackwell, 1992), pp. 232ff.

54   H.L.A. Hart, *Punishment and Responsibility: Essays in the Philosophy of Law* (Clarendon Press, 1968), p. 232.

55   John Cottingham, 'Varieties of Retribution', *The Philosophical Quarterly*, vol. xxix (1979), pp. 238–246, at p. 238.

56   Joel Feinberg, *The Moral Limits of the Criminal Law. Vol. IV: Harmless Wrongdoing* (Oxford University Press, 1988), p. 159.

57   Antony Duff and David Garland (eds.), *A Reader on Punishment* (Oxford University Press, 1994), p. 6.

58   All from p. 14. (It should perhaps be added that Bennett has himself written an article called, 'The Varieties of Retributive Experience', *The Philosophical Quarterly*, vol. lii (2002).)

59   And from yet others typically referred to as retributive. For instance: the idea that the offender must 'pay for what he has done', must 'pay his debt to society'; the idea that the offender must be 'paid back' for what he has done; the idea that punishment is justified merely because the offender *deserves* it. See, for example, C.L. Ten, *Crime, Guilt and Punishment* (Clarendon Press, 1987), p. 46; Nigel Walker, *Why Punish?* (Oxford University Press, 1991), p. 67; Michael Moore, 'Justifying Retributivism', *Israel Law Review*, vol. xxvii (1993), p. 15, and *Placing Blame* (Clarendon Press, 1997); J. Angelo Corlett, 'Making Sense of Retributivism', *Philosophy*, vol. lxxvi (2001), pp. 77–110; the idea that punishment is a response to the *autonomous* nature of offenders (T.C. Liew, *The Soundest Theory of Law* (Marshall Cavendish, 2004)). (Liew also emphasizes desert, as do many who emphasize autonomy.)

60   One might, of course, *ignore* the call in the interest of mercy, or of some other value.

61   But for a defence of the view that the desire for revenge legitimates
      punishment, see Charles K.B. Barton, *Getting Even: Revenge as a Form
      of Justice* (Open Court, 1999).
62   David Boonin has argued that punishment should be completely
      replaced by restitution (see *The Problem of Punishment*); Michael
      Zimmerman has argued that legal punishment is always immoral
      and should be replaced by other 'tools' for the prevention of crime
      (*The Immorality of Punishment*); and Nathan Hanna has the begin-
      nings of a defence of abolitionism in 'Say What? A Critique of Exp-
      ressive Retributivism', and 'The Passions of Punishment', *Pacific
      Philosophical Quarterly*, vol. 90 (2009), pp. 232–250.

      But writers who recommend the abolition of punishment and the
      retention of the state are rare. Many who call themselves abolition-
      ists have as their goal merely the abolition of prisons, not the abol-
      ition of punishment. And there are many who would like to see a
      great deal of punishment replaced by some form of mediation
      between offender and victim (see, for instance, James Dignan,
      'Reintegration Through Reparation: A Way Forward for Restorative
      Justice?', in Antony Duff *et al.* (eds.), *Penal Theory and Practice:
      Tradition and Innovation in Criminal Justice* (Manchester University
      Press, 1994)); these views are, of course, quite different from
      recommending the abolition of punishment. For a brief critique of
      restorative theories, see Andrew von Hirsch, 'Penal Theories', in M.
      Tonry (ed.), *The Handbook of Crime and Punishment* (Oxford Univ-
      ersity Press, 1998), pp. 672ff.

      Utopian Socialists, such as William Morris, looked forward to a
      time when there would be no punishment — see, for instance, *News
      From Nowhere*, ed. Krishan Kumar (Cambridge University Press,
      1995), Ch. 12; but Morris saw that time as one in which there would
      also be no state.

      Michel Foucault, after his ponderous excavation of the modern
      practice of punishment, by turns fantastic and banal, does not seem
      to recommend its abolition; see *Discipline and Punish: The Birth of the
      Prison* (Peregrine Books, 1979).

      'Critical criminologists' are sceptical about the whole notion of
      crime, and favour conflict resolution quite generally as a response to
      the 'troubles' that western society 'constructs as crime'; but the dis-
      covery that most of the victims of crime are amongst the socially and
      economically disadvantaged, and that rape is not, after all, a revol-
      utionary act nor just a conflict to be resolved, turned some of them
      into 'Left Realists', who are less resistant to the idea of punishment.

      For a sympathetic and intelligent discussion of abolition, see
      William de Haan, *The Politics of Redress: Crime, Punishment and Penal
      Abolition* (Unwin Hyman, 1990). For a gently critical survey, see R.A.
      Duff, 'Penal Communications: Recent Work in the Philosophy of

Punishment', *Crime and Justice: A Review of Research*, vol. xx (1996), pp. 1–98.

63 Romans, xii.19. St Paul is, presumably, loosely quoting Deuteronomy, 32.35. Did the LORD lay claim to vengeance, or to retribution? Or do they coincide in His case?

Chapter Two

Simple Desert

'a mystic bond between wrong and punishment.'[1]

Perhaps, the most intuitively compelling of the internalist theories of punishment is, on the surface at least, very simple. I shall call it the Simple Desert Theory.[2] It has two parts, logically separable but intimately connected. First is the claim that 'we justly punish because and only because offenders deserve to suffer for their culpable wrongdoings';[3] and second that they should suffer in proportion to the moral gravity of their offences. There is no *further* reason why they deserve to suffer; it is not, for instance, that this will put things right with the victim, or with the world at large, or that it will help to reform them. A moral offence simply imposes a demand that the offender suffer in proportion to his offence. Michael Moore, who has given the most extensive and sophisticated justification of retributivism, characterizes it like this:

> By 'retributivist' I refer to one who believes that the justification for punishing a criminal is simply that the criminal deserves to be punished... Moral responsibility ('desert')... in such a view is not only necessary for justified punishment, it is also sufficient. Such sufficiency of justification gives society more than merely a *right* to punish culpable offenders. It does this, making it not unfair to punish them, but retributivism justifies more than this. For a retributivist, the moral responsibility of an offender also gives society the *duty* to punish. Retributivism, in other words, is truly a theory of justice such that, if it is true, we have an obligation to set up institutions so that retribution is achieved...

Punishment of the guilty is… for the retributivist an *intrinsic good*.[4]

We find similar sentiments in Igor Primoratz:

> The crucial tenet of retributivism [is]… a fundamental moral principle — fundamental in the sense of not being deduced from a more general ethical theory. A retributivist can put forward his basic thesis in this way, and then go on to explain it and to support it in a non-deductive way. By way of elucidating it he will say that punishment is just when it is deserved, and it is deserved by the commission of an offense. The offense committed is the sole ground of the state's right and duty to punish, and accordingly the measure of the severity of punishment as well. 'Justice' and 'just deserts' are not meant merely negatively, as constraints, but also positively, as demands for punishment of the guilty and full measure of proportion between the punishment and offense.[5]

Kant also spoke in similar terms.[6]

When we speak of an offence, we may mean either a legal offence or a moral offence. It may seem tempting to think that the most plausible version of the Simple Desert Theory will hold that it is only *legal* offences that demand punishment, because the law does not in fact punish people in virtue of having committed merely moral offences,[7] and, conversely, many legal offences are not, in themselves, moral offences. However, it is a *moral* offence that must justify punishment on the Simple Desert Theory.[8] That offenders deserve to suffer can mean only that they *morally deserve* to suffer. There is no philosophical question about whether offenders *legally deserve* to suffer; this would be merely an odd way of raising a question about legal liability. For what, then, do they morally deserve to suffer? It could hardly be a legal offence *merely as a legal offence*. A legal offence might also be a moral offence *merely in virtue of* being a legal offence (though it would take an unusual strain of legal fanaticism to make this view seem appealing), and it might then be held that *only* moral guilt which supervenes upon legal guilt can generate a desert to suffer. But that would surely be arbitrary and *ad hoc*;[9] further, no defender of the Simple Desert Theory is likely to think that the moral wrong for which murderers are punished so severely is merely their having broken the law, for others have done *that* and been punished much less severely. It may be replied that murderers deserve to suffer so severely not just because they have broken the law, but because they have broken *this particular* law. But this would simply raise the question why breaking *this particular* law should be such a serious matter, and the most obvious answer, for the Simple Desert Theorist, would be that murder is particularly immoral. In any case, an exclusive focus on *legal* offences will not respect the intuitions that lie at the base of the theory.

The best version of the theory, then, will hold that punishment is justified simply because the offender deserves to suffer in proportion to the moral seriousness of his offence.[10]

Do the Guilty Deserve to Suffer?

A theory of punishment must tell us why it is justified to inflict suffering on offenders. The Simple Desert Theory will reply that it is because they deserve to suffer. There is, of course, a vast and unsettled literature about the concept of desert.[11] For now, and for the sake of the argument, Let us simply concede that we have an intuitive sense that wrongdoers deserve to suffer because of their wrongdoing. But many will then find it inescapable to ask *why* offenders deserve to suffer. And the Simple Desert Theory refuses an answer: offenders deserve to suffer just because they have done wrong, and there is no further reason to be given. There is nothing incoherent about this; a moral system may permissibly be based upon some propositions that are not derived from further, more basic propositions. But if these propositions are widely contested, then some reason should be given as to why we should accept them. We shall return to this question later.

Who is Permitted to Punish?

The Simple Desert Theory holds not only that the guilty deserve to suffer. It holds, in addition, that *someone*, perhaps everyone, has an obligation (or at least a permission) *to make* them suffer. This is a further step; what is supposed to justify it?[12]

It is a further step, not because although someone may, *prima facie*, deserve something, there may be overriding reasons for not giving it to him.[13] It is a further step because 'x deserves to φ' does not, even *prima facie*, generally entail 'There is a y who ought to bring it about that x φs'.[14] 'Pirie deserves to win the race', for instance, does not entail that anyone, let alone everyone, has an obligation, or even a permission, to see to it that he does so. Pirie himself has a permission to do all that he fairly can to try to win; but he does not have that permission in virtue of the fact that he deserves to win; even undeserving competitors are normally entitled to win races. Again, 'Pirie deserves to be disqualified' does not entail that someone ought to disqualify him. The rules of the game may have made no provision for disqualification; or they may not, by an oversight, cover this case. In both cases, further premises would be needed for the entailment to go through. There seems no reason to think things different with 'x deserves to suffer'. Sometimes, of course, the further premises need no explicit statement; the surroundings already make them clear or at least point in the general direction of what they would be. But 'He deserves to suffer, therefore there is someone who ought to make him suffer' does not seem to be like that. A developed legal system may, of course, specify officials whose job it is to see to it that offenders get their deserts, and then the existence of that system can serve as an unspoken, missing premise. But that cannot help the Simple Desert Theory because that theory is supposed to supply a moral basis for such a system, not to ride upon its back.

That people should get what they deserve might be thought to be a matter of justice. We might, then, add a premise to the effect that everyone has a duty to do what is just. This would give us the desired conclusion, but the additional premise is problematic. The only sense in which it is uncontroversial that we all have a duty to do what is just is that we all have an agent-relative, *prima facie* duty *to refrain from doing injustice*. It is certainly far from uncontroversial that we have a general duty to prevent injustice wherever we can, let alone a duty to promote justice wherever we can. Of course, some unjust states of affairs cry out for positive rectification, and impose a positive duty on all of those who could rectify them. But that is because injustice usually generates other morally relevant considerations. Where, for instance, resources are distributed unjustly with the result that some people lead lives that are barely worth living, it is plausible to think that here we have a duty to act (though many people seem to deny even this). But it is also plausible to think that here it is the quality of the lives involved that generates the moral duty, rather than the simple injustice. Where people lead lives of misery simply because, say, there are no resources to distribute (and not because of any injustice), our duty to help is equally clear and strong. And, conversely, there can be injustice amongst the affluent, but it is not at all clear that an unjust distribution of luxuries cries out for rectification; perhaps no one cares about it.

Typically, it is the suffering involved in distributive injustice that makes it plausible to hold that the injustice in such cases is everyone's business. In the case of retributive justice, in the way that this is understood by the Simple Desert Theory, this is not so. No one suffers merely because a wrongdoer does not get his just deserts. There is merely an abstract principle at stake. Why is it my business, or the business of anyone else, to take care of that principle? Without a satisfactory answer, the theory will seem to fail in one of the ways mentioned on p. 30: it will involve an unacceptable moral judgment.

Punishment and The State

A theory of punishment must also explain why it is justifiable for *the state*, and, for the most part, only the state, to punish offenders. After all, it is not clear that the state has the right to pursue every legitimate moral aim. The Simple Desert Theory can explain this in either (or both) of two ways.

One could simply hold that the state has a right, and perhaps a duty, to pursue moral aims simply for their own sake, aims which have nothing to do with the welfare of citizens. Exacting retribution might be one of these aims.[15] But this would involve an acceptance of the purest form of legal moralism, and few people, including conservative political theorists, are attracted to such a view.[16]

The second strategy holds that giving the state the right to exact retribution would serve a legitimate instrumental purpose: it would simply be the fairest and most economical way of ensuring that retribution were exacted as generally as reasonably possible.[17] Punishment by the state would then be justified—in principle—by the demands of justice. But the justification would only be in principle. As Douglas Husak has pointed out in this connection, in the real world the criminal justice system is extremely costly, and not merely in financial terms; and given a desire to exact retribution generally, consistently, and fairly, this is surely inevitable. And it is not clear that these costs are justified merely by the duty, if there is one, to exact retribution.[18] Even if the costs were much less great than they are, one might still wonder whether the duty to exact retribution for moral wrongdoing were stringent enough to justify the costs.

The Problem of Commensurability

It is often said that what an offender deserves is suffering that matches his offence. But a punishment can match an offence in any number of ways. Trivially, any punishment that is prescribed by the criminal justice system for an offence can be said, in one sense, to 'match' that offence; the Simple Desert Theory obviously requires more than that. The word 'match' may suggest 'an eye for an eye, and a tooth for a tooth'; but this adage is itself less informative than might appear. Clearly, it suggests 'like for like'. But that merely raises the question: 'Like for like *in what respect*?' Evidently, the idea cannot be that a punishment should match the offender's act in *every* respect. We are presumably to focus on some morally salient aspect of what he did. Often an act description may be thought to carry the morally salient aspects with it, as, arguably, with such act descriptions as 'rape' and 'murder'. But 'causing the loss of a tooth' does not. And if the adage simply informs us that we should put out the eyes and teeth of those who have put out the eyes and teeth of others, most people will not think that this captures a suitable conception of desert.[19]

The notion of matching must be cashed in terms of proportion: what an offender deserves is punishment proportional in its severity to the moral gravity of the offence. But the idea that there can be any sort of suitable *proportion* between the severity of a punishment and the moral gravity of an offence is surely doubtful.[20]

The doubt would be laid to rest if a simple theory were correct, namely the theory that offence and punishment are commensurable on a scale of *utility*: we can measure the moral gravity of an offence in terms of the harm (disutility) it caused, and we can compare this with the severity of a punishment measured in terms of the disutility to the offender.[21] This assumes, of course, that utilities are measurable and interpersonally comparable; but, given that, we should then have a way of comparing the severity of a punishment with the moral gravity of the offence, and thus a precise, and coherent, interpretation of the idea that the punishment should match the crime.

But there is no prospect of this being correct. For one thing, punishments standardly and acceptably impose considerably greater loss of utility than do the offences for which they are imposed. Unsuccessful attempts provide the most obvious examples (even when the costs of detection and conviction are factored in). But the pattern is pervasive. 'Surely the average person, even the average thief, would prefer to have his car stolen than to be confined for a month or two… Not very many people would prefer spending six months in a typical American jail to receiving a serious beating that left no long-term disability.'[22]

It is also worth pointing out that, since offenders' utility scales differ enormously, any system which approached what is required here would have to allow almost unfettered discretion to sentencing authorities, discretion the exercise of which would inevitably involve immense guesswork, and which would probably be politically quite impossible.[23]

But there is a more fundamental objection: this theory makes no reference to the mental state in which the offence was committed. Without that, no one will think that we have an appropriate notion of moral gravity. The moral gravity of an offence is a compound of the *wrongness of the action* and the *culpability of the agent* in committing it.[24] And, whatever account we give of culpability, two things seem clear. First, it cannot be measured simply in terms of utility; second, it comes in degrees: action-types which are otherwise identical can be performed more and less culpably. But if the severity of a punishment is measured in terms of utility, and the moral gravity of an offence is measured, in part at least, not in terms of utility, then we should surely doubt whether there is an appropriate common scale on which the severity of a punishment can be more than, or less than, or equal to the moral gravity of an offence.

This is not, of course, to deny that there are common scales on which we may measure and compare the severity of a punishment and the moral gravity of an offence — assuming both to be real properties. The members of *any* pair of measurable properties are commensurable on some or other trivial scale. The question is whether they are commensurable on any *appropriate* scale, a scale that is suitable for the purpose for which the measurements are being made and is at least broadly consistent with our intuitions. And this is more doubtful. An action's having a certain moral quality might be causally connected with a rise in the blood pressure of ordinary observers; so too might the severity of a punishment. Or perhaps there might be some causal connection between the moral gravity of an offence, the severity of a punishment, and public reactions of approval and disapproval. But it is surely obvious that such measurements and comparisons as these would not be appropriate for a theory offering a *moral* justification of punishment.

But though moral gravity may not itself be a psychological reaction, may it not be measured by psychological reactions, in the way that temperature, say, is measured by the movement of a column of mercury? But the analogy is faulty. We measure temperature by observing how it moves a column of mercury because temperature just is (a measure of) mean kinetic energy. But whatever moral gravity may be it is not identical with, or a measure of, or reducible to public or private sentiments. We might, conceivably, hold that such sentiments are good guides to the proportion between a punishment and the moral gravity of an offence.[25] But we could do that only after we had explained what exactly it *meant* to talk of a proportion here; and that we have yet to see. If there is a suitable common scale on which the severity of a punishment may be compared with the moral gravity of an offence, we have not yet discovered it.[26]

Accepting this, a weaker version of the Simple Desert Theory might simply hold that we can at least *rank* offences in terms of moral gravity, and that we can rank punishments in terms of severity, and that we can, in some suitable way, pair off values on those two scales.[27] This weaker theory could take different forms. The most minimal, a 'thin' version, would require only that we rank offences and punishments in a purely ordinal manner, and then require that 'the serious offences [be] punished more relative to the less serious ones'[28] (we may take 'serious' here to mean 'morally grave'). A less minimal theory, a 'thick' version, would rank offences and punishments on an interval scale, ensuring that the *magnitude of difference* between any two offences is reflected in a similar magnitude of difference between the punishments assigned to them.

Unsurprisingly, since it offers only ordinal comparisons, the 'thin' version is unresponsive to even the most basic intuitions about punishment. On this version of the theory, all that an offence deserves is a level of punishment more severe than would be given for a less morally grave offence. This requirement would be satisfied if, for instance, aggravated murder were punished by torture and death whilst non-aggravated murder, and all lesser offences, were punished by graded, but small, fines. Anyone attracted by the Simple Desert Theory will hold that we have a conception of desert according to which such a system would not give offenders what they deserve; the thin theory has no ability to articulate this conception.

The 'thick' version hopes to remedy this, in part at least. Some may perhaps doubt whether its talk of 'magnitudes of difference' really makes sense here. But even if it does, it does not ensure that 'serious offences should be punished severely and minor offences leniently';[29] it would be consistent with a system in which *all* of the punishments would strike us as too lenient, or too severe, so long as the magnitude of the interval between the seriousness of two offences were matched by the magnitude of the interval between the severity of the corresponding punishments. The parking violator would have got his just deserts *whatever* his punishment so long as those whose offences were morally more grave than his received a correspondingly more severe punishment. This should not strike us as an acceptable moral theory of punishment.

We have so far questioned only whether the severity of a punishment and the moral gravity of an offence may be commensurable, having accepted, for the sake of the argument, the two notions themselves. We should now, however, query the notion of the moral gravity of an offence. As so far characterized, this is a compound of (at least) two things: the wrongness of the action and the culpability of the agent.[30] But why should we think that wrongness and culpability are themselves commensurable? Both, after all, surely come in degrees. Some actions are more wrong than others. And some agents are more culpable than others. But, as I have said, the wrongness of an action is typically measured partly in terms of the disutility caused to victims; culpability is not measured in those terms.[31] If so, the problem about the commensurability of offence and punishment seems likely to reproduce itself here as a (more fundamental) problem about the commensurability of wrongness and culpability, and so about the notion of moral gravity itself. This in turn would prevent even the weakest ordinal ranking of offences.

This may seem surprising, and C.L. Ten tries to defend the notion by means of an analogy:

> [T]he construction of an ordinal scale of crimes is a project that seems capable of being carried out. Those who are sceptical should look at analogous cases. Thus when tutors and teachers rank the essays of their students, they do not have only one relevant feature to look for. There are a number of different features — originality, understanding of the issues discussed, lucidity of presentation, etc. — which each makes a contribution to the quality of the essay. An essay may be strong in one dimension but weak in another, and yet it is possible to make an overall assessment of the essay as being better or worse than another. Indeed it is also possible to argue that one essay is only marginally better than another essay, whereas it is considerably better than a third essay. Of course such judgements are sometimes controversial, but a teacher knows how to argue for his or her judgement by pointing to relevant features of the essays and the relative weights to be given to each feature in the context of the work as a whole. Now the problems faced by retributivists in ranking offences are not very different from those confronting teachers in ranking essays.[32]

But what is supposed to make it clear that teachers really do know how to weigh the different factors involved in assessing an essay? Of course, teachers are often *quite confident* that they are making comparisons of the sort Ten mentions. But that doesn't establish much; after all, many people are often quite confident that they can make the disputed judgments about moral gravity too. If this confident belief is called into question it will be of little avail to appeal to a different sort of case where — again — we had nothing more than the confident belief that we successfully perform the activity in question.

Any scepticism we might harbour about whether teachers really can make the sort of judgments in question would be reasonably dispelled by an account of how such judgments are actually made. But such an account would leave in place any scepticism we might harbour concerning our judgments about moral gravity. All that would dispel *that* scepticism would be an account of how *those* judgments are supposed to proceed. After all, it was never in doubt that there are cases in which we arrive at genuine rankings on the basis of two independent variables. Uncontroversially, for instance, we commonly do this for temperature and humidity, giving what is known as a heat index.[33] But knowing how we do it in that case throws no light at all on how we are supposed to do it in the case of moral gravity. And it does not seem likely that an account of how it is done in the case of a teacher ranking students' essays will throw any more. There are numerous ways in which this might be done. Assume, for instance, that the notion of general intelligence is a suitably straightforward notion, and can itself be fitted onto an appropriate scale; we might then, conceivably, be able to compare the lucidity and originality of two essays for how much intelligence each displays. Again, in principle, an appropriate scale might be generated by a concern for certain sorts of predictions; we might want to know, for instance, how successful in some sphere will be someone who can achieve *this* degree of lucidity and *this* degree of originality, and the two dimensions may be measurable and comparable by reference to this predictive concern.[34] But this account will tell us nothing about how to compare the quite different elements supposedly involved in the notion of moral gravity, just as an account of how we measure the heat index will tell us nothing about how to compare two students' essays.

It is tempting, perhaps, to reply that we all think that someone who deliberately murders has done something morally more grave than someone who steals from a shop, and that this is as good a judgment as any. But this is not clear. The thought alluded should not be confused with the thought that he has done something morally more wrong, or something more harmful. It goes beyond that, or so the Simple Desert Theory says, and aggregates, or somehow combines, the two properties, wrongness and culpability, to produce a third property, moral gravity. We are surely owed some explanation as to how this judgmental feat is accomplished. And with no explanation we are surely entitled to be sceptical.

Why Should We Accept the Theory?

Given all of these questions, we are surely justified in asking for some reason to believe what seemed intuitively obvious, that punishment is justified because offenders deserve to be punished for their offences.

Self-evidence

It might perhaps be suggested that it is self-evident, unable to be understood without being accepted. But this seems weak.[35] There are, after all, many sensitive and intelligent people who claim precisely that they do not accept that the guilty deserve to suffer.[36] One could say that this is a failure of understanding on their part. Possibly so, but they typically manifest competence elsewhere with all of the constituents of the proposition: as far as one can tell, they know what guilt is, what desert is, and what suffering is. The mere assertion that they do not, after all, understand these concepts should be based upon more than their disputing the very question at issue.[37]

More would be provided if it could be shown that the proposition seemed to have the sort of centrality in our thought that makes it more or less inescapable. Think, by contrast, of the judgment that, normally at least, one ought not deliberately to kill innocent people.[38] The depth of our commitment to this judgment is not merely psychological, but a matter of its place in a whole web of moral thought, and it is hard to see how any of the web could survive if that judgment were given up. If the value of one's life generated no restrictions on the behaviour of others then it is hard to see what else could sensibly do so. A moral system in which theft, say, was prohibited but murder was not would seem bizarre. It would strike us either as containing a crippling inconsistency or as being merely a set of taboos. The judgment that the guilty deserve to suffer, on the other hand, is not like that; it can be extracted from the web of our moral thought leaving the rest of it more or less, perhaps entirely, intact.

Consistency

Another suggestion might be that the theory is simply one instance of a quite general principle of desert, a unitary principle whose instances include, e.g. both that the guilty deserve to suffer for their wrongdoing, with no benefit to anyone, and that the tortfeasor deserves contract sanctions against him (Michael Moore's example).[39] But if there is such a principle, it is unlikely that the Simple Desert Theory is an instance of it, because that theory requires comparisons that are conceptually impossible; most other desert conceptions would be able to resist this charge. Many, for instance, do not involve real *comparisons* at all. For instance, we may say that he who has put the most effort into a competition, other things being equal, deserves to win; but there is no comparison here, except in a degenerate sense. And we might say that the one who put in most effort deserves to win *more than* does the one who put in the next most, but again there is no real comparison here: this would be merely a misleading way of saying that only the one who put in the most effort deserves to win (the one who put in the next most effort does not deserve to win at all; what he deserves is to come second).

Of course, certain comparative notions may get a hold here too. We may say that one winner in a competition deserved to win more than did another winner in another competition. Both deserved to win, but perhaps one had put in a much larger amount of effort. But now we are dealing with comparisons that we can actually make. The degree of desert here is, say, a function of the margin of victory and the amount of effort. There is no incoherence in the idea that these things can be measured and compared. We should need, of course, to decide how to weight these two dimensions. But that will be given by our goals in having this sort of competition at all. (Compare the way in which educational aims supply a way of comparing the different dimensions along which students' essays can be evaluated.)

We find the same thing in many other cases that involve comparisons: the comparisons involve commensurable quantities. This is often the case when we are speaking of reparation and compensation, for instance. If you injure my property, then your liability is in proportion to my loss; this comparison can usually be carried out uncontroversially in, for instance, monetary terms.[40] Sometimes, perhaps, it cannot. People sometimes say that their loss is immeasurable. Often, this just means that it is greater than any possible compensation. That is perfectly coherent and perfectly possible. But it is itself a comparison, and without the possibility of genuine comparisons we have no grip on the notion of just compensation.

We should in any case question whether there is such a thing as a unitary principle of desert. Compensation, after all, surely has everything to do with the notion of putting things right; that is what compensation *means*. (In most jurisdictions, compensation awards are often intended to have a deterrent effect too.) Whatever principle that derives from, if any, it seems unlikely to have the same source as the claim that those who have culpably done wrong deserve to suffer when this does not put things right and indeed benefits no one in any way.[41]

The Principle of Abduction

Michael Moore also suggests a different sort of justification, one that appeals to the 'principle of abduction'.[42] That principle might suggest that we should accept the Simple Desert Theory because it is the best explanation of a range of particular judgments, or emotions, reactions that are widely and deeply held.[43] Michael Moore, for instance, describes some particularly brutal crimes, crimes sure to evoke strong condemnation in almost any reader, and suggests that the best explanation of these reactions is an objective quality of *desert*, an 'objectively existing' property, which 'causes' these 'retributive' reactions in us.[44]

If that is how the argument is to go, then we should require, first, that the phenomena be accurately and carefully described and, second, that the theory that explains them be, according to some plausible metric, the best available explanation. There is surely doubt about both of these.

Moore says that the judgments in question are shared by 'me and most people I know'.[45] As a set of phenomena to be explained abductively by the presence of an objective property of desert, this is a pretty poor sample. Who are 'most' of the 'people' that Moore knows? Law professors and law students? Middle class Americans? A more random sample of Americans? A random sample of humanity? And what is to be said of the few people who, it is implied, Moore knows but who do not share these judgments? Perhaps they are self-deceived or have a corrupt sensibility. Perhaps; but something will have to be said about them. Moore points out that, often, people are repelled by 'retributivism' because it is associated in their minds with disreputable emotions, or based upon fallacious arguments, neither of which provides good grounds for rejecting the theory. This is no doubt true, but leaves it open that others reject the principle for perfectly good reasons.

Moore also challenges us to imagine the judgments that we would make if we had *ourselves* committed awful crimes. No doubt he is right that we should feel guilty; but it is too quick to claim, as Moore does, that the sense of guilt involves the sense that one ought to suffer for what one has done: '[T]o feel guilty is to judge that we must suffer.'[46] Whether this is true as a psychological generalization is not, of course, relevant; all that is relevant is the conceptual claim, and that is surely doubtful.

Second, there is surely doubt about the correct interpretation of the judgments in question. The initial judgment is that someone should suffer for what he did, with, on pain of circularity, no thought of *desert*.[47] But, so far, this could be simply the expression of a vicarious desire for revenge.[48] The desire for revenge is, of course, a personal matter in a way that judgments about retribution are not.[49] I can take revenge only on someone who has injured *me* or *my family* or, in general, *my x*; and only I, or my agent, can do that. However, I do not myself have to have been injured directly in order that it be appropriate to speak of my seeking revenge; it is enough if the injury is suffered by someone with whom I identify in an appropriate way.[50] This sort of identification is typically mediated by close personal ties, or merely family ties. But there are other vehicles of identification; for instance, we readily identify with the victims of particularly awful crimes;[51] and people may feel personally aggrieved, more or less consciously, that offenders have offended when they themselves have refrained;[52] such phenomena make it appropriate to speak of *revenge* here. And it should be no surprise if, in a culture which exalts justice and denigrates revenge, there are those who wish to express such desires in the language of justice rather than of revenge. So the so-called 'retributive' reactions may plausibly be thought to be, as many have suggested, no more than the desire for 'vengeance in disguise'. Those who, in the first person, claim to judge that they themselves should suffer for their crimes could hardly be accused simply of the desire for vengeance. But it is not difficult to think of these responses as motivated by the deep desire for consistency between their judgments of others and their judgments about themselves.

Even if we were to agree that the phenomena had been correctly described, the story would not be over. We should still want to know that the Simple Desert Theory is the best explanation of them. And there must surely be serious doubts about this. Moore labours mightily to answer these doubts,[53] but they surely remain. His whole metaphysical structure is highly disputable, and disputed, at almost every turn. This is not, of course, to say that it is not correct. But, as is well known, many writers, such as John Mackie,[54] have tried to give a less metaphysically freighted, evolutionary, explanation of our tendency to make these judgments, one which, if it were plausible, might seem to undercut Moore's argument. Moore does not deny the plausibility of such accounts.[55] He simply replies that one may give a perfectly good evolutionary account of, say, the physical sciences without this undermining our 'beliefs in the physical sciences'; why, then, should the availability of an evolution-

ary account of our retributive judgments undercut his own
account of them? But it is important to note here that evolutionary explanations of human belief-forming capacities are
not usually thought to compete with such justifications as we
ordinarily offer for the beliefs we form. They are usually
taken to explain why such belief-forming capacities generally
result in justified beliefs.[56] By contrast, the sort of theory
envisaged by Mackie clearly *does* compete with Moore's
theory because it leaves out, as unnecessary, the crucial
causal story that Moore tells linking our moral judgments to
a supposedly objectively existing property. And if Mackie's
explanation is otherwise as plausible as Moore's, then the
demands of economy surely dictate that we accept Mackie's
explanation, or a similar one.

Heuristic guides

A fourth suggestion, one we also find in Moore, supposes
that there is a weaker connection between the 'retributive'
judgments we make and the principle that is supposed to
explain them: our emotions are *good heuristic guides* to the
moral truth.[57]

Emotions, Moore points out, have a propositional (or
proposition-like) content (one is angry *that p*, for instance)
and are constrained by requirements of proportionality (it
makes sense to judge that someone is *too* angry or *insufficiently* angry). They thus have a form suitable for acting as
guides to the truth.

It is true that, without these characteristics, emotions
could hardly function as heuristic guides at all; but that does
not imply that, with them, they are good heuristic guides.
And that they are in fact so Moore gives no real argument
for; he simply appeals to the well-known phenomenon that,
having dealt with a moral dilemma by having done what, all
things considered, one thinks was the right thing to do, one
might still feel guilty about that's having, say, required one
to violate someone's rights: one might, for instance, have had
to sacrifice one innocent person to save a great many more.[58]
The residual feeling of guilt, it might be thought, is a pointer
to the moral truth that one, perhaps justifiably, did someone
a moral wrong. But plainly, to argue from such phenomena
to the claim that the emotions are good moral guides is

simply to assume what has to be proved. Such situations, after all, present *dilemmas*: one did what, all things considered, seemed right and yet one is left with a feeling of guilt at the way one had to treat someone. Now if one were to *assume* that the emotions were good moral guides in such cases, then one should of course accept that, in some sense, one had not acted rightly. But, the cases in question *being dilemmatic*, one might, alternatively, think that the emotions were here *poor* guides to the moral truth, and that one had, after all, acted entirely rightly. That would not in itself be surprising. Everyone should admit that, in all sorts of cases, including cases of this sort perhaps, our emotions float free of what even we ourselves take to be morally correct. So too they might float free of what we think morally correct in the case of what Moore identifies as the 'retributive' emotions.

Natural and appealing though the Simple Desert Theory may seem to be, there is, I have tried to suggest, little to be said for it and much to be said against it. Anyone attracted to an internalist theory should, then, look elsewhere.

---

[1]   Oliver Wendell Holmes, *The Common Law* (Boston, MA, Little, Brown, 1963 (1st ed. 1881)), p. 37.

[2]   Jesper Ryberg also uses this phrase, although for a slightly different theory: he interprets the proportionality requirement merely in terms of an ordinal ranking (see *The Ethics of Proportionate Punishment: A Critical Investigation* (Kluwer, 2004)); the theory really requires a cardinal ranking of both offences and punishments.

[3]   Michael Moore, 'A Tale of Two Theories', *Criminal Justice Ethics*, vol. xxviii (2009), pp. 27–48, at p. 31. See also his *Placing Blame* (Clarendon Press, 1997).

[4]   *Placing Blame*, pp. 84, 87f., 91, footnotes omitted; cf. 'The Moral Worth of Retribution', in Ferdinand Mount (ed.), *Responsibility, Character and the Emotions* (Cambridge University Press, 1987), pp. 181f; and 'A Tale of Two Theories', pp. 27–48.

Note that Moore here seems to conflate two different questions: (1) whether the theory gives merely a necessary condition for the justification of punishment, or both necessary and sufficient conditions, and (2) the question of whether it justifies merely a permission to punish or an obligation. Nicola Lacey also confuses these distinct issues in *State Punishment: Political Principles and Community Values* (Routledge, 1988), p. 16. Moore's considered view is that moral wrongdoing gives a necessary and sufficient condition of a *prima facie* duty to punish (*prima facie* because of the possibility that there may be countervailing considerations which might override the justification; sufficiency conditions are, as he puts it, 'contextual' ('Justifying Retributivism', *Israel Law Review*, vol. xxvii (1993), pp. 34f.; and *Placing Blame*, pp. 173f.)).

5   *Justifying Legal Punishment* (Humanities Press, 1989), pp. 147f. Primoratz also holds an expressive theory of punishment; see his 'Punishment as Language', *Philosophy*, vol. liv (1989), pp. 187–205.

6   See *The Metaphysical Elements of Justice: Part 1 of the Metaphysics of Morals*, translated by John Ladd (Macmillan, 1965), pp. 331ff. It is, however, very hard to know just what Kant's theory of punishment is. See Thomas E. Hill, Jr., 'Kant's Anti-Moralistic Strain', *Theoria*, vol. xliv (1978), pp. 131–151 (rp. in Thomas E. Hill, Jr., *Dignity and Practical Reason in Kant's Moral Theory* (Cornell University Press, 1992)); and Jeffrie Murphy, 'Does Kant Have a Theory of Punishment?', *Columbia Law Review*, vol. lxxxvii (1987), pp. 509–532.

7   This is not, of course, to deny that legislators sometimes make behaviour illegal simply because it is, in their view, immoral; but it is then punished because it is illegal.

8   Cf. H.L.A. Hart, *Punishment and Responsibility: Essays in the Philosophy of Law* (Clarendon Press, 1968), pp. 231f.; and Moore, *Placing Blame*, pp. 184ff.

9   Antony Duff argues that at least some offences exhibit what he calls 'civic arrogance' and are thus moral offences (R.A. Duff, 'Crime, Prohibition, and Punishment', *Journal of Applied Philosophy*, vol. xix (2002), pp. 97–108). For a careful explanation of why this will not do the work required, see Douglas Husak, '*Malum Prohibitum* and Retributivism', in R.A. Duff and Stuart Green (eds.), *Defining Crimes: Essays on the Special Part of the Criminal Law* (Oxford University Press, 2005).

10   So, for instance, Moore, *Placing Blame*, pp. 209, 254, 256, *et passim*.

11   George Sher, *Desert* (Princeton University Press) is still a good general discussion. But the literature in general seems even more than is usual in philosophy to depend upon contradictory intuitions. (Cf. Brian Barry, *Political Argument: A Reissue with a New Introduction* (Harvester Wheatsheaf, 1990 (1st ed. 1965)), p. 107. Barry's scepticism about the usefulness of desert remains robust in the later edition of the book.)

12   Cf. Brian Barry, *Political Argument*, p. 106; David Lyons, *Ethics and the Rule of Law* (Cambridge University Press, 1984), pp. 150f.

13   This issue is raised by David Dolinko, 'Some Thoughts About Retributivism', *Ethics*, vol. ci (1991), pp. 537–559; Moore replies to it in *Placing Blame*, pp. 172ff.

14   Moore seems to overlook this in *Placing Blame*; see pp. 172ff.

15   Cp. Moore: '…because an action is morally wrong is always a legitimate reason to prohibit it with criminal legislation' (*Placing Blame*,

p. 70); see also 'A Tale of Two Theories', p. 31. But Moore places considerable restraints on legislation motivated by legal moralism; their 'upshot is that legal moralism hardly justifies much of the criminal legislation already on the books' (*ibid.*, p. 33). (He holds that 'our most obvious and most stringent moral obligations are about causing serious harms to others' (*Placing Blame*, p. 662).)

16 So-called legal moralism often turns out to have a consequentialist base which would be quite alien to the Simple Desert Theory. J.F. Stephen, for instance, is often taken to hold a form of legal moralism, but in fact his views have a firmly utilitarian basis, a version of what we would today call motive-utilitarianism (see *Liberty, Fraternity, Equality* (Cambridge University Press, 1967)). Again, when Lord Devlin famously spoke of the right of the state to enforce morality, what was being granted was the right to uphold the *generally accepted* morality, on the ground that this is, in various ways, in the interest of the state's security (see Patrick Devlin, *The Enforcement of Morals* (Oxford University Press, 1968)). See also H.L.A. Hart, *Law, Liberty and Morality* (Clarendon Press, 1963); and Ronald Dworkin, *Taking Rights Seriously* (Duckworth, 1977), Ch. 10. Differently, legal moralism is often confused with a sort of intrinsic majoritarianism but this, again, is utterly alien to the Simple Desert Theory.

17 Moore holds this too; see 'A Tale of Two Theories', p. 42.

18 Douglas Husak, *Overcriminalization: The Limits of the Criminal Law* (Oxford University Press, 2008), pp. 203ff.

19 Nor is it clear that it was meant to in, for instance, *Exodus* 21:22ff., *Leviticus* 24:17ff., *Deuteronomy* 19:16ff. But for the claim that the *Lex Talionis* is what is required by desert, see Jeffrey Reiman, 'Justice, Civilization, and the Death Penalty; Answering van den Haag', *Philosophy and Public Affairs*, vol. xiv (1985), pp. 115–148.

20 See, for instance, Hastings Rashdall, *The Theory of Good and Evil*, vol. 1 (Clarendon Press, 1907), p. 289; H.L.A. Hart, *Punishment and Responsibility: Essays in the Philosophy of Law* (Clarendon Press, 1968), p. 161; C.L. Ten, *Crime, Guilt, and Punishment* (Clarendon Press, 1987), pp. 150ff.; Nicola Lacey, *State Punishment: Political Principles and Community Values* (Routledge, 1988), pp. 20f.; Michael Davis, 'Harm and Retribution', *Philosophy and Public Affairs*, vol. xv (1986), pp. 236–266 (esp. pp. 252ff.); and Ted Honderich, *Punishment: The Supposed Justifications Revisited* (Pluto Books, 2006), pp. 30ff.

21 There are, of course, more and less complicated ways of measuring that (for a more complicated way see, for instance, Andrew von Hirsch, *Censure and Sanctions* (Clarendon Press, 1993), Ch. 4).

22 Warren Quinn, 'The Right to Threaten and the Right to Punish', *Philosophy and Public Affairs*, vol. xiv (1985), p. 352. See also Alan Goldman, 'The Paradox of Punishment', *Philosophy and Public Affairs*, vol. ix (1979), pp. 42–58. The point was made by Hugo Grotius, *De Jure Paci ad Belli*, Bk. II, Ch. 20, § xxxii.

[23]   Cf. 'Subjectively, three years' imprisonment may mean very different things to a twenty-three-year-old gang member, for whom it is a
rite of passage; a forty-year-old employed husband and father, for
whom it will likely destroy the material conditions of his and his
family's lives; a frightened, effeminate twenty-year-old middle class
student, for whom it may result in sexual victimization; or a
seventy-year old, for whom it may be life imprisonment' (Michael
Tonry, 'Proportionality, Parsimony, and Interchangeability of Punishments', p. 73, in Antony Duff *et al.* (eds.), *Penal Theory and Practice:
Tradition and Innovation in Criminal Justice* (Manchester University
Press, 1994)). This point is discussed in detail in Jesper Ryberg, *The
Ethics of Proportionate Punishment: A Critical Investigation* (Kluwer,
2004).

   The point is also made by T.H. Green: see *Lectures on the Principles
of Political Obligation, and other writings*, p. 147.

[24]   So Moore: 'desert is a function of two things — 'how wrongful was
the act done, and how culpable was the mental state of the actor
who did such a wrong' ('A Tale of Two Theories', p. 37); cf. also
Placing Blame, p. 180.

   Jurisdictions routinely require that, in sentencing, both the
seriousness of the offence and the culpability of the offender be
taken into account. For numerous examples, see Julian V. Roberts,
Punishing Persistent Offenders (Oxford University Press, 2008), Ch. 5,
but also *passim*.

[25]   So Moore, *Placing Blame*, Ch. 3.

[26]   Moore is a (metaphysical) realist about moral properties, but the
doubts I express about the genuineness of the notion of a proportion
here are not doubts about that realism; even an Expressivist will
want his moral responses to be responses to real comparisons
between real properties.

[27]   Ten, *Crime, Guilt, and Punishment*, pp. 158ff. Ten, it should be said,
does not intend this as a substitute for the Simple Desert Theory. For
him, as for many others, it is intended to provide constraints upon
an otherwise broadly utilitarian framework for punishment. 'The
constraints imposed by the principle on the pursuit of utilitarian
aims rule out the kinds of exemplary punishments considered
earlier in which a minor offender received a heavy penalty. They
also rule out a small fine for certain types of murder even if this can
be justified on utilitarian grounds' (pp. 159f.). In terms of the distinction that I made earlier, for Ten this is only (part of) a theory of
sentencing, not a theory of punishment. This does not, of course,
make it any more responsive to our intuitions.

[28]   Ten, *Crime, Guilt, and Punishment*, p. 158.

[29]   Ten, *Crime, Guilt, and Punishment*, p. 158.

[30]   I assume for the sake of the argument that the moral gravity of an
offence really is a function of just these two properties. This seems

most unlikely. But the addition of any further properties will not make the problem more tractable; quite the reverse.

31 Though the disutility to the offender of not performing a prohibited action can sometimes lessen culpability.

32 *Crime, Guilt, and Punishment*, p. 155.

33 For a formal account, see D.H. Krantz, R.D. Luce, P. Suppes and A. Tversky, *Foundations of Measurement. Vol. 1: Additive and Polynomial Representations* (Academic Press, 1971), pp. 17f. Indeed, there is an indefinite number of ways, but none of them appropriate, in which we could do it for the elements of moral gravity (assuming them to be severally measurable).

34 I assume that lucidity and originality are here straightforward, scalar properties.

35 Cf. Christopher Bennett, 'The Varieties of Retributive Experience', *The Philosophical Quarterly*, vol. lii (2002), p. 148.

36 Here are four examples:
'[T]he old conviction still lingers in the popular view of Criminal Justice: it seems still to be widely held that Justice requires pain to be inflicted on a man who had done wrong, even if no benefit result either to him or to others from the pain. Personally, I am so far from holding this view that I have an instinctive and strong moral aversion to it' (Henry Sidgwick, *The Methods of Ethics* (Macmillan, 7th ed. 1907), p. 281);
'[T]he only thing that human beings 'deserve' in this life is *good*,... no matter what evil a person has committed, no one is justified in doing further evil to her' (Jean Hampton, 'The Moral Education Theory of Punishment', *Philosophy and Public Affairs*, vol. xiii (1984), p. 237);
'We are against pointless suffering, even of murderers' (John Braithwaite and Philip Pettit, *Not Just Deserts* (Clarendon Press, 1990), p. 175).
'I believe very strongly... that no one could ever deserve to suffer' (Derek Parfit, *On What Matters, vol.* 2 (Oxford University Press, 2010), p. 455).

37 A point, it seems to me, overlooked by Michael Moore, *Placing Blame*, pp. 221, 223f.

38 Even primitive 'warrior societies' have restrictions on killing the innocent.

39 Cf. Michael Moore, *Placing Blame*, pp. 170ff.

40 There are, of course, immense complications in the notion of just compensation, but none that touch the present point.

41 (Moore admits on p. 171 (fn. 3) that he is 'regimenting the use of' 'desert' in his claim that there is a unitary principle of desert, though I think he is regimenting it in ways he does not recognize.)

42 *Placing Blame*, pp. 162, 176ff.

43 *Placing Blame*, pp. 98f., 163. Moore speaks indifferently of 'judgments' and 'emotions'. His considered view is, or should be, I think, that the *emotions* are good heuristic guides to the *judgments* that we should make. Cf. *Placing Blame*, pp. 131ff., 181ff.

44 *Placing Blame*, pp. 162, 176ff. Moore's strategy has what seems to me to be the unfortunate result of tying the Simple Desert Theory to a disputable objectivism in ethics.

45 *Placing Blame*, p. 163.

46 *Placing Blame*, p. 148. Richard Joyce seems to claim this too: see *The Evolution of Morality* (MIT Press, 2006), p. 103.

47 Moore, *Placing Blame*, pp. 167, 180, for example.

48 Cp. Holmes, *The Common Law*, p. 39: 'the feeling of fitness' between crime and punishment is really no more than 'vengeance in disguise'. James Fitzjames Stephen, of course, did not think that the desire for vengeance was even disguised (*Liberty, Equality, Fraternity*, pp. 152–154).

49 See, for instance, Ted Honderich (ed.), *The Oxford Companion to Philosophy* (Oxford University Press, 1995), p. 772; Igor Primoratz, *Justifying Legal Punishment* (Humanities Press, 1989), p. 71; Robert Nozick, *Philosophical Explorations* (Clarendon Press, 1981), p. 367; C.L. Ten, *Crime, Guilt, and Punishment*, p. 43 (relying on Nozick); C.K.B. Barton, *Getting Even: Revenge as a Form of Justice* (Open Court, 1999), pp. 52–69.

This commonly held view has been rejected by Michael Davis in 'Revenge, Victim's Rights, and Criminal Justice', *International Journal of Applied Philosophy*, vol. 14 (2000), pp. 119–128, and further in 'Victims' Rights, Revenge, and Retribution', *Australian Journal of Professional and Applied Ethics*, vol. 3 (2001), pp. 45–68.

50 Compare Mill's account of the desire to punish in Ch. V of *Utilitarianism*.

51 This explains, what T.H. Green noticed, that certain sorts of offence (pre-eminently horrific assaults and offences against children) generate a demand for 'retributory' punishment more readily than others.

52 Cf. Ted Honderich, *Punishment: The Supposed Justifications Revisited*, Ch. 3.

53 See, e.g. Moore, 'Moral Reality', *Wisconsin Law Review*, 1982, pp. 1061–1156; and 'Moral Reality Revisited', *Michigan Law Review*, vol. 90 (1992), pp. 2424–2533.

54 See J.L. Mackie, 'Morality and the Retributive Emotions', *Criminal Justice Ethics*, 1982, pp. 3–10; and *Ethics: Inventing Right and Wrong* (Penguin, 1977) for a more general sceptical account of ethical properties.

55 'There is undoubtedly much truth in Mackie's explanation of our retributive reactions to culpable wrongdoing. Yet as thus far stated, there is nothing in Mackie's explanation that excludes an explanatory role for an objective moral property of desert. After all, a good,

survival-related evolutionary explanation can be given for our beliefs in the physical sciences, yet such explanation of those beliefs does not exclude a supplemental in terms of the reality of physical objects and their properties' (Moore, *Placing Blame*, p. 178).

[56] Whether in fact they eventually do so is another matter. Cf. Alvin Plantinga, *Warrant and Proper Function* (Oxford University Press, 1993), Ch. 12.

[57] *Placing Blame*, pp. 131ff., 181ff.

[58] 'Moral dilemma' here is something of a technical term; for the topic generally, see H.E. Mason (ed.), *Moral Dilemmas and Moral Theory* (Oxford University Press, 1996).

Chapter Three

A Just Distribution

The Simple Desert Theory refuses a substantive answer to the question why offenders deserve to suffer. The Just Distribution Theory, propounded most famously by Herbert Morris, gives us a substantive answer.[1] Morris aims to make sense of the thought that an offender has *a right to be punished*. His view is that *punishing* an offender is a fitting response to his *personhood* in a way that treatment based on, for instance, the model of medical treatment would not be; and the right to be punished, he argues, is derived from the general right to be treated as a person. But in the course of this argument he gives a justification of punishment that has attracted many followers.

According to Morris, punishment is 'a social practice with a highly overdetermined justification' which supplies a number of reasons for punishing offenders.[2] Some of these are of a broadly utilitarian character. But one is not utilitarian. A system of punishment proscribes certain sorts of behaviour, and compliance with these proscriptions provides benefits for all:

> These benefits consist of noninterference by others with what each person values, such matters as continuance of life and bodily security. The rules define a sphere for each person then, which is immune from interference by others. Making possible this mutual benefit is the assumption by individuals of a burden. The burden consists in the exercise of self-restraint by individuals over inclinations that would, if satisfied, directly interfere or create a substantial risk of interference with others in proscribed ways. If a person fails to exercise self-restraint even though he might have and gives in to such inclinations, he renounces a burden which others have voluntarily assumed and thus gains an advan-

tage which others, who restrained themselves, do not possess. This system, then is one in which the rules establish a
mutuality of benefit and burden and in which the benefits of
noninterference are conditional upon the assumption of burdens... A person who violates the rules has something
others have — the benefits of the system — but by renouncing
what others have assumed, the burdens of self-restraint, he
has acquired an unfair advantage. Matters are not even until
this advantage is in some way erased. Another way of putting it is that [the offender] owes something to others, for he
has something that does not rightfully belong to him.[3]

The offender, then, does not shoulder his share of the burden
of the self-restraint that makes possible a desirable society.
He has thus gained an unfair advantage, and punishment
rectifies this, re-establishing a fair distribution of benefits and
burdens. His advantage is, so to speak, nullified, and so punishment is a form of the annulment often spoken of by theorists of punishment. It is this that I shall refer to as the Just
Distribution Theory.

The Just Distribution Theory includes a requirement of
proportionality: punishment can achieve its aim only by
imposing a burden proportional to that which the offender
refused to bear.[4] So we may wonder whether the Just Distribution Theory can offer a better account of proportionality
than the Simple Desert Theory.

There is perhaps no problem if we are thinking merely of
balancing burdens with burdens. The offender failed to carry
the burden distributed to him by the system; his punishment
is the requirement to carry an equivalent burden. On the
assumptions that utility is appropriately measurable, and
that the idea of a burden is suitably interpreted, the idea of
an equivalence here does not seem to be incoherent. The
measurement may be carried out in a familiar way: if the
offender, or an average citizen, say, would be indifferent as
between the two burdens, then they are equivalent. Given
the measurability of utility, this is not incoherent.

However, a familiar problem looms when we try to take
account of the *culpability* of the offender, as we surely must.
As Morris points out, provision is made, and reasonably
made, for a variety of legal defences related to the offender's
mental state:

A person has not derived an unfair advantage if he could not have restrained himself or if it is unreasonable to expect him to behave otherwise than he did. Sometimes the rules preclude punishment of classes of person such as children. Sometimes they provide a defense if on a particular occasion a person lacked the capacity to conform his conduct to the rules. Thus, someone who in an epileptic seizure strikes another is excused. Punishment in these cases would be punishment of the innocent, punishment of those who do not voluntarily renounce a burden others have assumed.[5]

If the offender could not avoid his offence, or if it were unreasonable to expect him to do so, then, in the relevant sense, he has committed no offence because he has derived no unfair advantage. He has not failed to carry a burden that he had any duty to carry.

Things may seem unproblematic where someone literally has no control over his actions, as in Morris's case of the epileptic seizure.[6] But such clear instances are rare. Control comes in degrees, as Morris's mention of children makes clear; and so does reasonableness. Someone may be coerced into, say, exploding a bomb in a crowded market, but the degree of coercion, or the unreasonableness of not performing the action, can vary. From the moral point of view, it is one thing to be coerced by a threat to murder one's family, another thing to be coerced by the threat of a mild beating. And, morally speaking, it is one thing to be coerced into exploding a bomb in a crowded market, quite another to be coerced into participating in a small bank robbery. Culpability varies along with the degree of control that the offender has over his action and the degree to which it is reasonable to expect him to resist the coercion. That is, it is a function of two independent variables.

Morris tends to speak as if an offender were either culpable or not. If he is, then what he deserves is a simple function of what he illegitimately gained from his offence. If he is not, then he is innocent and does not deserve punishment. But if culpability comes in degrees, this surely cannot be right; what an offender deserves must be punishment whose severity is proportional to his illegitimate gain and his degree of culpability.[7] And, as with the Simple Desert Theory, we should be sceptical about the notion of proportionality here.

We shall return to this issue briefly later. For the present, we shall concentrate on what the theory claims to be the benefit gained by an offender in his offence.

Unfair Benefits?

The theory speaks of the benefits that an offender derives from his offence. We must be clear about what this means.[8] I shall suggest that there is no interpretation of the idea which will yield a satisfactory theory of punishment. All will yield quite unacceptable judgments about the appropriate level of punishment for offenders. The theory will thus fail to respond satisfactorily to the third query that a theory of punishment must respond to: it will be inconsistent with our deepest intuitions.

The benefits in question here cannot be the 'ill-gotten gains' that a thief may acquire through his activities, for there are too many offences which bring no such benefit: unsuccessful attempts, for instance, pointless acts of violence, and careless driving. In any case, Morris speaks only of the offender's unfair advantage having to be given back. No one thinks that depriving a thief of what he has stolen would be a just punishment.

So perhaps we should think of the benefit in more *psychological* terms: typically, offenders will gain some sense of satisfaction from their offences, sometimes from their material gains, sometimes simply from the action they have performed.[9] This will be satisfaction to which they are not entitled by the system of reciprocity. We might say, then, that the offender's punishment should be proportional to the satisfaction he gained from his offence. But the suggestion that a just punishment for, say, a brutal rape would be proportional to the satisfaction that the rapist gained from it would be wholly unbelievable. It would have the consequence that a just punishment would be one such that the rapist would, as far as his satisfactions are concerned, regard the punishment as a rational trade, and it is incredible that even the most obsessive rapist would voluntarily trade a few years in prison for a single act of rape.

Perhaps we should move, then, to a more abstract conception. We might say that the benefit the offender takes is, purely and simply, the rejection of the burden of self-restraint, the illegitimate exercise of freedom:

> [W]hen someone, who really could have chosen otherwise, manifests in action a preference (whether by intention, recklessness, or negligence) for his own interests, his own freedom of choice and action, as against the common interests and the legally defined common way-of-action, then in and by that very action he gains a certain sort of advantage over those who have restrained themselves, by the law. For is not the exercise of freedom of choice in itself a great human good?... [P]unishment rectifies the disturbed pattern of distribution of advantages and disadvantages throughout a community by depriving the convicted criminal of his freedom of choice, proportionately to the degree to which he had exercised his freedom, his personality, in the unlawful act.[10]

If we are thinking of incarceration, and execution, perhaps, then this might seem plausible. But its fit with corporal punishment — surely the vast majority of punishments administered throughout history — is surely a strain. Corporal punishment no doubt deprives the offender of his freedom, since he is forced to bear something he would not freely bear, but that is hardly what makes it a punishment.

We should also add that, though it is untypical for offenders to be punished willingly, it is no more than that; punishment may be voluntarily embraced, with all of its pain,[11] and in such circumstances it is hard to see how it thwarts the will.

We should also ask how we are supposed to measure the exercise of freedom.

Perhaps the idea is that we can measure how much one would have had to restrain one's will in order not to have committed an offence, then measure how much a given punishment would restrain one's will, and then match them up. Let us agree that we have rough intuitions about these measures (we surely could not claim more?); if so, the idea would give us an interpretation no more plausible than the last: failing to restrain one's lawless impulses is, in itself, a benefit, but one that hardly seems commensurate with the restraints involved in, for instance, legitimate prison sentences.

We should also have another other odd result. Those who are more strongly tempted to commit crimes will attract more severe sentences — independently of the nature of their offences — since they secured a greater exercise of freedom. The need for deterrence may furnish some reason to punish more tempting offences more severely. But the mere demands of justice surely suggest the very reverse.

George Sher suggests a different understanding:

> [T]he degree of the wrongdoer's benefit is a function of the degree of wrongfulness of his act; and the more wrong the act, the more stringent the requirement not to do it; and so 'as the [stringency] of the prohibition increases, so too does the freedom from it which its violation entails'.[12]

The problem here lies in understanding the notion of the 'stringency' of a requirement, which is supposed to enable the transition from the taking of freedom to wrongness. 'Stringency' here cannot refer to the number of exceptions allowed by the law to an offence, or to the thoroughness with which legal authorities will pursue the offence, or to the severity with which it will be punished. These would be conceptual claims about the law, and Sher's claim is about morality, not about the law. But as far as morality is concerned, it is hard to see what it means for one requirement to be more stringent than another unless it *just is* for the prohibited action to be more wrong. That being so, to say that someone has taken more freedom in his offence than has someone else in another offence is just to say that he has done something more wrong; the notion of freedom plays no independent role. But that leaves us with the bare proposition that the punishment should be proportional to the wrongness of the act. But that is the notion to be explained and justified, not the explanation or justification.

The interpretation apparently favoured by Morris is different again:

> A person who violates the rules has something others have — the benefits of the system — but by renouncing what others have assumed, the burdens of self-restraint, he has acquired an unfair advantage. Matters are not even until this advantage is in some way erased.[13]

So the offender's unfair benefit is what he derives from others' obedience to the law.

But does 'obedience to the law' refer to others' obedience to *the particular law* that the offender broke, or to others' obedience to *the law in general*.[14]

Richard Burgh has argued that, on the first interpretation, there are many laws that the theory cannot justify:

> Consider laws that prohibit embezzlement. The sphere of noninterference which they define protects only those who are in a position from which they can be embezzled. Yet clearly the fact that an embezzler happens not to be in a position to be embezzled from should be irrelevant to the question of whether he deserves punishment.[15]

But this is surely a mistake. Even those who cannot be embezzled from are likely to gain, indirectly, from laws prohibiting embezzlement; it is just that they will gain less. So the case of laws to which the theory has no application would be merely the limiting case of a more general problem, namely that different people gain widely different benefits from the general obedience to particular laws, differences that would not be reflected in any acceptable sentencing policy. Those who own much property, for instance, gain more from laws against theft than those who own little; those who wish to voice their thoughts on contentious matters gain more from laws protecting freedom of speech than those who have no such inclination; and so on. Indeed, it is hard to imagine laws of which this is not true. One might reply that it is the law that is at fault here, not the theory, and that we should indeed punish in accordance with the theory. But a tough customer prepared to take his chances in a society in which rape was not illegal would derive little benefit from laws prohibiting rape. It will hardly strike anyone as morally appropriate that his punishment for raping should be correspondingly small.

The second interpretation holds that the offender's benefit is what he gains from society's obedience to the law's requirements in general.

It has been argued[16] that, on this interpretation, the Just Distribution Theory would have the unwelcome conclusion that all offences should receive the same severity of punishment, since everyone receives the same benefit, namely the obedience of others to the law. In a thin sense, it is indeed true that everyone receives the same benefit. But in another sense it is not, for the protection of the law may not be an equal benefit to all. The weak, for instance, derive more benefit from the protection of the law than do the strong. So the theory can hold that the relevant benefit is not the protection of the law *simpliciter*, but the actual benefit derived by the offender from that protection. But on this interpretation, a different problem looms again: the theory will require unacceptably different levels of severity in the punishment amongst offenders, differences which have nothing to do with the nature of their offences. That is simply because different people gain different amounts of benefit from the protection given by the legal order. One reason for this is that the law protects, in a large degree, the social structure, and that the social structure of almost any society gives different people different stakes in it. This point is sometimes made in Marxist, or quasi-Marxist terms, as by Jeffrie Murphy in a notorious article.[17] But the point does not require this sort of political analysis, and is best separated from it. In any society, different people will derive different levels of benefit from the social order that the law makes possible. On the present version of the Just Distribution Theory, this will require differences in the severity of punishment that have nothing to do with the serious of the offences as that is normally understood.

The Principle of Fair Play

Unlike the Simple Desert Theory, the Just Distribution Theory purports to give an informative answer to the question *why* an offender deserves to suffer. The idea is that punishment is merely the application of a more general principle of justice that, in a cooperative venture, there should be an equitable distribution of the costs and benefits involved. And this in turn may suggest that the Just Distribution Theory will have a satisfactory answer to the further question: why it is legitimate for *the state* to punish. According to this theory, punishment is simply the rectification of injustice, and rectifying injustice may seem to be a paradigmatically legitimate exercise of the state's power. These answers may indeed be informative, but they are not, I shall suggest, acceptable.

We could hardly question the very general principle that, in a cooperative venture, there should be an equitable distribution of the costs and benefits involved. Certainly, if we were setting up such a venture, the idea would have immediate appeal, and we should certainly want to ensure such a distribution. For one thing, it would probably make the venture go better, since inequities, if known about, would be likely to produce resentment and consequent inefficiency. But even apart from this instrumental reason, the demands of justice alone would be likely to motivate us in this direction; we should be unhappy to countenance a situation in which some would benefit at a cost to others which they should bear themselves. And, similarly, in an ongoing such venture we should generally want to rectify any inequities of this sort, and for the same reasons. So if the system allowed an imbalance of costs and benefits then we would want to improve the system to prevent this in the future. And if benefits had fallen where they ought not then they should, as far as was reasonably possible, be returned to where they ought to have fallen. But we shall have to take this intuitively appealing idea considerably further than so far elaborated if it is to support the Just Distribution Theory.

The intuitive idea was articulated most famously by H.L.A. Hart in his 'Are There Any Natural Rights?',[18] where it was intended to form the basis for a theory of political obligation.[19] It is now generally referred to by the name given it by Rawls, the 'Principle of Fair Play'. The core of it is as follows:

> [W]hen a number of persons conduct any joint enterprise according to rules and thus restrict their liberty, those who have submitted to these restrictions when required have a right to a similar submission from those who have benefited by their submission. The rules may provide that officials should have authority to enforce obedience... but the moral obligation to obey the rules in such circumstances is *due to* the co-operating members of the society, and they have the correlative moral right to obedience.[20]

The most natural interpretation of Hart's own words here would yield simply the principle that cooperators have the right to compel cooperation from would-be free riders: if there is work to be done, then they may be compelled to work; if monetary contributions are required, they may be compelled to contribute. And it would be a short and uncontroversial step to cutting off benefits to those who, for whatever reason, could not be compelled to contribute. No more than this is suggested by Hart or by Rawls.[21] Now, with some additional premises, this might generate a theory of punishment, but it would not be the Just Distribution Theory. Viewing the social order as a cooperative venture involving costs and benefits, the principle might suggest that those who benefit could legitimately be compelled to pay some of the costs, and punishment might be seen as part of this process of compulsion. But this would lead only to an externalist theory emphasising, pre-eminently, deterrence.

A slightly more expansive interpretation would license cooperators to seize payment after the fact from those who benefited from the cooperation but did not participate. Whether this would be a plausible claim is a matter of dispute,[22] but we need not enter that dispute, because, again, this principle will not yield the Just Distribution Theory.

What the Just Distribution Theory requires is a yet more expansive interpretation. It requires not just that payment may be seized from those who have benefited from a cooperative venture without contributing to it, but that, when payment cannot be seized, unproductive burdens may be imposed in order to neutralize such benefits. This is a far cry from the intuitively plausible principle with which we started; it is not entailed by it, nor is it simply an uncontroversial extension of it. The intuitive principle, as envisaged by Hart and Rawls (p. 97), requires that the costs and benefits *of the system* should be distributed fairly, and its plausibility surely derives largely from the thought that respect for it would prevent contributors from having to contribute more than their fair share by supplying benefits to others who should, but do not, pay for them themselves. The burdens that are legitimated by the Just Distribution Theory of punishment, however, are not costs *of the system* at all, costs that must be incurred in order to secure the benefits; they are costs borne *in place of* costs that were not borne when they should have been. Imposing such costs contributes nothing towards the production of the benefits realized by the system, nor anything towards ensuring that contributors do not have to contribute more than their fair share — other than by their deterrent effect.[23]

Furthermore, though relatedly, the principle of fair play in Hart and Rawls is a principle about what those who benefit from a cooperative system owe *to those who participate* — a point specifically emphasized by Hart. Despite sloppy talk of offenders paying their debt to society, punishment is not normally thought of as the payment of a debt owed to others. It is certainly a natural thought, though not an inevitable one, that a citizen owes a duty to other citizens *not to offend*, a duty arguably deriving from the principle of fair play, or something like it. But it would not follow from this that if he does offend he then owes a further duty to his fellow citizens, a duty to suffer in order not to have benefited from his offence. The root intuition is simply that participants in a cooperative enterprise owe it to others *to pay their fair share*. It may or may not be thought to follow from this that they may be *forced* to pay for their fair share. But it certainly does not follow that, if payment cannot be extracted from them, they owe it to other citizens to bear unproductive burdens instead. And, of course, when it has been decided that an offender should be punished, he may owe it to other citizens to undergo that punishment, if only because refusing to do so may impose unjust costs on them; but that duty arises only when the justification for punishment has already been generated, and so cannot generate the justification itself. And an offender will normally owe it to other citizens to avoid offending in the future; this would uncontroversially generate a duty to undergo punishment if — but only if — we were to believe some version of the Reform Theory. And an offender typically owes something to his victim; but that is a matter of compensation, not punishment (this is not to deny that victims sometimes feel compensated by seeing the offender suffer). In sum, no duties that an offender can be thought to owe to other citizens will be repaid by punishment. The confusion is nicely illustrated, I think, by a remark of Herbert Morris. Echoing Hart, he says that

> [the offender] owes something to others, for he has something that does not rightfully belong to him. Justice... restores the equilibrium of benefits and burdens by taking

from the individual what he owes, that is, exacting the debt.[24]

This surely is a confusion. If the offender 'owes something to others', merely *taking it from him* will go no way towards setting *that* right. Requiring him *to pay them what he owes them* is all that could do that, and that is what is suggested by the original version of the principle of fair play. Certainly, restoring 'the equilibrium of benefits and burdens' by taking from the offender what he should not have will not, in itself, do so.

We have spoken so far of the principle of fair play as generating a duty *to other participants* to pay one's fair share. But one might also think of it as generating, not a duty *to* others, but, in addition, simply *a duty* to pay one's fair share — not a duty *to* anyone. In many cases this is clearly plausible, on the grounds that not doing one's bit towards a cooperative endeavour from which one benefits would often show a substantial meanness of spirit. But now it is not so clear that such a duty, if we wish to call it that, would justify coercion, and so it is again unlikely to yield a justification of punishment. Rational adults presumably have every right to their meanness of spirit, though not, of course, to all of the actions to which it may point them. It is not, normally at least, the business of someone else, and especially not of the state, to use *coercion* to try to make mean people less mean. And even if it were, forcing them to pay their share is hardly a sufficiently well-grounded strategy to justify coercion. Still less so is forcing on them an unproductive burden which, only by an illegitimate metaphor, could be spoken of as making them pay their fair share.

The Principle of Fair Play and the Prisoner's Dilemma

As I have already suggested, the justification for punishment offered by the Just Distribution Theory should not be confused with a quite different one. The Just Distribution Theory holds that punishment is justified merely because it restores a just balance of benefits and burdens in society; its central thrust is to subsume what Aristotle called retributive justice within the theory of distributive justice. A central thought in this justification is that the legal system is a cooperative enterprise. But that thought, simply taken by itself, could go in a quite different way.

The legal order is a massive public good, indeed a precondition of pretty well any social goods whatever; and it is one which could not be supported without a decent contribution from most of those who benefit. And thinking of the legal order in this way may suggest the idea that compulsion is justified by the need to avoid a disastrous Prisoner's Dilemma. On one version, this justification would have two parts. Without compulsion, it may be thought, each would do best for himself by not complying with the law. The result would be that no one would comply with the law, a result worse for everyone than if everyone complied. To get the second best option, on which (pretty well) everyone complies with the law, we need compulsion. In its most familiar version, the Hobbesian, this compulsion is provided by the state. That, highly schematically, is the first part of the justification. The second part is to point out that the compulsion is actually in the interest of those who are compelled. This may seem to make the justification all the more satisfying.

We could, of course, dispute the principle on which the second part of the justification seems to rest: we might hold that the fact that compulsion is in the interest of those compelled is not normally any sort of justification for the compulsion. But even if we did not dispute that, there would be a problem; it is by no means clear that the compulsion is actually in the interest of all of those whose participation would be compelled. It may be, as I have said, that there are some whose preference structures do not satisfy the conditions for a Prisoner's Dilemma—they may prefer the non-cooperation of all to the cooperation of all. In that case, compulsion would not be in their interest, and so the part of the justification that was supposed to make the compulsion more palatable would not be available. The second part of the justification would then fail.

We might still, however, have a justification, even without the second part. Urgent need to avoid a Prisoner's Dilemma might be—itself—sufficient justification, for it is arguable that urgent need can sometimes generate enforceable duties. We would then not need to make the further claim that the compulsion is in the interest of all of those compelled. It would be enough to make the claim that, without general compulsion, sufficient cooperation would not be possible, for those who preferred the cooperation of all would not themselves cooperate unless they had some assurance that enough others would cooperate.[25] This might be thought sufficient to generate a justification to compel participation on the part of everybody, including those who would thereby incur a net loss. Those who did incur a net loss might be thought to have had their rights violated, and incompensably so. But this could be held to be a justifiable overriding of rights. So the first part of the justification might itself do all of the work, if it were correct.

We shall not pause to enquire whether it is correct. For our purposes it is sufficient to note that it is a quite different justification from that offered by the Just Distribution Theory, for little, if any, part is played in it by the idea of distributive justice, let alone the more specific Principle of Fair Play.[26] In its second part it appeals not to the principle that those who have benefited from a cooperative enterprise should bear some of the costs but to the quite different idea that its being in the interest of the person compelled is a partial justification of compulsion; and this latter idea has nothing to do with distributive justice. Without its second part it appeals merely to the principle that sufficiently urgent need may justify compelling cooperation; it is doubtful whether this principle has anything to do with distributive justice, save in the most trivial sense; it certainly has nothing to do with the Principle of Fair Play.

---

[1]   The most well-known account is that of Herbert Morris in 'Persons and Punishment', *The Monist*, vol. lii (1968) (rp. in *On Guilt and Innocence: Essays in Legal Philosophy and Moral Psychology* (University of California Press, 1976), from which edition all of my quotations are taken). Versions of the theory are also found in, for example, Jacob Adler, *The Urgings of Conscience: A Theory of Punishment* (Temple University Press, 1991); Michael Davis, *To Make the Punishment Fit the Crime* (Westview, 1992) — but for stringent qualifications, see his 'Punishment Theory's Golden Half-Century', *Journal of Ethics*, vol. xiii (2009), pp. 73–100, at pp. 92ff.; John Finnis, *Natural Law and Natural Rights* (Clarendon Press, 1980); Jeffrie Murphy, *Retribution, Justice, and Therapy* (Reidel, 1979); W. Sadurski, *Giving Desert Its Due* (Reidel, 1985); George Sher, *Desert* (Princeton University Press, 1987); and Andrew von Hirsch, *Doing Justice* (Hill and Wang, 1976).

2   Herbert Morris, 'Guilt and Suffering', *Philosophy East and West*, vol. xxi (1971), pp. 419–434 (rp. in *On Guilt and Innocence*; the quotation is from p. 104). See also Morris, 'The Decline of Guilt', *Ethics*, vol. 99 (1988), pp. 62–76, at p. 65. Finnis takes the same view, though he holds that the aim provided by the Just Distribution Theory is what makes a legal sanction a *punishment* (*ibid.*, p. 262).

   If the reasons overdetermine the justification, not all of them are necessary. But Morris is not explicit about the formal relations between these overdetermining reasons.

3   'Persons and Punishment', pp. 33–34.

4   'Persons and Punishment', p. 39.

5   'Persons and Punishment', p. 35.

6   But, even here, things are not completely straightforward: did the 'offender' fail to take medicine that controls seizures? If so, why?

7   However, he says on p. 39: 'with punishment, there is an attempt at some equivalence between the advantage gained by the wrongdoer —partly based upon the seriousness of the interest invaded, partly on the state of mind with which the wrongful act was performed — and on the punishment meted out.' This suggests, but does not entail, that culpability comes in degrees.

8   Richard Burgh has also pointed out that there are a number of different interpretations here. My classification partly parallels his. See Richard Burgh, 'Do the Guilty Deserve Punishment?', *The Journal of Philosophy*, vol. lxxix (1982), pp. 193–210.

9   'Guilt and Suffering', p. 95.

10 Finnis, *Natural Law and Natural Rights*, pp. 263f.

11 A point much emphasized by Jacob Adler — himself a proponent of a version of the Just Distribution Theory — in *The Urgings of Conscience: A Theory of Punishment*.

12 *Desert*, p. 82.

13 'Persons and Punishment', p. 34.

14 Cf. Burgh, 'Do the Guilty Deserve Punishment?'

15 Burgh, 'Do the Guilty Deserve Punishment?', p. 205.

16 Burgh, 'Do the Guilty Deserve Punishment?', p. 206.

17 *Retribution, Justice, and Therapy* (Reidel, 1979), p. 106. Murphy no longer holds the view put forward in this article (see Jeffrie Murphy, *Retribution Reconsidered: More Essays in the Philosophy of Law* (Reidel, 1992), p. ix).

18 H.L.A. Hart, 'Are There Any Natural Rights?', *Philosophical Review*, vol. lxiv (1955), pp. 175–191. See also, *Essays in Jurisprudence and Philosophy* (Clarendon Press, 1983), p. 119. The principle is also found in various versions in the work of Rawls.

19 Michael Davis denies that the theory of punishment need rest on a political theory (*To Make the Punishment Fit the Crime*, Ch. 2). But the Principle of Fair Play is not itself a political theory.

20 'Are There Any Natural Rights?', p. 185.

21   Hart offers the principle as a route to the idea of political obligation, and this interpretation of the principle is all that is required for that purpose. Rawls, on the other hand, does not think that the principle will generate political obligations, for 'the average citizen' at least (*A Theory of Justice* (Harvard University Press, revised ed. 1999), p. 97), but does think that it will generate all requirements that are not 'natural duties'. Precisely what the principle is supposed to imply, however, is not clear. On p. 96 he says, 'We are not to profit from the cooperative labors of others without doing our fair share'. How this is supposed to relate to the immediately preceding paraphrase of Hart is not elaborated; it may be yet another paraphrase, or it may be supposed to be the underlying thought from which the principle of fair play derives. Nor does Rawls tell us anything about what precisely it means. On one interpretation of 'one is not to profit from' it would indeed support the Just Distribution Theory, but whether that is how Rawls intended it there is, I think, no saying.

22   On the one side, see, e.g. Richard Arneson, 'The Principle of Fairness and Free-Rider Problems', *Ethics*, vol. 92 (1982), pp. 616–633; Michael Davis, 'Nozick's Argument FOR the Legitimacy of the Welfare State', *Ethics*, vol. 97 (1987), pp. 576–594; and George Klosko, *The Principle of Fairness and Political Obligation* (Rowman and Littlefield, 1992). On the other side, see Daniel McDermott, 'Fair-Play Obligations', *Political Studies*, vol. 52 (2004), pp. 216–232.

23   One could, perhaps, accept this, and hold that the Just Distribution Theory is simply a theory about the appropriate level of sentences, not a theory about the justification of punishment. But this would still leave in place the criticisms levelled in the first part of the chapter.

24   'Persons and Punishment', p. 34.

25   Cf. H.L.A. Hart, *The Concept of Law* (Clarendon Press, 1961), p. 193; Michael Taylor, *The Possibility of Cooperation* (Cambridge University Press, 1987), p. 136.

26   There have been quite different attempts to bring the theory of punishment under the principles of distributive justice. See, for instance, Daniel M. Farrell, 'Deterrence and the Just Distribution of Harm', *Social Philosophy and Policy*, vol. xii (1995), pp. 220–240.

Chapter Four

Reform

'It is not, then, the function of the just man, Polemarchus, to harm either friend or anyone else.'[1]

Punishment involves inflicting suffering on an offender for his offence. It is natural to think that, from the standpoint of the offender, this suffering is a genuine evil; that, of course, is the source of most of the pressure to give a justification of punishment. But some theories deny this. They hold that if a punishment, with all of the suffering that it entails, is to be justifiable then it has to be a good for the offender. Such a thought naturally leads one to the idea of reform.

The good of the offender has, of course, not always been the controlling focus of reform theories. Mostly, they have been straightforwardly externalist theories, holding that the point of punishment is to reduce crime; that reforming offenders is an effective way of doing so; and that punishment is, contingently, an effective method of reform.

Just how punishment is supposed to effect reform, however, is far from obvious, and that question has been a dominant theme through the history of the reform theory. The optimism about the reformative potential of punishment that we find in the early prison reform movement may now strike us as naïve, but it was not silly:

> The prison was stern but effective medicine. Men turned to crime because of their defective background, their weak wills, their bad society. The prison cured these problems. It provided the missing training, the missing backbone.[2]

Here, there is no mystery about how that suffering is supposed to reform, for it is not strictly the suffering that does that; suffering is just the largely unavoidable concomitant of the isolation, labour, and discipline that are supposed to do it. And we could certainly imagine that the conditions imposed in the model prisons of the nineteenth century might indeed have reformed offenders. But in fact they did not, or not to any significant degree anyway.

A different conception of reform focuses on what is known as 'individual deterrence'. Here the thought is that the offender has not been deterred by the threat of punishment because he has an insufficiently lively sense of what the punishment involves. What he needs is to experience the thing at first hand, and he will then want more strongly to avoid it in the future. Again, this is not a silly idea. Unfortunately, the empirical data give it little significant support.

A different sort of reformative theory was famously advocated by Barbara Wootton. In one of her most influential works[3] she argued that the sole aim of the law should be preventive. There was no place whatever for 'retributive' considerations, which she regarded as little more than the religious superstitions of a passing era. Though seeming to accept that there is some place for deterrent considerations in penal theory, she strongly emphasized the reformative aspects of the law. She made no attempt to explain how offenders could successfully be treated. Her view was that this was a question for psychological research, and offenders should be treated in whatever manner should turn out to be most effective.[4] However, she tended to take the view that punishment, as normally understood, is unlikely to be a successful form of treatment. Her view, then, was more aptly described as the view that, in so far as we are concerned with reform, punishment should be superseded by treatment, rather than the view that the aim of punishment is reform. On this view, prisons become, rather than a form of punishment, places in which punishment's successor may be carried out. One might call such theories, at the limit, theories of punishment, but, strictly, they do not aim to justify punishment, and so they do not fall under our purview. Even so, we may remark that, so far as we know, no one has yet discovered any generally effective 'treatment' of offenders.[5]

Externalist reform theories do not usually give the offender's own good a special role. Our concern in this chapter will be with theories that do so.

When we think of such theories, we inevitably think of Plato. He accepted that punishment may have a deterrent aim,[6] but the centre of his theory of punishment is reformative. To be used as an example for the deterrence of others is a fate reserved for the incurably wicked.[7] We must 'cure' criminals 'whenever we can'; only this is the work of a 'perfect law'.[8] Only when that condition is satisfied may we move to a consideration of the public good and punish the criminal in order to educate and deter others.

In Plato, this view of punishment is connected with two more general thoughts. One is that wrongdoing is the result of disorder in the soul.[9] The other is the thought that it is never right to harm anyone, that is, to make anyone 'more unjust' or 'worse as a man'.[10] This latter view entails that no punishment will be justified if it harms the offender. We may thus seek to deter by punishment so long as the offender does not, in his punishment, suffer a net harm; and this means that, for someone who is not incorrigible, there must be some improvement in his soul to make up for the suffering that he undergoes in his punishment.[11] But neither view entails that the *aim* of punishment is reform; nor do the two together.

If these views do not entail a reform theory, they may nonetheless suggest it. But Plato gives little explanation as to why, if we wish to improve the souls of offenders, causing them to suffer is the appropriate means. In the *Gorgias*, wrongdoing is identified with intemperance, lack of restraint. The ambiguity in the Greek word *akolazein* — which can mean either 'restrain' or 'punish' — then makes it easy for Socrates to argue that punishment improves the soul by restraining it and thus ridding it of intemperance (504a–505b). This, of course, is no better than a pun. One might drop the pun and simply claim, as an empirical matter, that those who are subjected to restraint generally acquire the virtue of self-control — perhaps through the habituation that Aristotle thought necessary for the practice of virtue. No doubt this is what many nineteenth-century penologists thought. But it seems to be false.

One response would be one that we have already noticed: we might eschew the notion of punishment as traditionally conceived, and think instead of 'punishment' as simply providing the *opportunity* to educate offenders, as has been done with some prison regimes. That, however, was not Plato's view — not, anyway, according to the eschatological myth in *Gorgias*. There we read that the benefit that comes to offenders through punishment 'comes to them through pain and sufferings both here and in Hades — for there is no other way to get rid of injustice'.[12] But why, we may ask, are pain and suffering necessary means to that end? To this, Plato has no adequate reply. Nor, I shall suggest, do any of those who follow his general view.

With God, of course, all things are possible. And so the evident lack of reformative power that attaches to earthly punishment need not be thought to attach to divine punishment. It is therefore the less surprising to find a reform theory of divine punishment espoused by Christian thinkers, particularly those with a Platonic background.

The combination of Platonism and Christianity that we find in, for instance, Origen, and Clement of Alexandria, seemed to demand this. Since the love of God is infinite, His punishment, they thought, could have only a reformative purpose and Origen held, or so it seems, that even Satan would eventually be purified by the fires of Hell. How this purification is to work, however, is not entirely clear. For Origen, the fires of Hell were metaphorical, the misery consequent upon a realisation by the sinner of his separation from God. Here, at first sight, we may seem to have a basic thought that will recur in the history of reformative thought — punishment will bring the offender to see the wrongness of what he has done — but with a backing that more secularized versions would lack, for Origen, being both a Christian and a Platonist, is entitled to the claims that God will bring it about that sinners will eventually perceive the good, and that, perceiving it, they must needs love it. But if, as Origen tells us, the fires of Hell are simply a metaphor for the sinner's suffering at the sense of separation from the good, then it must seem that when he suffers them the reform must have taken place, and there is then nothing further for the pains to accomplish—nothing reformative, at any rate; how, or what, they are to purify is thus not clear.

Augustine too entertains the thought that after death there may be, for some, 'a kind of purgatorial fire',[13] but throws no more light on how such purging is to work. All he tells us is that the fire will burn up the sinner's sinful desires; but how this metaphor is to be cashed is unclear.

The Early Church Fathers had inherited the idea that after death there would be punishment by fire, and considerable thought was given to the question of where this fire would be, and how it would work.[14] In addition, they had inherited from St Paul the idea that some people might be saved 'though as through fire',[15] and that text dominated the development of the doctrine of purgatory.[16] But if there was a problem in understanding the idea that one might be eternally punished in Hell by fire, it was greatly compounded in the idea that one might be *saved* by fire. For how is being set afire supposed to contribute to one's salvation? One response, the one we have looked at briefly, was to think in reformative terms; but this, instead of answering the question, merely relocates it. Another was to think of the fire as expiatory, purifying the sinner by purging him of his guilt. This is, perhaps, not a reformative idea, and so not relevant to our present purposes. It is, in any case, no easier to understand.

Moral Education

Why then, if one wants to reform offenders, is punishing them an appropriate means? Few now accept the simplest answer, that as a matter of empirical fact this is the most effective way of reforming them. So perhaps such theories will do better if they hold that the connection between punishment and reform is not merely contingent, that punishment is, as a conceptual matter, required for the sort of reform that is morally appropriate. Is that possible? Jean Hampton seems to suggest that it is.[17]

Hampton accepts that the ultimate aim of punishment is the prevention of crime.[18] However, in pursuing this aim it must be bound by a number of constraints. One is that the rational autonomy of the offender must be respected. Another is that the offender who is punished must not be merely being *used* for the good of society at large. And another is that punishment must be a good to the offender: 'the only thing that human beings "deserve" in this life is *good,...* no matter what evil a person has committed no one is justified in doing further evil to her.'[19]

These requirements, according to Hampton, rule out a simple deterrence theory. On such a theory, punishment is to be used coercively; it does not appeal to the individual's reason, allowing him the freedom to act in accordance with the moral law or to reject it. She says, with Hegel, 'if we aimed to prevent wrongdoing only by deterring its commission, we would be treating human beings in the same way that we treat dogs'.[20]

The only system of punishment that would respect the autonomy of offenders would be one which aimed to educate, but left it to the individual whether he followed the instruction he was given. Thus, if the aim of punishment is the prevention of crime, then this must be accomplished through education. Hampton's theory 'maintains that punishment is intended as a way of teaching the wrongdoer that the action she did... is forbidden because it is morally wrong and should not be done for that reason'.[21] '[P]unishment is justified as a way to prevent wrongdoing insofar as it can teach both wrongdoers and the public at large the moral reasons for *choosing* not to perform an offense.'[22]

So far, however, the theory could be a purely externalist one. The proper response to crime is to prevent it, and to do so through education. What would make the theory an internalist one would be the claim that the education at issue necessarily involves punishment, where the necessity claimed is not merely psychological. And that seems in fact to be Hampton's view:

> [T]he infliction of pain is *necessarily* connected with the promotion of the goal of moral education... [P]ainful experiences of a particular sort would seem to be necessary for the communication of a certain kind of moral message. (p. 224; Hampton's emphasis)

How is this claim to be made out?

If someone has done wrong, the most natural response might seem to be to *tell* him so, to tell him that there is a moral boundary which he has crossed, and why there is such a moral boundary; but this, Hampton says, will not be 'effective':

> The way to communicate to such people that there is a barrier of a very special sort against these kinds of actions would seem to be to link performance of the actions with what such people care about most — the pursuit of their own pleasure. Only when disruption of that pursuit takes place will a wrongdoer appreciate the special force of the 'mustn't' in the punisher's communication. So the only effective way to 'talk to' such people is through disruption of their own interests, that is, through punishment. (p. 226)

And to get the offender to appreciate the reasons why there is such a boundary:

> Someone who (for no moral reason) violates her (perfect) moral duty to others is not thinking about the others' needs and interests, and most likely has little conception of, or is indifferent to, the pain her actions caused another to suffer. Hence, what the punisher needs to do is to communicate to the wrongdoer *that* her victims suffered and how much they suffered, so that the wrongdoer can appreciate the harmfulness of her action. How does one get this message across to a person insensitive to others? Should not such a person be made to endure an unpleasant experience designed, in some sense, to 'represent' the pain suffered by her victim(s)?... By giving a wrongdoer something like what she gave to others, you are trying to drive home to her just how painful and damaging her action was for her victims, and this experience will, one hopes, help the wrongdoer to understand the immorality of her action. (p. 227)

What wrongdoing demands, then, is punishment; only punishment can get the wrongdoer to appreciate the harm suffered by the victim, and the wrongness of what he has done.

Hampton seems to assume that the immorality of an offence derives from its disregard of the suffering that it causes its victims. This seems natural enough when one considers such things as theft and physical assault, but considerably less natural for many other sorts of offence. Take, for instance, fraudulent claims on insurance companies. No one may suffer, in real terms, from any such particular act. The costs of such fraud will, of course, be passed on to others; but these extra costs accruing to the individual may be, literally, insignificantly small. Perhaps we should add up all of the insignificant costs, and sum them over all of the affected individuals; we may then find that they add up to something significant.[23] It is by no means clear that this is the right way to capture the wrongness of such actions, but leave that aside. The suffering of the offender in his punishment is sufficiently far removed in its nature from this aggregate 'suffering' (which is not actually experienced by anyone) that the former could hardly 'represent' the latter in any way that could be thought educationally illuminating. There are also many offences, such as speeding, that are in particular cases wholly victimless (at least in the sense that no suffering is actually imposed on anyone). Is the idea, then, that speeding wrongfully endangers others' well-being, and those who are put at risk are the victims? But speeding does not necessarily endanger anyone's well-being, and, in any case, it is not clear how a fine, say, is supposed to 'represent' the wrong that is done by merely being put at risk of injury.

This point is important, for the assumption that the immorality of all legal offences lies in the suffering caused to a victim makes Hampton's task seem easier than it really is. So long as we assume this, then we can at least tell a story, and one that is not *a priori* implausible, about how punishment is supposed to teach offenders the immorality of their actions: the offender's own suffering brings home to him the hurtful nature of what he did to his victim. But once we drop the assumption, that story is no longer available, and the process then becomes shrouded in mystery.

This brings us to a second question. Even on the assumption that the wrongness of offences can be understood in terms of the suffering they cause, what reason have we for thinking that inflicting suffering on the offenders is required to teach them the relevant lesson? Hampton seems to think that the offender's failing is, at bottom, cognitive:[24] offenders do not fully understand the extent of their victims' suffering. But surely their failure may be, on the contrary, that they understand it well enough but don't care about it (or sometimes even welcome it). Indeed, the suggestion that offenders generally do not really understand the suffering that they cause is surely quite implausible. They presumably know well enough what suffering is, since they will have experienced it themselves; and they know well enough what effects their actions have on their victims. What reason have we, then, for saying that they do not understand their victims' suffering? One can, of course, make it a tautology that anyone who really understands the suffering of others must care about it. Occasionally, people proclaim this odd view in the name of Wittgenstein. But nothing in his work supports it, and indeed there is nothing to be said for it.

The assumption that the offender's failing is cognitive is, however, absolutely crucial to Hampton's position: any plausibility that this sort of reform theory has derives from it. If we assumed that, for instance, burglars burgled only because they did not realize that being burgled was the sort of thing that one would have reason to object to, then we might think that what they needed was to be deprived of some of their own property, so that they would learn how it feels. But if we assumed that they understood perfectly well how their victims felt, but simply did not care about it, it would be mysterious why making them suffer in a similar way would be required to improve *that* situation.

Without the assumption that an offender's failing is cognitive, then, Hampton's claim that the infliction of suffering is 'necessary' for her 'moral growth'[25] is implausible. But even *with* the assumption it is not clear why it is forced upon us. How is it supposed to follow from the fact that offenders do not understand their victims' suffering that punishment is required in order to make them do so?

Hampton remarks that an account of how moral concepts are acquired is necessary in order to see this.[26] She does not explain the point, but perhaps her thought is that one cannot understand what suffering and pain are like without experiencing them, just as one cannot know what red is like without having seen it. We need not enquire whether this is true, for it is doubly irrelevant. Someone who had led a painless life could have a grasp of the concept adequate for understanding its role in moral reasoning—which is the point at issue—for he may know as well as anyone that it is something which there is typically, perhaps essentially, reason to avoid. In any case, offenders have not typically led painless lives.

The reform theory, in the versions we have looked at, does not seem very promising;[27] but we shall return to the theory in Chapter 6.

---

1 Plato, *Republic*, 335a–e.
2 Lawrence M. Friedman, *Crime and Punishment in American History* (Basic Books, 1993), p. 80.
3 Barbara Wootton, *Crime and the Criminal Law* (Sweet and Maxwell, 1963).
4 As she recognized in her major work, *Social Science and Social Pathology* (Allen and Unwin, 1959), this move potentially poses a severe practical problem for those, like herself, who believe that the law should also aim to deter: there is no reason whatever to think that the treatment that might reform actual offenders will also deter potential offenders.
5 There are, of course, still a few rehabilitation theorists; they usually do not expect *punishment* to do very much work. See, for instance, Edgardo Rotman, *Beyond Punishment: A New View of the Rehabilitation of Offenders* (Greenwood, 1990).
6 'Now it is fitting for everyone undergoing vengeance and rightly suffering vengeance from another either to become better and be benefitted, or to become an example to the rest, so that then others see him undergoing whatever he undergoes, they will be afraid and become better' (*Gorgias*, 525b; Irwin's translation).
   For a different view, see Mary Margaret Mackenzie, *Plato on Punishment* (California University Press, 1990).
7 'But those who commit the ultimate injustices and because of such injustices become incurable, the samples are made from them. And they no longer gain benefit themselves, since they are incurable. But others are benefitted who see that for their faults they are undergoing the greatest, most painful, and most frightening suffering for all time, simply examples hung up there in Hades in the prison, spectacles and reproofs for the unjust arriving at any time' (*Gorgias*, 525c; Irwin's translation).
8 *Laws*, 862c–d.
9 Cf., e.g. *Gorgias*, 479. 'The remedial conception is closely bound up with the Socratic view that delinquency is in a sense "involuntary"' (E.R. Dodds, *Plato: Gorgias. A Revised Text with Introduction and Commentary* (Clarendon Press, 1959), p. 254).
10 Cf. *Republic*, 335a–e, where Socrates concludes: 'It is not then the function of the just man, Polemarchus, to harm either friend or anyone else.'
11 Terence Irwin, however, argues, on grounds of consistency, that Plato must hold that incurables may be used as examples only after death (*Plato: Gorgias* (Clarendon Press, 1979), p. 245).

[12] 525b, Irwin's translation. However, in *Laws*, 862, Plato recognizes means other than pain and suffering.

[13] *The Enchiridion*, Ch. 69. Cf. also *The City of God*, Bk. 21. Ch. 26.

[14] For a famous example, see St Augustine's *The City of God*, Bk. 21.

[15] I Corinthians, 3.12–15.

[16] For an informative history of the doctrine of purgatory up to the fourteenth century, see Jacques Le Goff, *The Birth of Purgatory* (University of Chicago Press, 1984; French, 1981). Hobbes was still wrestling with the text in *Leviathan*, Ch. 43.

[17] 'The Moral Education Theory of Punishment', *Philosophy and Public Affairs*, vol. xiii (1984), p. 215.

[18] 'The Moral Education Theory of Punishment', p. 211. (I assume that this is what Hampton means when she says that we must accept 'the deterrence theorist's contention' that the justification of punishment is 'connected with' the necessity of preventing crime.)

[19] 'The Moral Education Theory of Punishment', p. 237. Hampton does not explore the relations between these constraints. The first two have a Kantian source and the third a Platonic, but, suitably interpreted, the last may be held to entail the first two (which in turn may be held to have an entailment relation, or even to be identical).

The thought that punishment must be aimed at the offender's good also motivates Herbert Morris's theory in 'A Paternalistic Theory of Punishment', *American Journal of Philosophy*, vol. xviii (1981), pp. 263–271.

[20] 'The Moral Education Theory of Punishment', p. 211.

Hegel's famous pronouncement is in *The Philosophy of Right* (Clarendon Press, 1952), Addition 62, p. 246.

[21] 'The Moral Education Theory of Punishment', p. 212.

[22] 'The Moral Education Theory of Punishment', p. 213 (Hampton's emphasis). She refers to the public at large because she holds that punishment has an educative effect there too.

[23] Cf. Derek Parfit, *Reasons and Persons* (Clarendon Press, 1984), Ch. 3.

[24] In fact, she says, as though the difference were of no account, that the offender 'has little conception of, or is indifferent to, the pain her actions caused'. The tenor of her argument is generally consistent with the first of these formulations, which makes the matter cognitive rather than affective. (Cf. also p. 230 for a recognition of the general problem of understanding what wrongdoing consists in.)

[25] 'The Moral Education Theory of Punishment', p. 224.

[26] *Ibid.*

[27] For further cogent criticism of Hampton, see David Boonin, *The Problem of Punishment* (Cambridge University Press, 2008), pp. 180–192.

Chapter Five

Denunciation

'The ultimate justification for any punishment is not that it is a deterrent but that it is the emphatic denunciation by the community of a crime.'[1]

Introduction

Lord Denning's view of the point of punishment, given in evidence to a royal commission inquiring into capital punishment, has been widely shared amongst judges, and has become increasingly popular amongst legal theorists and philosophers. But why should we wish to denounce offences? And, more particularly, why should we expend the enormous resources of the criminal justice system in order to do it? Yet more particularly, why should we inflict suffering on people (indeed, kill them, in Lord Denning's view) merely in order to do so?

Most of the theories that emphasize the denunciatory aspect of punishment are externalist, and they answer these questions by claiming that denouncing crime will help to reduce its incidence. For instance, it may be thought that denouncing crimes will serve to inculcate the sense that the behaviour in question is wrong,[2] or perhaps just that it will not be tolerated. Or it may be thought that potential offenders will be deterred by the sense of shame that is induced by the condemnation expressed by punishment.[3] In addition, many crimes cause outrage in the public at large; punishment should enable them to express this outrage vicariously, and if it does not then they are likely to express it directly in behaviour which is a danger to all.[4] Yet another sort of theory claims that expressing disapproval of crime will tend to promote traditional moral values, and thus tighten the bonds that hold society together.[5]

The foregoing theories are externalist. It has been argued by Joel Feinberg that punishment is *inherently* expressive, that its expressive role is a defining purpose of punishment:[6] the 'reprobative function must be part of the *definition* of punishment.'[7] Feinberg's article caused considerable stir because it was widely thought to have injected a positive 'retributive' element into the theory of punishment at a time when this was unfashionable.[8] However, Feinberg did not suggest that punishment is *justified* simply in virtue of its denunciatory impact. As he recognizes, the denunciatory aspect of punishment actually increases the requirements on a justification since it adds another layer of 'hard treatment'. And in *The Moral Limits of the Criminal Law*, Feinberg is explicit that the ultimate aim of punishment is 'to reduce the number of wrongful harms inflicted on individuals by one another'.[9] He says little about the role of condemnation in this, but seems to endorse Neil MacCormick's view that the role of condemnation is to 'vindicate' the morality that prohibits certain harmful actions.[10] Since the 'ultimate aim' of punishment is to prevent such actions, we are presumably to think that vindicating the appropriate morality plays a role in this by '*creating* and endorsing moral consensus'. In the respects relevant to our purposes, then, Feinberg's view does not differ significantly from those mentioned in the previous paragraph.

All of the theories so far mentioned hold that the point of denouncing crime is to prevent it. They thus provide a sensible answer to the first of the questions distinguished on p. 28f. But if it is the *denunciatory* aspect of punishment that does this, then we may wonder why, in order to denounce crime, we need to use punishment. As Hart put it: 'The normal way in which moral condemnation is expressed is by *words*, and it is not clear, if denunciation is really what is required, why a solemn public statement of disapproval would not be the most "appropriate" or "emphatic" means of expressing this. Why should a denunciation take the form of punishment?'[11] The answer must be that the denunciation expressed by punishment is, *as denunciation*, more effective in preventing crime than denunciation expressed in other ways.

But denunciation is denunciation, and if punishment is more effective in preventing crime than stern words from public officials there is at least the suspicion that this must be due to some of its other aspects. The claim is, of course, an empirical one. But no one has yet succeeded in finding any empirical evidence to support the view that the denunciatory aspect of punishment, separated from its other aspects, has any measurable impact on the level of crime.[12]

Condemnation for Its Own Sake

Andrew von Hirsch adopts Feinberg's view that punishment is inherently condemnatory.[13] 'Punishing someone consists of visiting a deprivation (hard treatment) on him, because he supposedly has committed a wrong, in a manner that expresses disapprobation of the person for his conduct.'[14] However, his view also differs from the view that we seemed to find in Feinberg, for he holds that the condemnatory aspect of punishment is not subordinate to the further aim of preventing crime. His view is that punishment has two separate purposes, each necessary to justify it, but neither alone sufficient. One of those purposes is to discourage crime, mainly through deterrence; its other purpose is to express condemnation of the offender. Our attempt to discourage crime needs little justification; as to the latter purpose, it is simply intrinsically appropriate to condemn wrongdoing. If the state were to 'penalize adult criminal conduct in as morally neutral a way as possible', with no 'implied claim that there was anything wrong with the perpetrator's acts', this would be a '*morally* inappropriate response', quite independently of any ill effects that might or might not follow.[15] Forming an adverse judgment on wrong behaviour is, quite generally, part of what it is to have a morality, von Hirsch says, and one would withhold the overt expression of such a judgment 'only if one had special reasons for not reproving the actor'.[16] Von Hirsch's view is thus an internalist one. Wrongdoing cries out for condemnation, and punishment is a way of expressing that condemnation; it is therefore guaranteed to be an appropriate response to wrongdoing.[17]

We find the same view in Antony Duff, who is explicit that it is a

conceptual point that to mean what we say in condemning
some conduct as wrong is to be committed to censuring
those who engage in it (assuming that we have the standing
to do so)...[18]

Is it in fact intrinsically morally appropriate, or conceptually
demanded, to respond to wrongdoing with condemnation in
the way suggested by von Hirsch and Duff? It does not seem
obvious. The strongest conceptual claim that could be made
— one far too strong for many philosophers — would be that
overt condemnation is *one of a range* of types of conduct
proneness to some of which would be a criterion for a moral
belief. But that claim would not support the thesis of von
Hirsch and Duff. Nor does it seem more appealing as a
simple moral thesis. However much one feels like sounding
off when someone has done something of which one dis-
approves, one typically ought to have a better reason for
doing so — such as, for instance, that it may get him to desist
from such actions in the future, or even just that it will help
him to understand the wrongfulness of what he did (as Duff
goes on to argue).

In *Censure and Sanctions*, von Hirsch invokes an idea of
Strawson's:

> The capacity to respond to wrongdoing by reprobation or
> censure, he [Strawson] says, is simply part of a morality that
> holds people accountable for their conduct. When a person
> commits a misdeed, others judge him adversely, because his
> conduct was reprehensible. Censure consists of the expres-
> sion of that judgment, plus its accompanying sentiment of
> disapproval. One would withhold the expression of blame
> only if there were special reasons for not confronting the
> actor: for example, doubts about one's standing to challenge
> him.[19]

But nothing in Strawson legitimates the last sentence of this
quotation; and indeed Strawson's argument gives no real
support to von Hirsch's position. Strawson argues that such
reactive attitudes as resentment and moral condemnation do
not depend upon the falsity of determinism for their rationality; those attitudes are inescapable for us, and it makes no
sense to question their rationality globally on the basis of a
general metaphysical thesis. Nothing in the argument
licenses the move from the claim that the general tendency to

feel moral condemnation is beyond rational appraisal to the further claim that expressing it needs no justification.

Telling people what we think of them typically needs some justification.[20] And that is even more evidently so when, as in the case of punishment by the state, one's manner of telling them is to inflict suffering on them, at considerable cost to them and to others. And this brings us to a second question: if we are to censure offenders, why do so by inflicting suffering on them?

To this von Hirsch has a candid answer. The condemnatory aspect of punishment is necessary for its justification; but it is not sufficient. He admits that if all we wanted to do was to *condemn* offenders then we should indeed use a means that did not involve the infliction of suffering, for the condemnatory function is not, by itself, sufficient to justify the suffering. What justifies *that* is the preventive function of crime. In so far, then, as a theory of punishment must explain why it is justifiable *to inflict suffering on offenders*, von Hirsch's *denunciatory* theory would offer no help.[21]

Duff gives a different answer, and we shall turn to it in due course.

Reconnecting With Correct Values

A more ambitious, and ingenious, expressive theory has been propounded by Robert Nozick in what he refers to as an attempt to articulate a 'framework for retribution'.[22] According to Nozick, we should denounce the offender because it *reconnects him with correct values*. 'It is not that this connection is a desired further effect of punishment: the act of retributive punishment itself effects this connection.'[23]

At the centre of Nozick's theory is the idea that 'retributive punishment' has a certain structure. I quote:

> Under retributive punishment for S's act of A (I speak here of the fullest and most satisfactory case):
>
> (1) Someone believes that S's act has a certain degree of wrongness
> (2) and visits a penalty upon S
> (3) which is determined by the wrongness H of the act A, or by $r \propto H$,[24]
> (4) intending that the penalty be done because of the wrong act A

(5) and in virtue of the wrongness of A

(6) intending that S know the penalty was visited upon him because he did A

(7) and in virtue of the wrongness of A,

(8) by someone who intended to have the penalty fit and be done because of the wrongness of A

(9) and who intended that S would recognize (he was intended to recognize) that the penalty was visited upon him so that 1–8 are satisfied, indeed so that 1–9 are satisfied.[25]

The structure of actions and intentions here is, of course, exactly parallel to the structure that H.P. Grice claimed to constitute meaning in an utterance,[26] and Nozick draws the conclusion that '[r]etributive punishment is an act of communicative behavior'.[27] The message to be communicated is, 'roughly', 'This is how wrong what you did was'. The best point of communicating this message would be, for Nozick, to reform the offender, but he is sensibly pessimistic about punishment generally having such an effect and so he settles for something less. 'The wrongdoer has become disconnected from correct values, and the purpose of punishment is to (re)connect him.'[28] More accurately, this purpose is a necessary condition of justified punishment; reform of the offender would be a valuable 'intensification'.

To be connected to value is for value to 'have effect in our lives' —and to have effect *qua value*, not merely adventitiously.[29] And this occurs under (at least) three circumstances. First, value has effect in our lives when we do things because they are right, or good. Second, value has effect in our lives when, having failed to do what is right, we repent. And, third, value has effect in our lives when we are punished for wrongdoing.[30] For value to have effect in someone's life in the third way is less valuable than for it to have effect in the first two ways. 'Yet still, it is of some considerable value, much better than if the correct values qua correct values had no effect on him at all.'[31]

We might question Nozick's claim that 'retributive punishment' must have the Gricean structure (even in 'the fullest and most satisfactory case'), in particular that it requires conditions (6)–(9). Proponents of at least some of the theories we have so far discussed are perfectly at liberty to reject these conditions. The Simple Desert Theory, for instance, has nothing in it that requires those conditions; nor does the Just Distribution Theory. We should also note that Nozick's theory will run straight into the problem of commensurability that I have earlier discussed. The message that punishment is to communicate is 'This is how wrong what you did was'. The 'this' here must refer to the suffering involved in punishment. That suffering is not, however, itself 'wrong' — obviously, for that would make no sense — nor is inflicting it necessarily wrong. More fully spelled out, then, the message must presumably be 'This degree of suffering is proportional to the wrongness of your act'. And we saw reason in Chapter 2 to think that this is not a coherent message.

But let us ignore these problems. Expressive theories have two other questions to answer. First, we need to know why we should bother to denounce an offence. Second, we need to know why, if we are to do this, we should do it through the infliction of hard treatment.

Nozick's answer to the first question is that it is appropriate, sometimes even 'called for', to denounce the offender because this connects him with correct values, and such connecting is intrinsically good.[32]

But it is not obvious that there is anything intrinsically good about correct values' merely *having effect* in one's life. This can happen in all sorts of ways, some of them good, some of them bad, and some of them neutral. Just as one can do what is right because it is right, so one can do what is wrong because it is wrong — or so many people think. Correct values, in such a case, have effect in one's life, but it is hardly obvious that this is 'good in itself', 'much better than if the correct values qua correct values had no effect on [the offender] at all'.[33] Less controversially, someone may instruct me in correct values and I may reject the instruction; here, correct values have had effect in my life, but one that is presumably, from the point of view of value, quite neutral.

In this last case, is it true that correct values have had effect in my life 'qua correct values'? That depends upon what precisely this means — a matter to which Nozick devotes little attention, though the qualification is clearly intended to do significant work. But, whatever it means, if it is satisfied in the case of punishment (as Nozick asserts) then it will clearly be satisfied when someone simply *tells* me what are the correct values, for it is, according to Nozick, merely the Gricean structure of meaning that guarantees that correct values have effect in punishment 'qua correct values',[34] and if the Gricean account is correct its conditions could hardly fail to hold in the case where someone merely tells me something. Of course, one could reject the Gricean account of meaning; but then we should have lost the reason Nozick gave us to think that punishment is communicative in the first place.

There is, then, nothing intrinsically good about the mere fact that correct values have had effect in one's life. In order to generate any intrinsic goodness, the values must have had effect *in the right way*. It seems at least plausible to think that when one acts rightly because of a commitment to correct values, then correct values have had effect in the right way, and there is something intrinsically good about the situation. It is surely far less clear that there is anything intrinsically good about the situation in which someone is made to suffer simply because he has flouted correct values and knows this. I do not say that someone cannot sensibly take this view, though I find it hard to see its appeal. I merely say that one can sensibly reject it. And one might have hoped for a better answer to the question why punishing someone is intrinsically good than the bald, 'That's just the view I take'.[35]

In fact, Nozick also undertakes to give a better answer than this:

> [I]n seeing retribution alongside the other phenomena of connecting or linking with value, namely, acting rightly and repenting, in seeing it share some of their characteristics and also in seeing all such connections with value as part of an even more general category which includes the connection of knowledge, of belief tracking the truth, we place retribution in its widest context; in so seeing how it resembles other things of value, falling under the very same general categories, we do more than simply repeat that retribution is deserved.[36]

Certainly, subsuming a phenomenon under a more general category is sometimes an acceptable form of explanation. In this particular instance, however, it is not enough to see that 'retribution' shares with acting rightly and repenting 'some of their characteristics'. What it must share are the *right* characteristics. In particular, what we must see is that punishment, like acting rightly and repenting, connects the offender with correct values *in the right way*. And that is just what we have not yet seen.

Even if we were to grant that being 'connected with correct values' is intrinsically valuable, we should still have to explain why we use *punishment* in order to effect this connection. Nozick claims that the relation is an internal one. Being reconnected with correct values, correct values having effect in one's life, is not some further end contingently brought about by the punishment that effects it; 'the act of retributive punishment itself effects this connection.'[37] But still this leaves our question. Nothing yet has precluded the possibility that other processes — friendly instruction in correct values, for instance — might also effect the connection in question, and do so no less contingently. Why, then, favour punishment?

Nozick (implicitly) raises this question. In answer, he replies that punishment 'is needed for the effect to be significant (this would not be served merely by telling [the offender] that he was wrong)'.[38] But this is surely no answer. Instructing the offender in correct values must surely be significant: it is a paradigm case of connecting the offender with correct values, having correct values affect his life. Would executing him or sending him to prison be *more* significant? Certainly, that would have a more dramatic effect on his life, and we could express this by saying that in such circumstances correct values have had a greater effect on his life. But now we may wonder why that greater significance should tell in favour of punishment rather than mere instruction. Presumably the theory does not have a hitherto concealed component which requires that punishment should *maximize* the effect of correct values on people's lives — otherwise it would impose no constraints whatever upon how severely an offender may be punished. In fact, as we saw earlier, Nozick makes a gesture towards a requirement of proportionality: the message that punishment is to communicate is '*This* is how wrong what you did was'. But that requirement of proportionality does not appear out of the

blue; it is motivated by the thought that punishment is supposed to communicate to the offender the wrongness of what
he did. But in that case, 'this is how wrong what you did
was' could be followed as well by an explanation as by an
object lesson, and it remains unclear why the effect of the
former should be less 'significant' than the effect of the latter.

Nozick has a further answer: '[T]he role of suffering in
punishment is not merely to ensure a significant effect in
people's lives, but... to negate or lessen flouting by making it
impossible to remain as pleased with one's previous anti-
linkage.'[39] Let us imagine, then, that the offender does indeed
become less pleased with his 'anti-linkage', that he comes to
regret that he did what he did—but purely because things
have turned out badly for him. This may go a little way
towards satisfying our vengeful reactions towards him, since
regret is an unpleasant experience, and we may feel some
satisfaction from his undergoing it; but—unless we are simply to appeal to the Intrinsic Desert Theory, which Nozick's
theory is supposed to go beyond—it is not obviously of
intrinsic value. After all, in these circumstances regretting
that he did what he did is, presumably, regretting that he did
it at the time that he did it, or in the place, or manner in
which he did it, thoughts that are not significantly different
from the regret that he got caught. He may, of course, go
further than this; he may come to wish that he did not have
the desires that led him to do the act in the first place. But if
this is motivated merely by self-interest rather than by a
perception of the evil of the desires then it is again not clear
that there is anything intrinsically valuable about it (though
it may have great instrumental value). If, on the other hand,
it is indeed motivated by a perception of the evil of the desires that had previously motivated him then this is becoming
too much like reform to suit Nozick's purposes.

Vindicating the Value of the Victim

We shall turn, finally, to another sort of expressive theory,
that of Jean Hampton.[40] For her, as for Nozick, the theory has
its place as part of an attempt to support what she calls a
retributive theory of punishment. She rejects the Intrinsic
Desert Theory. Retribution is not, she thinks, a 'foundational'
idea, but is in fact teleological.[41] She also rejects what I have

called the Just Distribution Theory, which, though an internalist theory, might be thought of as teleological. In her view,
retributive punishment is to be understood as 'the victim's
value "striking back" and in this way proving itself'.[42]

How are we to spell out this metaphor?

According to Hampton, retributive punishment achieves
its aim in two ways. The first, briefly stated, is this. Wrongdoing sends a message to the effect that the victim is of lesser
worth than the offender. Punishment annuls that message.
The second way is this. Society protects its members against
crime through the institution of punishment, and just how
much protection it gives to different sorts of people is a
function of the value it places on them; this 'in turn can be
viewed as an indication of how valuable one really is'.[43] So
'people who long for a high valuation may come to demand
punishment [for those who victimize them]... because they
want the expression of what this legal protection symbol-
izes'.[44] Like Hampton, we shall mainly focus on the first of
these ideas. Punishment, according to the second, has a clear
enough end, but one that has no essential connection with
punishment. It is thus an externalist theory and not essentially different from the sorts of mentioned at the start of this
chapter. The first idea is, however, quite different.

Central to Hampton's theory is an account of the *wrongness* to which punishment is a response. As she points out,[45]
what makes an action a wrong is not merely the harm that it
does, for we could always imagine identical harm occurring
without any wrong having been done. What makes an action
a wrong, Hampton claims, is that it does not accord its victim
the respect that he deserves. Let us begin by spelling this out
more fully.

The central notion is that of human worth, or value,
which, Hampton says, may be thought of either instrument-
ally or intrinsically. The most familiar version of the latter
sort of conception is that of Kant, according to whom we
humans 'by virtue of having the property of rationality... are
intrinsically valuable as ends-in-ourselves, so that we are all
equal in worth'.[46] And since our value depends wholly and
only upon our rationality it cannot, in the ordinary course of
events, be lessened or lost (it is, presumably, wholly possessed once some threshold of rationality is passed). Hampton

thinks that the correct conception of human worth is indeed the Kantian one, and, for the most part, she spells out her theory in terms of it, though she thinks that some other theories (though not instrumental ones) are also available to the retributivist.[47]

When someone does me a wrong my worth is threatened. I am *demeaned* by the action: that is to say, I am forced to endure treatment that is too low, inappropriate to my value; when I am thus treated, I may feel pain from such treatment, but, whether I do so or not, I have been demeaned, and therefore wronged.

When someone demeans another they

> incorrectly believe or else fail to realise that others' value rules out the treatment their actions have accorded the others, and they incorrectly believe or implicitly assume that their own value is high enough to make this treatment permissible. So, implicit in their wrongdoings is a message about their value relative to that of their victims.[48]

'A retributivist's commitment to punishment' is a commitment to countering this message, 'a commitment to asserting moral truth in the face of its denial'.[49] 'By victimizing me, the wrongdoer has declared himself elevated with respect to me, acting as a superior who is permitted to use me for his purposes. A false moral claim has been made. Moral reality has been denied. The retributivist demands that the false claim be corrected.'[50] But how does punishment counter the message? Punishment conveys *defeat*, and thus the message that the offender is not, after all, superior to the victim. Indeed, retributive punishment 'is a symbol that is conceptually required to reaffirm a victim's equal worth in the face of a challenge to it'[51]—'conceptually' because the victim's equal worth can be reaffirmed only by defeating the offender, and '*any... method*, so long as it was still a method for *defeating* the wrongdoer, *would still count as punishment*'[52] or 'retribution'.[53]

Does Hampton's theory satisfactorily explain, as a theory of punishment must, why it is legitimate to inflict suffering on offenders?

Our aim in punishment, according to Hampton, is to vindicate the worth of the victim, to send a message to the effect that the offender is no more valuable than the victim.

But surely, it may seem, punishment is not the only way in which we could do that. Why not, for instance, celebrate the victim's worth with a ticker tape parade? Here is Hampton's reply: 'Still the fact that [the victim] had been mastered by the wrongdoer would stand. He would have lost to her, and no matter how much the community might contend that he was not her inferior, the loss counts as evidence that he is.' Punishment, however, in its mastery of the wrongdoer, counters that evidence, and this is no mere contingency for *'any... method,* so long as it was still a method for *defeating* the wrongdoer, *would still count as punishment'* or 'retribution'. Thus, if this is correct, so long as we have a satisfactory answer to the question why we should wish to vindicate the worth of the victim, the question why we should do so through punishment cannot not arise.

But the claim that any method, painful or otherwise, which defeats the wrongdoer 'would still count as punishment' is surely not correct. When one nation defeats another in a war it would be simply wrong to hold that the defeated nation has thereby been punished. Similarly, when police prevent a criminal from carrying out his criminal intent they have defeated him but he has not been punished. Elsewhere she weakens the claim, suggesting that any method that inflicts defeat on the wrongdoer is *retribution*, but that retribution is a broader notion than punishment.[54] But this claim too is false, and for just the same reason.

Unfortunately, the claim is crucial to Hampton's enterprise. Without it, she is not in a position to explain why, given that there is good reason to convey a message to the effect that the offender is of no more worth than the victim, punishment is necessarily the appropriate means of doing so.

Even if Hampton could explain this we should be left, of course, with the prior question: is there indeed good reason to convey such a message?

Hampton holds that there is. The offence itself sends a message, the message that the offender is superior to the victim; and we have an obligation to counter this message. Does this seem plausible?

It is important here to distinguish a number of different claims which such words as 'express' and 'convey' may tend to obscure. Let us agree for the moment, for the sake of the argument, that a crime does indeed *embody* a message about the offender's attitude to the victim. This need mean no more than that something of the offender's attitude to the victim can be inferred from it. Let us also say that, when the crime is committed, that message is *sent*, in something like the way that a message is sent when a flag is lowered to half-mast. However, when a message is sent, it may not be *received*: it may or may not be heard; if it is heard, it may or may not be understood. And even if the message is heard and understood it may or may not be *believed*. So when Hampton talks about a crime 'sending' or 'conveying' a message, which part(s) of this process is she talking about: the embodying, the sending, the receiving, the believing, or all of these?

Hampton's language sometimes suggests that it is just the first three parts of the process that are at issue, the embodying, the sending, and the receiving. The 'criminal actions convey the idea',[55] she says. But if that were all that were at issue it would hardly seem to generate a sensible theory of punishment. Take the clearest case of a message being sent and received. Imagine that someone falsely *says*—in the normal sense of that word—that he is superior in worth to me; and that people hear and understand what he says. Does this call for action? Not necessarily.[56] It may be that no one believes what they have heard. In that case most people would think that the sensible course of action would be to ignore it. And if there is great cost attached to doing anything about it, as with the criminal justice system, that is even more evidently so. Hampton, however, sometimes speaks as if there is a duty simply to counter falsehoods. 'A retributivist's commitment to punishment is... a commitment to asserting moral truth in the face of its denial... A false claim has been made. Moral reality has been denied. The retributivist demands that the false claim must be corrected.'[57] 'A false moral claim has been made. The moral facts have been denied. The punisher who inflicts retribution on such a wrongdoer... wants to reassert those facts and vindicate the value of the victim.'[58] But I imagine that most people would think that if there is indeed a duty to counter falsehoods then this is a duty to prevent people from believing them, or being offended or annoyed by them, or at least being affected by them in some way detrimental to someone's interests, rather than a duty simply to counter them when uttered. Moreover, even if there were such a duty, it is hard to see how it, with all links to human welfare severed, could plausibly be vested in the legal system; this would require an extreme version of legal moralism that would appeal to few.

Hampton, in fact, sometimes speaks as if there were indeed more substance at issue, as if the nub of the matter were, not merely that a message is *sent*, but that we have some tendency *to believe* the message. 'Whatever the wrong-doer's intentions or purposes, *we read his action as* one that simultaneously "humbles" the victim and "elevates" the action's perpetrator'; 'the one who has effected this humbling *seems to have* won a kind of victory over the victim'; 'at his hands *she is made to look* inferior.'[59] The wrongdoing is (read by us as) 'evidence' that the victim is of lesser worth than the wrongdoer; and 'the evidence of value loss provided by the crime is nullified by the new evidence provided by the sub-ordination effected through punishment'.[60] So, let us say, the message is not merely sent and received; it is also, to some degree, believed.

The problem with this is surely that, except for a few special sorts of case, it is wholly fantastic. When someone is raped, for instance, virtually no one sees this as evidence that the rapist is superior in worth to the victim.[61] Of course, the rapist has in one sense dominated the victim, but this obv-iously does not make the rapist more admirable, let alone superior in human worth (the relation between these two different judgments we shall turn to briefly in a moment). The same is true for almost all wrongdoing. Wrongdoing can occasionally become glamorized, of course, but we should not dwell on these atypical cases. It is enough to observe that, normally, no one takes wrongdoing as evidence for sup-erior human worth.

This claim is, of course, empirical, and it may be that Hampton thinks that it reflects a simplistic understanding of the relevant psychology. Much of what she says seems to depend upon the idea that human worth, our own as well as others', is something that we have deep doubts about. Having remarked that, on a Kantian theory, human worth is possessed by everyone equally, and cannot, ordinarily, be lost, she goes on:

> Nonetheless, however popular the Kantian insistence on equality of worth is among people reflecting upon such matters, the way in which human beings' sense of worth is threatened by crime, and the way in which so many of us attack others in an attempt either to augment or maintain our own standing suggests that at least emotionally, if not intellectually, most people are non-egalitarian in their views about their worth relative to others.[62]

If this were correct, then, we might indeed have reason to speak of a need to vindicate the worth of the victims of wrongdoing. But it is surely not correct.

First, Hampton says that 'emotionally' 'people are non-egalitarian in their views about worth'. If this means that they have emotions whose propositional content is a commitment to non-egalitarian views, then this is not to the point, for these may be emotions from which they are wholly alienated, emotions whose content they are not the least inclined to assent to. That is a common enough phenomenon. We might compare it to, for instance, irrational guilt feelings, which can linger when all rational commitment to them has gone; even in the emotional grip of such feelings one may have no serious inclination to believe them. If that is the sort of 'commitment' that is at issue, then talk of vindication, and so on, is quite out of place. One can vindicate an idea only if it has been put under suspicion, and that has not occurred in cases such as these. But perhaps 'vindication' is the wrong concept. Perhaps what the victims of crime need is *reassurance* about their human worth. But if we are talking about trauma caused in part by irrational feelings then some system of post-victimisation counselling would seem more appropriate than the elaborate, necessarily impersonal, machinery of the judicial system.

There is a second, and more important, confusion, one generated by words such as 'worth' and 'value'. When men are violently robbed in the street they typically suffer a sense of humiliation. But it is important to note that the fact that one may feel humiliated by wrongdoing does not suggest that one doubts one's human worth in any sense relevant to the present discussion. A Kantian can fully accept that he is not the man he may wish to be without thinking that this threatens his human worth; that, after all, is a central point of the Kantian conception of human worth. That I may feel humiliated by an attack in the street does not suggest in any way at all that I am committed to a non-egalitarian conception of human worth. My failure to deal with my assailant has no relevance to the assessment of human worth, on a Kantian conception at any rate.[63]

In fact, the same is true on virtually any plausible conception of human worth, intrinsic or instrumental. At the wrongdoer's hands, Hampton says, the victim 'is made to look inferior'.[64] But if this is true it is so in only the most trivial sense. If I am attacked and beaten in the street this may reveal me to be the inferior street fighter; but even on the most instrumental conception of human worth this could hardly look like reasonable evidence, all things considered, for thinking me the inferior *as a human being*. On any conception, that would be a more complex judgment than could be based upon my prowess in scuffles on the street.[65]

Typically, then, the message, if any, about the victim that one is likely to extract from wrongdoing will not be relevant to assessments of human worth. This is important. Hampton must insist on the claim that the message expressed by wrongdoing really is about human worth. After all, if the message sent by the offence actually were that I am of inferior worth as a human being one might at least begin to understand the moralistic desire that the message be countered. By contrast, there seems little plausibility in the idea that we should go to great pains to counter the message that I am an inferior street fighter. Who cares? And anyway *that* message is *true*.

We earlier granted for the sake of the argument that wrongdoing does indeed *embody* a message about the human worth of the victim. It is now time to question that.

There is no doubt that some offences are actually intended to convey a message, as with, for instance, cross-burning by the Ku Klux Klan. It might also be true of many crimes of violence.[66] Hampton knows that most offences at least are not like this, but she thinks that even when offences are not specifically intended to convey a message they do nonetheless *embody* a message.[67]

> [P]eople who believe their purposes warrant them in taking another's wallet, or another's savings, or another's life, are

people who believe their victims are not worth enough to require better treatment. Indeed, they are convinced enough about the importance of their own purposes — and thus of their own importance — to regard their behavior as permissible with respect to these others.[68]

This may be an accurate description of the mental state in which some offences are committed. But it is doubtful whether it is essential to all cases, for it seems to impute to offenders a cognitive state which there seems little reason to believe that they necessarily possess. It seems, after all, plausible to suggest that many offenders have no view whatever about their victims' worth, nor about whether their actions are 'permissible'. They may simply not think about such things.[69] If so, it is indeed not true that they believe their victims are worth enough to require better treatment. But this is not to say that they 'believe their victims are not worth enough to require better treatment'; we must not here confuse an external negation with an internal one. Alternatively, it may be that they do indeed think that their victims are every bit as valuable as they themselves, but simply commit their offences anyway.

Perhaps it might be replied that, though offenders themselves need not explicitly accept the thought that their victims are worth less then they, and that this legitimates their actions, we must nonetheless appeal to such thoughts in order to interpret their behaviour. Their actions alone show that they think little of their victims' worth, and that their actions are thus permissible. As it might be put, these, and similar actions, *are part what it is* to have such thoughts.

But here we must be careful. It is a familiar claim that accepting certain value judgments commits one to certain sorts of action.[70] But that has no relevance to the present issue. All that would be relevant here would be the converse view that performing certain sorts of actions commits one to accepting certain value judgments; and, unless one insists upon identity criteria for actions that make it trivially true, this view is clearly false: one and the same action can be performed for an indefinite number of quite different reasons, reasons sharing no relevant evaluation. One man, for instance, may kill his wife because he thinks she is worth no better. Another may kill his wife because he thinks that after a lifetime of love and affection he owes it to her to help her be rid of her suffering. Their actions, barely described, do not reveal their motivations beyond the desire to kill. Similarly, the actions of a criminal who steals someone's wallet need not reveal much about his motivations, certainly not the valuation that he places on his victim. As I have said, the case of the person who really does think that his victim is of less worth than himself and that this makes his behaviour permissible is perfectly intelligible. But so also is the case of the person who simply does not think about such matters. So also is the case of the person who thinks that the victim is worth as much as he himself, but steals the wallet anyway because he thinks that his *need* is sufficiently great, or merely because he cannot resist the temptation.

The claim that wrongdoing necessarily expresses a message about the relative worth of the wrongdoer and the victim is, then, one that we should reject — and with it Hampton's answer to the question why we should punish.

---

1 Lord Denning, evidence cited in the *Royal Commission on Capital Punishment, 1949–1953, Report*, Cmnd 8932 (H.M.S.O., 1943), § 53.

2 Cf. James Fitzjames Stephen, *A History of the Criminal Law of England*, vol. *ii* (Macmillan, 1883), pp. 79f.; *ibid.*, p. 81; Bentham, *An Introduction to the Principles of Moral and Legislation*, Ch. 14, note o; Lord Devlin, *The Enforcement of Morals* (Oxford University Press, 1965).

3 See, for instance, John Braithwaite, *Crime, Shame and Reintegration* (Cambridge University Press, 1989); John Braithwaite and Philip Pettit, *Not Just Deserts: A Republican Theory of Criminal Justice* (Clarendon Press, 1990), Ch. 6; and James Dignan, 'Reintegration Through Reparation: A Way Forward for Restorative Justice?', in Antony Duff *et al.* (eds.), *Penal Theory and Practice: Tradition and Innovation in Criminal Justice* (Manchester University Press, 1994).

4 F.J. Stephen also took this view: 'The laws which punish murder or theft are substitutes for private vengeance, which, in the absence of law, would punish those crimes more severely, though in a less regular manner' (*Liberty, Equality, Fraternity*, ed. R.J. White (Cambridge University Press, 1967), p. 59). As Stephen elsewhere makes clear (p. 82), by 'private vengeance' he means the 'public desire for vengeance'.

5 This is probably Lord Devlin's central thought in *The Enforcement of Morals*. Something of the view can also be found in Neil MacCormick's *Legal Right and Social Democracy: Essays in Legal and Political Philosophy* (Clarendon Press, 1982), pp. 30–34.

Émile Durkheim is the most famous exponent of such a view; see *Moral Education: A Study in the Theory and Application of the Sociology of Education* (The Free Press, 1961; French, 1925), Ch. 10.

6   'The Expressive Function of Punishment', *The Monist*, 1965 (rp. in Feinberg's *Doing and Deserving: Essays in the Theory of Responsibility* (Princeton University Press, 1970), to which edition my page references refer).

Feinberg holds the same view in *The Moral Limits of the Criminal Law, Vol. IV: Harmless Wrongdoing* (Oxford University Press, 1988); cf. pp. 149–150.

7   'The Expressive Function of Punishment', p. 98.

8   Feinberg held that his theory captured the core of 'moral common sense' that lay at the bottom of retributive theories ('The Expressive Function of Punishment', p. 118).

9   *The Moral Limits of the Criminal Law, Vol. IV*, p. 150.

10   *The Moral Limits of the Criminal Law, Vol. IV*, pp. 12f.

11   H.L.A. Hart, *Law, Liberty and Morality* (Oxford University Press, 1963), p. 66. See also Bernard Williams, 'Moral Responsibility and Political Freedom', *Cambridge Law Journal*, vol. lvi (1997), pp. 96–102, at p. 100 (rp. in Williams, *Philosophy as a Humanistic Discipline* (Princeton University Press, 2006)).

12   For a short discussion of the evidence, see Nigel Walker's *Why Punish?* (Oxford University Press, 1991), Ch. 3.

The lack of any substantial evidence of the social effects of punishment has not prevented many people from confidently telling us what they are. David Garland, for instance, remarks that the 'the data we have on this crucial issue… are woefully inadequate', but is quite happy to tell us that the institutions of 'penality' have a 'major impact' on how we think about, for instance, morality, authority, and the notion of the person (*Punishment and Modern Society: A Study in Social Theory* (University of Chicago Press, 1990)).

Faith in the educative effect of the law, however, seems to know no bounds. Consider the following, from a cabinet paper prepared by Chuter Ede, Home Secretary (the occasion was a forthcoming meeting of the cabinet to discuss whether the Government should take a position on capital punishment in the debate on the 1947 Criminal Justice Bill): 'There are some reprieved murderers whom it is right to release on licence after very short periods of imprisonment…, [but] it would be undesirable in such cases for a court publicly to pass a sentence of imprisonment for a few months or for a year or two, and thereby to create the impression that the taking of human life may in certain circumstances be no graver a crime than theft' (quoted by Lord Windlesham, *Responses to Crime, Vol. 2: Penal Policy in the Making* (Clarendon Press, 1993), p. 55). Even in the 1940s it was absurd to think that what happens in courts could create such an impression.

13   See Andrew von Hirsch, *Past or Future Crimes?* (Rutgers University Press, 1985), Ch. 5; *Censure and Sanctions* (Clarendon Press, 1993), Ch. 2.; and 'Penal Theories', in M. Tonry (ed.), *The Handbook of Crime and Punishment* (Oxford University Press, 1998).

14   *Censure and Sanctions*, p. 9.

15   *Past or Future Crimes?*, p. 52.

16   *Past or Future Crimes?*, p. 50.

17   Though, as always, that appropriateness may sometimes legitimately be overridden by other factors.

18   *Punishment, Communication, and Community* (Oxford University Press, 2001), p. 72; cf. p. 28. Duff, however, criticizes a central aspect of von Hirsch's theory, and has a more complex conception of the point of censure.

19   *Censure and Sanctions*, p. 9. Strawson's article is 'Freedom and Resentment', *Proceedings of the British Academy*, vol. xlviii (1962), pp. 1–25.

20   Cp. Christopher Bennett, *The Apology Ritual* (Cambridge University Press, 2008), pp. 141–142, 170; and, for a somewhat more nuanced version of this sentiment, David Boonin, *The Problem of Punishment* (Cambridge University Press, 2008), pp. 172–176.

21   John Tasioulas points out how uneasily the two aspects of von Hirsch's theory sit together in 'Punishment and Repentance', *Philosophy*, vol. lxxxi (2006), pp. 279–322, at pp. 290ff. His own view is that denunciation is the primary justification for punishment, and that denunciation must 'take the form of condemnation that involves hard treatment' because 'only punishment adequately conveys the blame the wrongdoer deserves'. We shall turn to this in more detail in the next chapter.

22   *Philosophical Explanations* (Clarendon Press, 1981), pp. 363–397.

23   *Philosophical Explanations*, p. 374.

24   In the formula 'r ∞ H', 'r' stands for—roughly—the degree of the agent's responsibility [AJE].

25   *Philosophical Explanations*, p. 369.

26   In H.P. Grice, 'Meaning', *The Philosophical Review*, vol. lxvi (1957), pp. 377–388.

27   *Philosophical Explanations*, p. 370.

28   *Philosophical Explanations*, p. 374.

29   I assume that this is part of the import of the passage on pp. 374f. It is, however, somewhat in tension with the passage on pp. 376f. where Nozick says, 'Retributive punishment is to effect two things: (a) connect the wrongdoer to value qua value (b) so that value qua value has a significant effect in his life, as significant as his own flouting of correct values'. The latter passage seems to suggest that being connected to value and value's having effect in one's life are two different things. If so, it is unclear just what the metaphor is supposed to mean.

30   *Philosophical Explanations*, p. 374.
31   *Philosophical Explanations*, p. 376.
32   *Philosophical Explanations*, p. 377.
33   *Philosophical Explanations*, p. 376.
34   *Philosophical Explanations*, p. 377.
35   Nozick's purported intention in *Philosophical Explanations* is, of course, merely to offer 'explanations' rather than 'coercive arguments'. I leave it to the reader to decide whether Nozick actually pursues only this aim, and indeed whether the aim, and the distinction upon which it is supposed to rest, are sensible.
36   *Philosophical Explanations*, p. 376, fn.
37   *Philosophical Explanations*, p. 374.
38   *Philosophical Explanations*, p. 377.
39   *Philosophical Explanations*, p. 384. 'Anti-linkage' is a pleasing conceit implying something more than merely being unlinked — though precisely what more it is difficult to say.
40   Hampton's theory is outlined in Jeffrey G. Murphy and Jean Hampton, *Forgiveness and Mercy* (Cambridge University Press, 1988), and 'An Expressive Theory of Retribution', in Wesley Cragg (ed.) *Retributivism and Its Critics* (Steiner, 1992).
41   *Forgiveness and Mercy*, p. 123.
42   *Forgiveness and Mercy*, p. 123.
43   *Forgiveness and Mercy*, p. 141.
44   *Forgiveness and Mercy*, pp. 141f.
45   *Forgiveness and Mercy*, pp. 44f.
46   *Forgiveness and Mercy*, p. 46.
47   *Forgiveness and Mercy*, p. 124.
48   *Forgiveness and Mercy*, p. 124. Hampton means, of course, that they incorrectly believe that others' value does *not* rule out this treatment.
49   *Forgiveness and Mercy*, p. 125.
50   *Forgiveness and Mercy*, p. 125.
51   *Forgiveness and Mercy*, pp. 125f.
52   *Forgiveness and Mercy*, p. 126; emphasis in original.
53   'An Expressive Theory of Retribution', p. 16.
54   'An Expressive Theory of Retribution', p. 16.
55   'An Expressive Theory of Retribution', p. 8.
56   Cf. Christopher Bennett, *The Apology Ritual* (Cambridge University Press, 2008), p. 170.
57   *Forgiveness and Mercy*, p. 125.
58   'An Expressive Theory of Retribution', p. 12.
59   'An Expressive Theory of Retribution', p. 13 [my emphases].
60   'An Expressive Theory of Retribution', p. 13.
61   Rape in men's in prisons, where it is often alleged to be relatively common, may provide an exception to this, for here it seems sometimes to be intended as little more than a form of mastery. But understanding the systems of values that one finds in those cultures

is no easy matter. In any case, this would be, at most, a special sort of case from which it would be foolish to generalize.

[62] 'An Expressive Theory of Retribution', p. 9.

[63] There are, of course, sensible conceptions of human excellence in which the physical and mental abilities required by such activities do play a role. But the relation between human worth and human excellence is not straightforward — they are not obviously identical notions — and it is human worth that Hampton is speaking of. In any case, the role they play would be nowhere near sufficiently large to validate Hampton's claims.

[64] 'An Expressive Theory of Retribution', p. 9.

[65] Perhaps there are cultures in which physical prowess is ranked sufficiently highly that this does not hold true. But these are not our cultures. And crimes of violence are a small part of the wrongdoing with which the law deals.

[66] The psychology is, however, not so pellucid as many make it seem. Hampton, for instance, says that some wrongdoers 'go out of their way to disparage their victims' worth; sometimes they *intend* their actions to be demeaning or degrading', and she contrasts such cases with those that are not actually intended to be 'insulting' ('An Expressive Theory of Retribution', p. 6). But the former sort of cases do not necessarily suggest the vocabulary of communication. Take the following instance, one of a type that is often mentioned in this context:

> 'Maybe six years later, I'm doing some running around and howdy-doody, I get my butt busted in some fucking tiny town in Arizona and these hicks put me in a cell with this kid, probably seventeen or so, and you know what I did? I fucked him. I beat the shit out of him first and then I rolled him over and I fucked his ass.
>
> And you know what, when I was doing it, I thought about how I'd been fucked, I sure did. I kept thinking about how it felt to be fucked in the ass, how much I had hated it, how humiliated I'd been.
>
> You see, I finally understood why those motherfuckers fucked me when I was just a kid.
>
> It really didn't have nothing to do with sex. It had to do with power. All my life, people been fucking me, and when I was fucking that kid, I hated what I was doing, but I loved it too, because it was me on top and there wasn't one fucking thing he could do to stop me. Nothing. I was in charge, complete control.
>
> I could have done whatever the fuck I wanted to him and it is a fucking amazing feeling when you feel that way.' (*The Hot House: Life Inside Leavenworth Prison*, by Pete Earley (Bantam Books, 1992)).

Here, the speaker presumably intends his action to be humiliating to the victim. But that — by contrast with cross-burning — is not because he wants to send any message to him. He merely wants to revel in the sense of power, and in principle one could achieve this if one's victim did not even know that he were a victim; one might have killed him, for instance.

67   'An Expressive Theory of Retribution', p. 5.
68   'An Expressive Theory of Retribution', p. 6.
69   Cf. Philippa Foot, *Natural Goodness* (Clarendon Press, 2001), p. 19.
70   The modern *locus classicus* for such a view is R.M. Hare's *The Language of Morals* (Clarendon Press, 1952).

Chapter Six

Condemnation, Penance, and Reconciliation

We shall turn now to a theory that marries the central focuses of the last two chapters: denunciation and reform.[1] Antony Duff argues that an acceptable institution of punishment must have four aims: repentance on the part of the offender, reconciliation between the offender and the victim(s) of his offence, reform of the offender, and the prevention of crime.[2] According to Duff, the last of these is 'the central aim of the criminal law',[3] but Duff's main interest is with the other three, the 'three Rs' as he calls them, because in so far as punishment aims to prevent crime, it should do so through the realisation of these other three aims, rather than through deterrence or incapacitation.[4]

The restriction to these aims is motivated by two commitments. The first is to the value of (a certain conception of) autonomy. The second is to a politics of liberal communitarianism, an ideal of political community structured by a commitment on the part of each citizen to certain shared values (liberal ones), and a moral commitment, there and binding whether one likes it or not, to other citizens as fellow citizens.[5] These commitments work in tandem in Duff's argument; in particular, as will become clear, there is no route to his conclusion from the liberal communitarianism alone unless that political conception has built into it the value of autonomy, suitably understood. Everything turns, then, on the issue of autonomy. So let us start there.

Duff's central thought is that people are to be treated as rational, autonomous agents. Indeed, his 'main aim is to explore the implications of the Kantian demand that we should respect other people as rational and autonomous moral agents—that we should treat them as ends, never merely as means—for an understanding of the meaning and justification of criminal punishment'.[6] This Kantian demand is, of course, consistent with our desire that wrongdoers change their ways. We can, at least sometimes, get them to do so through threats or some other sort of coercion, but such responses aim to *manipulate* rather than appealing to the wrongdoer's reason, and this is not consistent with the Kantian demand, because, according to Duff, it fails to respect the offender's rational autonomy.[7] What is called for is an attempt to get the wrongdoer to *understand* the wrong that he did, and this calls for condemnation which, we hope, will lead the wrongdoer to such an understanding.

The appropriate response of the legal system to an offender, then, is to express the community's condemnation of his offence with the intention that this should bring him to a repentant understanding of his wrongdoing. It does this, first, in the trial process, which Duff sees as 'a formal or institutional analogue of a moral process of criticism and blame'.[8] But it is not only the verdict which is a condemnation of the offender; on Duff's view, so too is the punishment:

> Punishment is... continuous in its meaning and purpose with the criminal trial and the criminal law: it seeks to communicate to the offender that judgment on, and that condemnation of, his conduct which his trial has justified and which his conviction also expresses; to bring him to accept that judgment, to condemn himself, and to modify his future conduct accordingly; and thus to persuade him not merely to *obey* the law, but to *accept* its justified demands and judgments.[9]

The government, then, must treat its citizens—even those who break the law—as ends-in-themselves, and not as tools to be used for the general welfare. We should certainly accept this. But whether it follows that punishment must aim primarily at repentance, reform, and reconciliation is another matter. I shall later argue that a system of deterrent punishment can respect this Kantian constraint, though only if offenders are not punished in order to deter others. But Duff thinks that a system of deterrent punishment falls at an even earlier hurdle, because a government, in issuing deterrent threats in the first place, is trying to manipulate the behaviour of its citizens by playing upon their fears, and that in this way it 'fails to treat the citizen as a rational and autonomous agent'.[10]

What reason is there to think this?

Here is one bad reason. Duff appeals to Hegel's famous pronouncement that deterrent punishment treats a man like a dog.[11] But despite the fame of the pronouncement, the analogy is altogether misplaced. Deterrent punishment works by giving the potential offender a reason not to offend. We need not scruple to call this a threat, for that is also what it is. Hegel latches onto this, and says, 'A threat presupposes that a man is not free, and its aim is to coerce him by the idea of an evil'.[12] The second part of this is true. And there is a conception of freedom under which the first part of this would be true too—though whether a coherent conception is another matter.[13] But there is nothing beyond his mention of this pronouncement to suggest a commitment on Duff's part to this demanding, Hegelian conception. On any less controversial conception, however, the first part of Hegel's pronouncement is simply false. A threat typically presupposes precisely that, in the relevant sense, a man *is* free, for it presupposes that he can contemplate the reason offered and act in the light of his valuation of it; and if he could not do this then the threat would normally be useless. It is true that some threats may be intended simply to induce panic and fear, and thus reduce the scope for rational action.[14] Others are perhaps meant to work by making the undesired alternative sufficiently undesirable as to be psychologically impossible to perform—if that means anything. But threats need not be of anything like these kinds, and the threat of punishment involved in our criminal justice systems certainly is not. Now, though a threat *presupposes* that its victim is, in one sense, free, it is of course intended to *render* him unfree to act as he wishes—but only in a quite different sense of 'unfree'. Exactly what it means to say that a threat renders a man unfree is not easy to spell out;[15] but it certainly does not mean that it is intended to get him to refrain by depriving him of his rational faculties, which would not, properly speaking, be *coercion* at all.[16]

The victim of a threat will sometimes say that the threatener left him with no choice, that he was not free to act differently. But if the case is a typical one — one in which the threat does not paralyse thought or action — all that this can mean is that the threatener so structured the situation as to leave the victim with no *reasonable* choice. But to be left with no reasonable choice is not to be left in a situation where one's actions are no longer guided by one's rational reflection — quite the reverse. On any normal conception of rationality, coerced action can be a paradigm of rational action.

Duff also appeals to an analogy between the deterrent threat of the law and that of a robber who threatens to kill his victim if he does not give him money; clearly, the latter does not show respect for the autonomy of the victim, but treats him merely as a means. The fact that the threat gives him, in some sense, a reason for acting one way rather than another, and then leaves the choice to him, does not alter this. And the problem here is not merely that the robber has no right to the money he is demanding, for according to Duff the situation would be no different if I threatened you with violence in order to get back from you money that you owed me.[17] What makes such threats objectionable has nothing to do with the worth of the end that is being sought; it is a matter of the means that are being used. More specifically, the person threatened is given *the wrong sort of reason* for acting, a reason that is 'inappropriate and irrelevant to the action'. But how, asks Duff, is a system of deterrent punishment any different? The penal system aims at persuading the potential offender not to commit offences; if it is to be morally acceptable then it must do so by 'good and appropriate reasons'.[18] And, according to Duff, the reason that we wish the potential offender not to commit offences is that his doing so would be immoral, so that would be a good and appropriate reason to offer him. If, on the other hand, we 'try simply to deter him from his conduct by making its consequences unpleasant for him' we simply 'offer him, indeed create for him, reasons which are inappropriate and irrelevant to the action'. 'In offering him that kind of reason I cease to treat him as a rational moral agent: for I no longer try to bring him to guide his conduct in the light of the appropriate kinds of moral consideration.'[19] As Duff puts it:

> [I]f what justifies me in trying to persuade someone to modify her conduct is (my belief) that she *ought* to do so, the relevant reasons I should offer her are precisely and only those moral reasons that justify my belief that she ought to do so and my attempt to persuade her to do so. If instead I offer her prudential reasons for behaving differently, and particularly if I *create* those prudential reasons by threatening to inflict harm on her if she remains unpersuaded, I cease to treat or to respect her as a rational moral agent; I am instead trying to manipulate or coerce her into obedience.[20]

> In offering [the potential offender] that kind of reason I cease to treat him as a rational moral agent: for I no longer try to bring him to guide his conduct in the light of the appropriate kinds of moral consideration; I instead use his morally irrelevant desires and anxieties as a means of controlling his conduct.[21]

The word 'controlling' here imports a rhetorical force to which, as should now be clear, the argument is not entitled. Nor is the reference to 'anxieties' justified. But much of what Duff says we need not object to. Deterrent threats do indeed operate by creating reasons deriving purely from the unpleasantness of the threatened consequences. The question is why it should be thought that the reason offered by deterrent punishment is not 'good and appropriate'. After all, the desire to avoid ill consequences is normally a perfectly good and appropriate reason for refraining from a course of action. To be sure, obeying the law in order to avoid punishment may not be the *best* reason for doing so; if, as we may accept for the sake of the argument, breaking the law is immoral. But from the fact that deterrent punishment does not offer the best reason it obviously does not follow that it offers a reason that is bad or inappropriate. The fact that some immoral conduct may work to one's disadvantage seems to be, if not the best reason, nonetheless both a good and appropriate reason to refrain from it.

Part of what troubles Duff seems to be that deterrent punishment *creates* a reason instead of appealing to one that already exists, and for this reason *manipulates* the potential offender.[22] But this too readily conflates 'manipulating' someone with failing to respect their rationality. To the objection that a system of deterrent threats manipulates the potential offender we can agree — not, for the moment, cavilling at the unwarranted rhetorical overtones of the word 'manipulate' — for it aims, in pursuit of ends that are not his, to get him to behave in a way that he otherwise would not by the creation of reasons that would not otherwise exist. But surely there can be nothing morally objectionable about that. It is the precise structure of many acceptable human transactions, such as rewards, or ordinary commercial transactions as, for instance, when I try to get you to sell me your car, for a purpose you do not share, by offering you a large sum of money for it. What is morally objectionable is manipulating people *in certain ways*. Contrary to a certain conception of Kant's ethics, there are many such ways; but we can, for the present, certainly admit that one way of manipulating people that is morally objectionable is the sort that involves not respecting their rationality. So if deterrent punishment manipulated people in this way, then it would indeed be morally objectionable. *But that is precisely what we have yet to see.* In other words, the claim that deterrent punishment *manipulates* people will have some moral bite only if we have an independent reason to think that, in doing so, it fails to respect their rationality. So we cannot appeal, as this line of thought does, to the claim that deterrent punishment manipulates the potential offender in order to explain why it fails to respect his rationality.[23]

It may perhaps be thought that if deterrent threats cannot be shown to respect the value of autonomy they nonetheless may still fall afoul of the communitarianism that Duff espouses explicitly in *Punishment, Communication, and Community*. He expresses the point like this: for a state to issue threats to its citizens in order to deter them from wrongdoing

> is to fail to address them as members of the normative political community whose law this is. As members of that community, they are supposed to share a commitment to its

central and defining values, which determine the content of
the criminal law. If the law is to address them as members of
the community, it must therefore address them in terms of
those values — the values that determine its content and that
should guide their conduct.[24]

The state 'must... address' its citizens 'in terms of' 'the central and defining values, which determine the content of the
criminal law'. It is not easy to know what this means. Taken
literally it is, surely, plainly false. Criminal laws never address the citizen in such terms, and we would not expect them
to. Typically, they simply declare that certain behaviour is an
'offence' (or a misdemeanour, or felony, or whatever), define
it, lay down certain procedural rules for its prosecution and
defence, and specify the penalty for it. To all intents and purposes, then, they simply issue peremptory prohibitions and
requirements; in so far as they 'address' the citizen, they do
so simply by issuing the threat of a sanction for non-
compliance.[25] Perhaps the thought is that the reason behind
these prohibitions and requirements must be based in the
community's defining values. That seems correct, but, by
itself, it does not imply that it would be illegitimate for the
government to use threats in order to get its citizens to obey
them. We might perhaps add that the methods used to
enforce the law's edicts must be consistent with 'the central
and defining values' of the society, and that an acceptable set
of such values will include a commitment to the value of
rational autonomy. That too seems acceptable, and if it were
the case that the use of threats necessarily flouted this value
then the argument would have its conclusion. But that claim
is precisely what the first part of the chapter has tried to
discredit.

Duff also holds that if the law addresses threats to its
citizens to deter them from wrongdoing, requiring them to
refrain merely because of the inherent authority of the law,
then it will lack transparency. 'The reasons it offers them are
different from the reasons that justify its demands on them.'[26]
But the talk of offering reasons is, I think, crucially unclear.
Laws typically do not 'offer reasons'. As we have seen,
deterrent threats *create* reasons, something which Duff objects to, but wrongly, as I have argued. They are also, usually,
based on reasons. It is a trivial point that the latter reasons

must be different from the former, but is hard to see why this should import a lack of transparency. It would be easier if we were thinking of a polity in which the citizens did not know the reasons why certain conduct was prohibited, but that is not the sort of polity that Duff is concerned with; and the fact that the law was intended as a deterrent would then anyway be irrelevant to the charge of opacity, for there would be no transparency for deterrent threats to sacrifice. In a more open society, deterrent threats are fully consistent with transparency. There is certainly nothing opaque about my saying to someone about to steal my car, in a society in which there is a shared commitment to the value of property, 'That's mine; touch it and it will be the worse for you'. My commitment to the value of property is not, it is true, revealed by my threat; but nor is it hidden by it.

Duff's argument seems to fail, then. The conclusion could, of course, still be true: it might indeed be that the only proper ends of the criminal justice system are repentance, reform, and reconciliation, as Duff argues follows from his communitarianism. Whether one should accept that communitarianism is a big question, and one I do not intend to go into. Nor shall we enquire whether his claims about punishment actually follow from it. Instead, we shall ask this: is it true that only punishment can achieve those three aims?

The central issue here is that of *repentance*, for Duff argues that the only appropriate forms of reform and reconciliation in this context are those based upon genuine and deep repentance. And Duff is insistent that it is not a merely contingent matter that the infliction of suffering is 'the appropriate way' to induce repentance:

> [I]t is not a contingent matter that punishment – the infliction of suffering on an offender for her offence – is the appropriate way of trying to achieve the kind of penitential reform which is its justifying aim: that aim can, of its nature, be achieved only by bringing the offender to suffer for what she has done.[27]

> [T]he relation between punishment and its aims is not... contingent and instrumental... but internal. The very aim of persuading responsible agents to repent the wrongs they

have done makes punishment the appropriate method of pursuing it.[28]

But how is this claim to be made out?

It is important not to be deflected from the precise question that must be addressed. We need to know why the infliction of suffering is demanded, conceptually demanded, if we wish to produce a repentant understanding in the offender. As Duff shows, we can make good sense of a repentant offender's desire to separate himself from his community; having betrayed its values he may feel that, perhaps temporarily, he can be no part of it.[29] And separation from one's community is a common form of punishment. But this is not what needs explaining; the desire for penitential suffering can occur only *after* the offender has achieved some degree of moral understanding of his wrongdoing; what needs to be explained is how the imposition of suffering can contribute to his acquiring that understanding in the first place — how, indeed, it is absolutely necessary for it.

Again, what needs to be explained is not how it is possible for the infliction of suffering to express condemnation, or undergoing it to express a repentant understanding, phenomena no more puzzling than the ability of, say, medals to express approval and admiration, or indeed of vocal sounds to express meanings and evoke emotions. Nor even is the question why it should be thought that the infliction of suffering 'more adequately' expresses our condemnation than would the use of mere words.[30] To say that the infliction of suffering is the most adequate way of inducing a repentant understanding is one thing; it is quite another thing to say, what is Duff's thesis, that it is conceptually required for this.

Another thought that Duff flirts with, and which is again not to the point, is that the infliction of suffering 'forces' the offender to contemplate his offence in a way that mere words would not. 'He is forced to attend to what he has done, by asking why he is being treated thus; he may thus... come to see and accept that he has sinned, and see how this penance can... help to restore him.'[31] Punishment is 'a way of trying to focus his attention on the crime'.[32] But, again, this is all beside the point; in so far as they amount to more than the trivial and irrelevant claim that suffering 'may' have this effect[33] these are empirical claims, and so not relevant here.

The real explanatory work is supposed to be done by the idea that punishment is a form of *penance*, which, we hope, 'will bring the criminal to repent his crime'.[34] But, of course, without further explanation this does not help. Does penance necessarily involve suffering? If it does not, then the connection with suffering has been lost. If, on the other hand, it does, our original question simply reappears as the question why we are obligated to use penance to try to bring about a repentant understanding. (Presumably we shall not be fooled by the mere sound of words into thinking that repentance can be produced only by penance.) Either way, we are not, as yet, any nearer to an explanation of the crucial claim that punishment is the appropriate method for bringing offenders to a repentant understanding of their wrongdoing.

Nor do we approach more nearly if we assert that the offender 'may intelligibly feel the need for a penance which will assist his penitential contemplation of his wrongdoing', or that the acceptance of suffering might play some part in this.[35] The problem is not just that what the offender may intelligibly feel the need of scarcely settles the question of how he should be treated, though that is presumably true. It is that we cannot simply take it for granted that those feelings—the latter in particular—are, as Duff asserts, intelligible. That the infliction of suffering can sensibly be thought appropriately to assist one's understanding of one's wrongdoing is part of what has to be explained. (The rest of the explanation—much the harder part, as it happens—concerns the question why the infliction of suffering should have a central, indeed, *definitive* role in this aim which punishment is supposed to pursue.)[36]

Indeed, I do not think that the crucial claim can be adequately explained. It rests, I believe, upon a confusion between a *process* and a *state*. There is certainly a sense in which it seems to be true that repentance 'can, of its nature, be achieved only by bringing the offender to suffer for what she has done'. Fully to grasp that what one has done is wrong, and to regret it on that ground, may be essentially painful. That is to say, the *state* of repentance is necessarily painful. In that sense, it may be true that one cannot bring someone to penitence without causing them suffering. And if this were all that Duff meant by saying that, 'the acquisition of such an understanding must of its nature be painful to the criminal',[37] that repentance 'can, of its nature, be achieved only by bringing the offender to suffer for what she has done', then we might perhaps have no objection. That, however, was not the point to be explained. What had to be explained was why the centrally appropriate *process* for bringing someone to a penitential, and painful, understanding must itself involve suffering, and that is an entirely different claim — and a claim which, if we distinguish it clearly from the different claims mentioned above, Duff says nothing to justify. And it does need justification. There are surely, in principle at least, numerous ways of getting someone to understand that what they have done is wrong, many of which do not, in themselves, involve the infliction of suffering (though, of course, the state of belief aimed at will typically involve suffering). I may, for example, merely explain the point to the offender. If he grasps it, he will typically find the understanding painful. One could say, in such a case, that the explanation caused him pain, and this would be true. But this does not mean, which would be false, that explaining to someone their wrongdoing is essentially painful to them. For one thing, the offender may not accept the explanation; for another, or so many people would think, he may accept it but not care. And if he does accept the explanation, and this causes him pain, it is not the explaining that has been painful but the acceptance.

It seems here, then, as if Duff, when speaking of 'the acquisition of such an understanding', is failing to distinguish two senses of 'acquisition', the process and the state.[38] The *mental state* achieved must be painful, we could agree; but it would not follow from this that the *process* by which one achieves it must also be painful. This distinction is not idle here. As Duff remarks, punishment and repentance are not logically connected in the sense that one could not have punishment without repentance, for one may be punished without repenting. But, equally, there seems to be no logical connection in the opposite direction either; it would seem that there are more ways than one of coming to repentance, and not all of them need be painful. Indeed, one may simply wake up one morning and find that one regrets having done something in the past. That this change of mind lacks the sort of history that such changes of mind usually have might make us suspicious of its reality. But it would certainly not entail that it was unreal. We can, conceptually, divorce the state from the process. That being so, it remains an open question whether, given the aim of reforming offenders, there is anything specially appropriate about punishing them.

We see the confusion again, I think, when Duff says that it is incoherent to think that 'some kind of drug or psycho-surgical technique' could bring about the kind of reform that punishment (properly) aims at.[39] Assuming that the kind of reform we are speaking of is merely the painful understanding of one's wrongdoing, there is in fact nothing incoherent about this. A drug might certainly free some of one's cognitive or affective processes with the result that one may acquire a radically different understanding of what one did. This is clear once one attends to the distinction between process and achievement. If it is not, then one has merely to contemplate the sorts of drugs, such as alcohol, that occasionally do precisely this. 'Psycho-surgical techniques' might, in principle, do it too. As Duff says, these techniques do not 'address the criminal... as a responsible moral agent'.[40] Indeed, they do not 'address' the criminal at all, and we may find this morally unattractive—sufficiently so, perhaps, to exclude them from consideration. But it does not follow that they are not attempts 'to solicit and arouse her repentant understanding',[41] nor that they may not succeed in this attempt.

We shall look at one last argument for Duff's position. Duff is very impressed with victim-offender mediation schemes, which attempt to foster reconciliation between an offender and his victim. So too he is impressed by probation schemes and community service orders. But these are not, he thinks, alternatives to punishment; they *are* punishment. That is because punishment, on 'the standard accounts of what punishment is' consists in

> something painful or burdensome imposed on an offender
> for an offense by someone with the authority to do so, and
> intended to communicate censure. A criminal mediation
> process is intentionally *painful or burdensome* in its procedure

and its outcome [for]… the process of being confronted with and having to listen to the victim should be painful for the offender, as is the remorse that that process aims to induce. The reparation undertaken must also be burdensome if it is to give real weight to the apology it is meant to express… [And] *censure* is central to the process: the offender is to 'receive a kind of blame that it would be very difficult to neutralise'.[42]

The same is to be said, we learn, of probation schemes[43] and community service orders. It is also to be said of penance.[44] Imposing a penance on someone is necessarily intended to be painful or burdensome: its end result is intended to be the pain of remorse, and the process itself will impose burdens on the offender. So penance too satisfies the definition of punishment.

Certainly, probation, penance, and so on *could* be ordered as punishment. But, as Duff himself points out, most people do not think of these things as punishment (pp. 96, 99). It is easy to see why. As I remarked on p. 15, punishment is an intentional notion. If one imposes probation or penance *as a punishment*, then it must *essentially* involve suffering or a burden of some kind; the suffering need not be one's ultimate aim, but it must at least be a subordinate aim. But, contrary to what Duff says in the passage quoted, none of the things listed *essentially* involve suffering or a burden; they may or may not involve coercion, or the threat of it, but that is different. So it is not hard to understand why people do not think of them as punishment.

In response, Duff says of his claim that we should see mediation programmes and the like as a form of punishment:

[M]y claim… is not merely the conceptual claim that it (more or less) fits standard definitions of punishment. It is, rather, the normative claim that criminal mediation *can* serve the appropriate aims of criminal punishment and *should* be thus understood, organized and justified — even if this requires us to modify conventional understandings of both mediation and punishment.[45]

But probation, criminal mediation, and the like, do not 'more or less' fit the 'standard definition of punishment'. They fit the definition precisely, so long as whatever suffering they involve is intended and not merely incidental; otherwise they do not fit it at all.

One might accept this, and say that we should favour probation, criminal mediation, and so on, but not thought of as punishment. But this is to give up the attempt to justify *punishment*, and that is assuredly not what Duff at least wants to do.[46] Nor should we, unless punishment in its 'conventional understanding' cannot be given a satisfactory justification. But it can, as I shall try to show in what follows.

---

1   See Antony Duff, *Trials and Punishments* (Cambridge University Press, 1986), and *Punishment, Communication, and Community* (Oxford University Press, 2001). See also his 'Retributive Punishment — Ideals and Actualities'; and 'Penal Communications: Recent Work in the Philosophy of Punishment', *Crime and Justice: A Review of Research*, vol. xx (1996), pp. 1–98.

2   *Punishment, Communication, and Community*, pp. 107ff.

3   *Punishment, Communication, and Community*, p. 112.

4   However, Duff does not usually speak as though his three favoured aims are subordinate aims, means to the achievement of the 'central aim'. Indeed, getting the offender to recognize his wrongdoing and apologize to the victim is referred to on p. 114 as 'a central aim of criminal punishment'. But then it is a little unclear what is meant by regarding crime prevention as '*the* central aim' (my emphasis).

5   The communitarianism is much more explicit in *Punishment, Communication, and Community* than in *Trials and Punishments*.

6   *Trials and Punishments*, p. 6.

7   Cf. also Deirdre Golash, *The Case Against Punishment: Retribution, Crime Prevention and the Law* (New York University Press, 2005), p. 100.

8   *Trials and Punishments*, p. 75.

9   *Trials and Punishments*, p. 238. Cf. *Punishment, Communication, and Community*, p. 81 *et passim*.

10 *Trials and Punishments*. See also 'Retributive Punishment — Ideals and Actualities', *Israel Law Review*, vol. xxv (1991), pp. 422–451; 'Penal Communications: Recent Work in the Philosophy of Punishment'; and *Punishment, Communication, and Community*, pp. 82ff.

Actually, in *Trials and Punishments*, Duff is less than wholly precise about what his view is. Sometimes he says that the use of threats, since it does offer reasons, does treat people as rational 'to that extent' (pp. 179, 298, for instance). At other times he says the use of threats does not treat them as rational agents (pp. 51, 180, for instance). Perhaps we should take the point to be the weaker one that threats do not treat someone fully as a rational agent. This will not affect the argument in the text.

11   *Trials and Punishments*, p. 180; *Punishment, Communication, and Community*, p. 85. For Hegel's pronouncement, see *The Philosophy of Right*, translated with notes by T.M. Knox (Clarendon Press, 1952), Addition 62, p. 246.

12   G.W.F. Hegel, *Philosophy of Right*, p. 246.

13   For a brief account of different senses of freedom in Hegel, see Michael Inwood, *A Hegel Dictionary* (Blackwell, 1992), pp. 311ff.

14   One might compare here Plato's failure, in the *Protagoras*, to distinguish between fear as an emotion and fear as a motive, a failure which is probably what led him to argue that one cannot act freely from fear (cf. C.C.W. Taylor's note in his edition of *Protagoras* (Clarendon Press, 1991), pp. 205ff.).

15   See Nozick, 'Coercion', in P. Laslett and W.G. Runciman (eds.), *Philosophy, Politics and Society* (Oxford University Press, 1972) (rp. in Nozick's *Socratic Puzzles* (Harvard University Press, 1997), pp. 15–44).

16   Cf. Hegel: 'As a living thing man may be coerced, i.e. his body or anything else external about him may be brought under the power of others; but the free will cannot be coerced at all (see Paragraph 5), except insofar as it fails to withdraw itself out of the external object in which it is held fast, or rather out of its idea of that object (see Paragraph 7). Only the will which allows itself to be coerced can in any way be coerced' (*Philosophy of Right*, § 91).

     However, compare Neil MacCormick, *Legal Right and Social Democracy: Essays in Legal and Political Philosophy* (Clarendon Press, 1982), pp. 232f.

17   *Trials and Punishments*, p. 179. Duff seems to think that though one may not threaten one's debtor one could permissibly use force to recover what is owed; in doing so, one is not 'trying to modify his behaviour by improper means' (*Trials and Punishments*, pp. 226f; cf. *Punishment, Communication, and Community*, p. 78). And, indeed, it is hard to see how Duff could avoid this implication: if one cannot threaten, what other recourse is there other than to acquiesce in his injustice? But the idea that though one may not threaten one may proceed directly to force would seem to me to be theory gone wild — criminally wild if applied, say, to international relations.

18   *Ibid.*, p. 50.

19   *Ibid.*, pp. 51f.

20   'Penal Communications', p. 14.

21   *Trials and Punishments*, p. 52.

22   *Trials and Punishments*, p. 52, esp. fn. 11; *Punishment, Communication, and Community*, p. 85.

23   For the view that Kant himself did not think that threats of punishment issued by a legitimate authority used those to whom they are issued, see B. Sharon Byrd, 'Kant's Theory of Punishment: Deter-

rence in Its Threat, Retribution in Its Execution', *Law and Philosophy*, vol xliv (1989), pp. 151–200. I do not appeal to those arguments here.

24   *Trials and Punishments*, p. 58 [italics omitted].

25   Statutes sometimes have a preamble which is occasionally couched in terms of 'the community's values', but these are usually held not to have much legal force.

Duff in fact seems to hold that the laws prohibiting *mala in se* do not in fact prohibit them but merely declare that they are wrongful (*Punishment, Communication, and Community*, p. 58). But I think that this cannot be right. Many people would hold that to declare something to be wrongful is necessarily to issue an imperative not to do it. Duff himself holds that such a declaration entails that those who ignore it should be censured (*ibid.*, p. 28), which surely comes very close to the same view. If we take this view, then the contrast is lost. If we reject it, then the law must do more than merely declare the wrongfulness of an action, for otherwise flouting the law need have no consequences – if a declaration that something is wrong does not in some way involve an imperative, then one is presumably free to ignore it. (However, the argument I make in the text is neutral as between these two ways of understanding the law.)

26   *Punishment, Communication, and Community*, p. 58.

27   *Trials and Punishments*, p. 262.

28   *Punishment, Communication, and Community*, p. 30, *et passim*.

29   *Trials and Punishments*, p. 68.

30   *Trials and Punishments*, p. 243. John Tasioulas also takes this view in 'Punishment and Repentance', *Philosophy*, vol. lxxxi (2006), pp. 279–322: denunciation is the primary justification for punishment, and that denunciation must 'take the form of condemnation that involves hard treatment' because 'only punishment adequately conveys the blame the wrongdoer deserves' ('Punishment and Repentance', p. 196). He offers no reason to think this, however, beyond the claim that it 'captures a widespread and deeply ingrained judgment' (*ibid.*). It is certainly a widespread and deeply ingrained judgment that offenders deserve to be punished; whether, as Tasioulas claims, the judgment that offenders deserve to be censured '*through* the infliction of hard treatment' is also widespread or deeply ingrained is another matter, and one about which there must be some doubt.

31   *Trials and Punishments*, p. 251; cf. pp. 246f. Cf. also: '[Y]ou cannot ignore a punishment, if it is severe enough. You cannot put it on one side; you must either assert that it is unjust, or admit that it is just' (J.M.E. McTaggart, 'Hegel's Theory of Punishment', *International Journal of Ethics*, vol. vi (1896), p. 489).

32   *Punishment, Communication, and Community*, pp. 107f.

33   Cf. '[H]ard treatment... *can* help direct the offender's attention onto what he has done and bring him to a more adequate moral grasp of its wrongfulness... Punishments... including those familiar in exist-

ing penal systems... *can* serve the same communicative purpose, *if* administered in the right spirit and context: they too *can* force the criminal's attention onto his crime... Such punishments *can* also assist, as well as stimulate, the further process of self-reform and reconciliation' ('Penal Communications', pp. 52–53) (the emphases on the word 'can' are mine).

34   *Trials and Punishments*, p. 245; cf. *Punishment, Communication, and Community*, p. 106.

35   *Trials and Punishments*, p. 251; cf. pp. 246, 247.

36   '[P]unishment – the infliction of suffering on an offender for her offence' (p. 262).

37   *Trials and Punishments*, p. 262.

38   John Tasioulas perhaps makes the same mistake: 'Even purely formal censure constitutes hard treatment, since condemnation is meant to be experienced as unwelcome' ('Punishment and Repentance', p. 295).

39   *Trials and Punishments*, p. 262; cf. *Punishment, Communication, and Community*, p. 80.

40   *Trials and Punishments*, p. 262.

41   *Ibid.*

42   *Punishment, Communication, and Community*, pp. 96f.

43   pp. 99ff.

44   pp. 106ff.

45   *Punishment, Communication, and Community*, p. 97 [emphases in original].

46   'An immanent critique begins with some existing, historically contingent practice. Ours must begin with the practice(s) of punishment within which we live – with criminal punishment as practiced in contemporary western societies, such as Britain and the United States, and with the normative understandings of punishment found within those practices. We then seek to transcend these particular practices, towards a set of wider political or moral values in terms of which we can ask whether and how such a practice could be justified' (*Punishment, Communication, and Community*, p. 16 [footnote omitted]). '[A]bolitionists are wrong to think that we must *replace* criminal justice and punishment by nonpunitive processes of reparation and reconciliation... [T]his [would reflect] an inadequate understanding of the possibilities of punishment – of what punishment can be and can mean' (*ibid.*, p. 34 [emphasis in original]).

Chapter Seven

Externalist Theories and Self-Defence

'[T]he sole end for which mankind are warranted… in interfering with the liberty of action of any of their number, is self-protection.'[1]

Externalism and Internalism

There are two thoughts that seem to make externalist theories of punishment unattractive.

First, it may seem that they interpret punishment as a technique for social management, and in doing so flout a general moral requirement that one ought *to treat all people as ends and never merely as means*.[2] What, precisely, this Kantian injunction means is not easy to say, and we shall return to it in due course. But it is the deterrence theory that is most commonly thought to fall foul of it, for in its most usual form this theory involves the claim that the main purpose of making the offender suffer is to modify the behaviour of others. But a denunciation theory will face the same problem if it holds that the point of denouncing offenders is simply to mould the behaviour of others.

Reform theories do not hold that the purpose behind the offender's suffering is to modify the behaviour of others, and so do not face precisely this problem. They may even stipulate that at least part of the concern in reforming offenders is their own good, and not simply the security of others. But even with such a stipulation, we may seem to be left with a related worry. The most plausible way to understand the idea that punishment may reform is through the idea of so-called 'specific deterrence'. But specific deterrence need have no particular interest in the offender's *understanding of the wrongness* of his offence; so long as the threat of further punishment achieves the desired end, it is of no great interest whether it does so by communicating an enhanced moral understanding or instilling abject fear. As we have seen, it has therefore seemed reasonable to some to say that this fails to respect the rational autonomy which generates the Kantian constraint, on the ground that it involves, or at least countenances, the unacceptable manipulation of the will of one by another.[3] But if specific deterrence is not the thought, then it is unclear how punishment is supposed to reform offenders at all. The only alternative seems to be that it does so by getting them to understand the suffering of their victims and thereby supplying an adequate motivation for refraining from crime in the future. This would perhaps circumvent the Kantian problem. But it is utterly implausible, because no one has yet been able to explain why causing offenders to suffer should be expected to lead to such an enhanced understanding, and all of the evidence indicates that it rarely does so.

We have spoken so far as if the ends of the offender and the ends of the judicial system necessarily diverge. That need not be so, of course; the ends of the judicial system may be the offender's ends too, and it is even possible for the offender to embrace his suffering willingly. In such circumstances, many people might think that the Kantian restriction can be observed.[4] But this is beside the point, for any worthwhile justification of punishment will hold that punishment is justified even when the offender does not share either its end or its means.

I shall later suggest that the deterrence theory, though not all externalist theories,[5] can rebut this first charge. But for now, let us notice a second motivation that may push one in the direction of internalist theories; it lies in the firm moral conviction that offenders should suffer for their offences; internalist theories guarantee the appropriateness of that conviction, whereas externalist theories do not.

The idea that offenders should suffer for their offences naturally generates the question, *Why?* Externalist theories can, given some empirical assumptions, provide an answer to this question. A deterrence theory, for instance, may say that it is morally permissible, perhaps obligatory, to try to prevent crime, and that a system of punishment will contribute to that end. But there is of course something conditional about this answer: a system of punishment will be a morally appropriate response to crime only so long as it is actually true that it makes a suitable contribution to preventing it; otherwise it will not. A reform theory, given some empirical assumptions, can also answer the question. But its answer is hostage to fortune twice over. Punishment may not reform at all; in that case, it will not be justified. It is also possible that, though it reforms, there may be some other, more efficient, way of reforming offenders; again, if that is so punishment will not be justified. But the conviction that offenders ought to suffer for their offences does not present itself as conditional in this way, and this might seem to suggest that we need some other way of giving it a morally appropriate articulation, one which reflects its unconditional nature. No externalist theory can offer that. Internalist theories, on the other hand, can. Perhaps the most obvious are those that hold specifically that offenders *deserve* to suffer and that it is the aim of punishment to see to it that they do so. The Simple Desert Theory, for instance, would guarantee, if it were true, that it is always, at least *prima facie*, appropriate to make offenders suffer. But we do not need to refer to desert. The Just Distribution Theory would also give us the same guarantee; it holds that an offence disturbs the just balance of benefits and burdens and that there is always a *prima facie* moral reason for rectifying such an imbalance. With the reform theories that we have considered, things are slightly different; they hold that the aim of punishment is to reform offenders in a certain way, and they cannot offer any guarantee that punishment, as we know it, will be effective in this aim. However, they must hold that even in these circumstances the infliction of suffering is still ultimately the appropriate response to an offence, for otherwise they would not be theories of *punishment*; they must hold that if punishment as we know it does not work then we should not give up the attempt to reform offenders, but seek ways in which the infliction of suffering will achieve that aim. All internalist theories guarantee that the appropriate response to an offence is, in the end, to make the offender suffer. If one of them were true, the legitimacy of our desire to see offenders suffer for their offences would wait upon no empirical claims about the effects of punishment; it would be guaranteed another, infallible, justification.

I do not think that a theory of punishment should respect this motivation. I believe that the conviction that offenders should be punished for their offences whether or not this achieves any further good is the expression of a desire for vicarious revenge. The desire may or may not be a useful one for humans to possess, but it is not, in my view, a morally attractive one. If it were, then I think that the difficulties that its theoretical articulation faces should lead us to resist those attractions.

If we are to justify punishment we must see it as a means to an external aim. What that aim should be is given to us roughly by the motto at the head of this chapter: I take it that the only reason for which it is in general justifiable to coerce, or harm, others is to protect oneself against aggression, by which I mean behaviour that injures or threatens one's interests or welfare and, by extension, to protect others against behaviour that threatens or injures their interests.[6] I shall refer to this as self-defence. If this is correct, it follows that the theory of punishment must be simply a special part of the theory of self-defence.[7] And as far as morality is concerned, I shall suggest that there is nothing special about punishment. It does not require any moral principles other than those that already motivate and constrain the use of force in self-defence generally. In the case of punishment, the constraints, arguably, have an effect different from those they have in other circumstances; in particular, as we shall see, in the theory of punishment the issue of culpability arises where it might not in other circumstances. But to understand punishment is simply to understand how those principles apply when the self-defence in question is the forceful prevention of crime.

Self-Defence

Punishing an offender may seem far removed from what many would regard as the paradigm case of self-defence, for the English phrase 'self-defence' naturally brings to mind an image with two salient features: that of someone defending himself against an actual, *ongoing* attack, and, furthermore, an attack on his *person*. And indeed this may have been the original sense of the phrase. But it is not, as a matter of usage, restricted in this way to such contexts. If I were to use force to protect my property from a robber, I would not be protecting my 'self', but it would be perfectly natural to refer to this as self-defence. And the phrase 'pre-emptive self-defence' is also perfectly natural (a Google search turns up more than 4000 instances of that very phrase).

More important, it would be arbitrary and obscuring to limit the idea of self-defence to contexts in which one defends one's person against an ongoing attack. There are many different sorts of interest that one may defend, many different sorts of circumstance in which one may act to protect one's interests, and many different methods that one may adopt. There is nothing conceptually special about the circumstance in which one uses force to defend one's *body* against an attack. Nor, despite the obvious dangers of pre-emption, is there anything special about an attack that is *ongoing* rather than merely anticipated, because the dangers of pre-emption accompany any form of self-defensive action: just as one may anticipate wrongly that someone is preparing an attack, one may judge wrongly that one is already under attack; or, again, it is always possible that one who really is preparing an attack may change his mind and not mount the attack, but the same is true even when someone has actually started his attack, because he may desist at any moment. The differences here are epistemic, not conceptual. Pre-emptive action, then, can legitimately be brought under the heading of self-defence.

So too can a form of action yet further removed from the use of actual force against a current attack, namely the use of threats of retaliation to deter potential aggressors. Again, it would be arbitrary to refuse to bring this under the umbrella of self-defence, for in issuing such threats one may be intending to protect one's welfare just as would be someone fending off an ongoing attack. Whether that could be said of any actual retaliation in the event of the threat's failing to deter is, of course, another issue, one to which we shall return in due course.

There is, then, no principled reason to restrict the notion of self-defence to the circumstances of an ongoing attack on one's person. The class of actions that is worth picking out comprises those actions that involve attempting to prevent behaviour that threatens one's interests. I shall have more to say about this later, but for now we may simply observe that any acceptable system of criminal law will involve something that at least resembles the issuing of threats of retaliation against offenders.

The idea of self-defence also tends to bring to mind the image of one defending oneself against an *aggressor*, by which I shall mean someone who violates a constraint whose point is to safeguard, directly or indirectly, individual welfare. But self-defence is not, of course, restricted to that. Aggressors, after all, usually defend themselves against their victims when their victims quite properly use force against them in self-defence. And most people think that one may legitimately defend oneself against those who threaten one's interests but could not properly be called aggressors. I am thinking of those who threaten one's interests without knowing that they do so, or those who threaten one's interests without taking any voluntary action.[8] We may sometimes use force to defend ourselves in these cases too. It has proved hard to find any very convincing justification for this, however, and indeed some writers deny that it is justified.[9] But most people do not take this view; they hold, rightly in my view, that it is often fully justifiable to defend oneself against such 'innocent threats'.[10]

It is not, as I have said, always justifiable to use force to defend one's own interests or welfare. But it is a necessary, though not sufficient, condition of any use of force that it be intended to enforce or uphold constraints whose point is to protect individual welfare. That condition is perhaps most obviously satisfied in cases where an agent is directly protecting his own interests against an ongoing attack. But it also extends to force used in assisting others to protect their interests. And it extends to force used to uphold constraints the violation of which *indirectly* threatens individual welfare, even though the particular violation may not itself directly harm anyone's interests. It does not, on the other hand, extend to the use of force to promote abstract moral goods, as when one might prevent someone from lying merely because lying is simply an intrinsically bad thing. Nor, obviously, does it extend to the use of force in retribution or revenge. Taking revenge might, of course, be in someone's self-interest, as might, conceivably, seeing retribution fall on someone's head;[11] but that is not to the point because what the Millian restriction rules out is the use of force for such things as revenge and retribution *for their own sakes*.

It has become customary to include in the idea of self-defence the defence of others. This is natural, but it is worth making some distinctions. When one person uses force to defend another from, say, a physical attack, this may be brought under a number of different principles. The law, for instance, typically recognizes as a defence to a charge of unlawful violence that one was aiding another as an exercise of citizen police powers. It is possible to regard this as a form of indirect self-defensive action, for the citizen may simply be intending to uphold the law which he sees as affording him general protections. Or it may be brought under a general duty to promote the good of others. Or, in principle, one might also think of it simply as upholding certain moral norms, perhaps because they are intrinsically worth upholding. But the most natural understanding, the one that I should think most accurately reflects the motives of most of those who go to the defence of others, is simply that one person is assisting another's *self*-defence. Presumably the right of self-defence must extend to allowing one to seek assistance, at least in some circumstances and in some ways, and the defence of others can generally be brought under that rubric. Sometimes, to be sure, it cannot. For instance, we may have the right to assist those under attack when they cannot actually seek our assistance. But even in such a case I assume that the most natural understanding is that one is acting to protect individual welfare, and for present purposes, no harm will come from including the defence of others under 'self-defence'.

The general prohibition on deliberately harming others can be overridden in cases of self-defence. A theory that derives the justifiability of punishment from the justifiability of self-defence thus has the beginnings of a satisfactory answer to the questions that we said at the outset that a theory of punishment must answer.

Just why self-defence can generate an exception to the general prohibition on deliberately harming others is a surprisingly difficult question, and one to which there is no generally agreed answer. If we focus on self-defence against aggressors, those who deliberately, and without justification or excuse, violate constraints that we are justified in upholding, then the legitimacy of counter-force—though not unconstrained counter-force—may seem to be explained by the aggressor's culpability. And this explanation may be mediated by an appealing principle of distributive justice: if harm must fall on someone, then it is just that it should fall upon the one who has voluntarily brought about this necessity.[12]

But the appeal to culpability would leave unexplained why it is sometimes legitimate, as most people think it is, to use force to defend ourselves against those who pose a threat to us but are in no way culpable (the insane, for instance, or those who pose a threat accidentally). Even in such cases, one may think that culpability still plays some role: one should, perhaps, if it is possible, avoid causing harm to a non-culpable threat, and would perhaps owe an apology or even compensation if one caused harm. But, obviously, it cannot be the culpability of a non-culpable threat that justifies the use of force when force is justified. And, the distributive principle just mentioned loses here all of the intuitive attractiveness it had in the case of culpable aggressors. Its defenders occasionally appeal, for an analogy, to a principle sometimes proposed in civil law, that where there is no culpability for harm caused, then the causer must pay. But if this has much appeal as a legal principle it surely has none as a moral principle.

Perhaps we can explain the point by simply deriving the right to self-defence from a more general right to refuse, within certain limits, to sacrifice ourselves for the good of others. This would seem to explain why it is legitimate, at least sometimes, to use force against non-culpable threats. But unfortunately it would leave unexplained something which seems as certainly correct as the idea that we may legitimately use force against culpable aggressors, namely that we may *not* use force against uninvolved bystanders in order to defend ourselves (by, for instance, seizing a hostage to use as a shield).

Whatever its precise shape, most people will think that the theory of self-defence must explain why it is sometimes justifiable to use force against both culpable and non-culpable threats, but not against uninvolved bystanders. That will require finding a morally significant difference between deliberately harming a non-culpable threat and, say, grabbing an uninvolved bystander to use as a shield or a hostage. That difference has proved hard to identify. I think myself that it rests upon the sense that it is wrong to use people as tool in matters of importance to them against their will, or even just without their consent, and one is doing that in seizing a hostage, but not when one defends oneself against a non-culpable threat.[13] But we do not need to settle that matter now.

The Limits of Self-Defence

Direct Self-Defence

Though the general prohibition on harming others can be overridden in cases of self-defence, there are of course restrictions on when the use of force is permissible and, when it is permissible, how much force is legitimate. These restrictions I shall refer to as the 'Restraining Consider-ations'. One we have already mentioned: it is normally impermissible deliberately to harm uninvolved third parties in pursuit of self-defence, for this would be unacceptably using them. For now, we shall be concerned with a different set of issues: the amount of force that it is permissible to use against an aggressor, or apparent aggressor; it must be *reasonably necessary* to use force in the first place,[14] and when it is permissible to use force the harm done to one's aggressor (and to any unfortunate third parties) must be in some suit-able *proportion* to the gravity of the threat of harm to one-self.[15]

There is considerable agreement about the broad shape of these Restraining Considerations. It is not incoherent to think that there are no moral limits whatever upon the response that one can make to an aggressor; but in fact virtually every-one thinks that whether force is reasonably necessary in self-defence, and how much force is proportional to the threat, are constrained by the distribution of the costs and benefits, broadly construed.[16] To illustrate, let us imagine that I have only three possible responses to an act of aggression already under way: doing nothing, rational persuasion, and counter-force. For each course of action, the primary benefit aimed at will be that the harm threatened by the aggression is avoided or minimized. So we need to know both how great the threatened harm is, and how likely it is to occur given each course of action.[17] If the threatened harm is slight and merely speculative (as when someone is in the act of throwing a paper dart at me), then normally the correct course of action will preclude the use of force, though in such circumstances there will usually be other alternatives than the three just mentioned. At the other extreme, a high probability of serious harm will usually justify the use of force.[18] But virtually everyone agrees that the victim of aggression should be required to forgo self-defensive force when there is a significant disparity between the harm threatened by the aggression and the amount of harm that it would be necessary to inflict on one's aggressor in order to thwart it (as when, for instance, the only way to defend oneself against a cuff to the side of the head would be by the use of lethal force). Similarly, most people will agree that, even when forceful self-defence is permissible, and the threat substantial, the victim of aggression may be required, at some sacrifice, to limit the use of force to what is proportional.

None of this is to deny that there is significant dispute about the more precise terms of these restrictions. Precisely how serious does a threat have to be to justify a forceful response? Just how significant does the disparity have to be between the harm threatened by the aggression and the amount of force required to thwart it before self-defensive force must be forgone? And, when self-defensive force is justified, what exactly is a proportionate response? Most people think that it is proportionate to use lethal force to ward off a sufficiently serious non-lethal threat; but how serious does it have to be?[19] As to what count as costs there will also be dispute. Some will consider the harm to the aggressor a cost, but others will not. Some may consider it a (moral) cost to oneself to indulge in violence, even if it is justified to do so, whereas others will not.

These disputes involve properties that are, in principle measurable and commensurable.[20] But they are probably nonetheless irresoluble. They involve differences about the relative moral weight to be attached to various aspects of human life and there is little prospect of definitively settling such disputes; I do not think that the resources exist to settle them, but if they do we do not know what they are. We may, however, say this. One of the motivations of the Restraining Conditions is to minimize the use of harmful force quite generally. This does not mean that in self-defence an individual must always take the course that involves the least harmful force. For one thing, the adoption of such a policy may not itself conduce, in the long term, to minimising violence. And there are no doubt other reasons why an individual, in defending himself, is not indefeasibly bound by such a restriction. But it does mean that, in the use of self-defence, minimising the use of violence must always be an important consideration. And it will be a particularly important consideration in the case of legal punishment: governments have an immense capacity for harmful violence, and the sorts of considerations that apply to individuals in direct self-defence and which release them from this restriction are almost entirely absent in the case of a government trying to prevent crime.

Beyond this, however, we must accept that there will be differences of opinion about the morality of self-defence, differences that we probably cannot settle. So the theory of punishment too will leave many questions about punishment unsettled. But that is as it should be. It is an important error to think that an acceptable philosophical theory of punishment will close questions about which there is in fact deep, and reasonable, disagreement. Such questions can be settled only by the normal political process, and they are to be lived and worked with as we live and work with intractable differences of opinion elsewhere in our political lives.

Self-Defensive Deterrence

We have been speaking so far of the direct use of force against an ongoing attack. But there is a more indirect form of self-defence, one that, if successful, does not involve the use of force at all, namely the use of deterrent threats. Faced with the possibility of aggression, I may threaten aggressors with retaliation in order to deter them. This may take different forms. One may, for instance, simply issue a threat to retaliate in the event of aggression, leaving it open whether or not one will in fact carry out the aggression. Or one may set up a system which, when triggered by an aggressor, will automatically carry out some retaliatory action with no further action necessary on one's own part. We might think of an electrified fence with a posted notice adverting to the electrification as an example of this.[21]

These two types of threatened retaliation differ morally, and we shall return to these differences later. But for now we may ignore them. Do we, then, have the right to threaten retaliation in order to deter? It seems plausible to think that, at least sometimes, we do; all else equal, it must surely be better to try to prevent aggression rather than to have to deal with it forcefully when it occurs. Of course, all else may not be equal. Greater force may have to be used to deter aggression than would be required to deflect it once it had started. Or the methods used to deter could be intrinsically unacceptable. Or the threat may have little chance of succeeding or even constitute a perverse incentive to potential aggressors. But in the absence of such factors, threats of retaliation are surely acceptable. Whether it is permissible to carry out the actual retaliation should the threat fail to deter is a more complicated question, one to which we shall turn in the next chapter. With automatic systems of retaliation, of course, that question cannot arise, but it is replaced by the question whether it is permissible to set up such systems in the first place; that too is a question to which we must return.

Imagine then that I have three possible responses to a threat of aggression: I may do nothing, I may try to persuade possible aggressors not to aggress, or I may threaten them with retaliation in order to deter them.

The situation is very different from the case of direct self-defence that we considered a moment ago; in particular, the limits on the amount of force one may use in direct self-defence and the limits on the amount of force it is permissible to threaten in self-defensive deterrence are different.

For instance, if a given level of assured retaliation is insufficient to deter an aggressor, then it may be permissible to increase the threatened retaliation; and, in some circumstances, it may be permissible to threaten more than would have been permissible in direct self-defence.[22] Indeed, at the extreme, and other things being equal, there would perhaps be no limit at all on what might be threatened if we could be absolutely sure that the threat would be effective.[23] Of course, other things rarely are equal.

On the other side, potential aggressors can often be deterred by the threat of much less force than would be required to prevent their aggression once it had started. If someone levels a gun at you with intent to kill you, it may be necessary to use deadly force to thwart this attack. But the threat of a less forceful retaliation would often be sufficient to deter such conduct in the first place. It might be sufficient, for instance, to let it be known that if someone were to kill you, your friends would give him a severe beating. More generally, all sorts of resources that might have been available in advance will not be available in the heat of the moment.

The issue of immediacy also raises the question of 'scatter'. If I booby-trap my house, and post a notice to this effect, the trap may still be triggered by innocent intruders who have not seen the notice. The problem of scatter is not confined to self-defensive threats, of course; it applies also to direct self-defence. But it is a more serious problem in the case of automatic systems of threatened retaliation, such as electrified fences and booby traps, than in most cases of direct self-defence, and requires a greater stringency in the restrictions governing the use of such systems.

But there is a deeper difference. Unlike an act of direct self-defence, a threat of retaliation is a speech-act directed to a class of people: perhaps just one person, perhaps everyone. If the threat is a justifiable one, then those who deliberately ignore it can have no complaint if they suffer the retaliation. But those who do not deliberately ignore it but still suffer the retaliation are owed a satisfactory explanation (and perhaps more than a satisfactory explanation). All that can justify retaliation is the fact that the threat was deliberately ignored by a person to whom it was justifiably addressed. And the innocent intruder has not ignored the threat if he has not seen it, or could not reasonably be expected to read it. If a 'threat' does not discriminate between those who can and those who cannot comply with it, it is not a threat but something completely different.

Collective Self-Defensive Deterrence

We have been speaking so far, tacitly anyway, of one individual defending himself. But of course groups may exercise self-defence collectively. Perhaps the most obvious example of that is when a nation goes to war to defend itself against aggression. But a group, including a society, can also undertake to defend one of its members against external aggression or aggression by another member of the group. When it does so through the deterrent threat of retaliation, we have the rudiments of a penal system.

Now, when we move from individual self-defensive deterrence to collective self-defensive deterrence on the part of society against those who aggress against its members, further complications come into view — empirical certainly, and arguably normative too. But the general structure of applicable principles is the same. A threat of retaliation may be a successful disincentive against aggression. But even when wielded by the government there are numerous reasons why it must be hedged around with restrictions. For one thing, governments typically have enormous capacity for visiting harmful force upon their citizens. And a government's agents are ordinary people, as likely to misuse such power as anyone else. And we view it with distaste when governments try to seek the cooperation of citizens by force, for this is a lapse from the ideal relationship between a government and its citizens; we are therefore reluctant to allow government to resort to it too easily. And even when serious punishment is completely justified, it is likely to foster an alienation from the government on the part of at least some citizens (the family and friends of the offender, for instance, who will often be prone to see the punishment as unjustified or excessive). There is also the question of likely harm to innocents: as well as the wrongly convicted there are others, such as the innocent families of properly convicted offenders. And the more serious the punishment we threaten, the greater the costs we shall feel constrained to pay in the attempt to avoid miscarriages of justice. The restriction to reasonable force, then, will require that government not use the threat of punishment to prevent crime if there is a reasonable, less violent alternative, and that it may threaten no more than is reasonably required for deterrence (and, of course, other externalist aims).

So, though the basic principles are the same, what it is permissible for an individual to do in direct self-defence will often diverge from what it is permissible for society to threaten in self-defensive deterrence. Overlooking this may make it seem that punishment and self-defence are morally separate phenomena:

> Proportionality in punishment—making the punishment fit the crime—is more rigorous than proportionality in self-defense. Using the death penalty for rape, for example, violates the principle of proportional punishment... Yet if a woman is threatened by rape, she may legally resist by killing the aggressor. Even legal systems that have abolished the death penalty permit the use of deadly force in the defense of vital interests. While proportionality in punishment requires that the sentence fit the crime, clearly more is permitted in self-defense.[24]

Fletcher speaks here of a distinction between what is permissible in self-defence and what is permissible in punishment. But I suggest that we should instead think of it as a distinction between what is permissible in direct, individual self-defence and what is permissible in collective, self-defensive deterrence. A woman faced with imminent rape faces an immediate, serious threat, which there may be no way of repelling short of killing her attacker. A legislature deciding upon the sentence for rape is also concerned with self-defence—that of the community in general against potential rapists—but it is not faced with the same problem as a woman about to be raped. Its problem is to deter potential rapists, and a threat of death does not seem necessary for this end; for the most part, the threat of lesser punishment achieves it. So an individual woman may kill in order to resist rape, whereas the state may not punish rapists by killing them.

But if *more* rapists could be deterred by the threat of death, would it then be justifiable to threaten the death penalty? In principle, it might. But the Restraining Consider-ations soon begin to bite, as is illustrated by the fact that, after all, one can, under stringent conditions, *generally* use lethal force to defend oneself against a sufficiently serious non-lethal threat—there is nothing special about rape in this respect—but we do not think it justified to try to deter such offences by the legal threat of death. The reasons are not hard to find. Most importantly, *immediacy* is crucial. When a woman is faced with imminent rape, the aggressor is right there, there is no doubt about his intentions, and, we may assume, there is no possibility of her killing the wrong man. The third of these considerations would weigh particularly heavily with most people considering the death penalty: the likelihood of wrongful capital convictions in a fallible legal system would strike most people as an unacceptable cost.[25] And, further, what we know about the psychology of deter-rence gives us little reason to think that most of those who are not deterred by the threat of the relatively heavy prison sentences that rape generally attracts would be significantly more effectively deterred by the threat of capital punish-ment.

It is, then, no surprise to find that in most legal systems a woman immediately threatened with rape may kill to protect herself. By contrast, in most civilized jurisdictions (though not, it is true, in all)[26] a woman may not, in order to deter potential rapists—or even potential murderers—prominently display a deadly weapon with intent to use it; and even those jurisdictions which allow the open carrying of firearms would, presumably, balk at a woman booby-trapping her body with a bomb which would explode if she were att-acked; these measures would pose an unreasonable threat to innocent people. The government, in adopting measures to deter rapists, is in the same position. We can see, then, that in order to explain the phenomenon remarked by Fletcher we do not need to postulate a set of principles of punishment intrinsically more restrictive than the principles of self-defence. The principles of punishment are, it is true, *in prin-ciple* no less restrictive either. Anything that it is permissible to do in direct self-defence will be permissible, in some imag-inable circumstances, in deterrent threats. So on a philos-opher's desert island, inhabited by only two people, one of whom is a determined rapist who can be deterred only by the genuine threat of death, it might be permissible to set up a deterrent threat of automatic, deadly retaliation.[27] But these are circumstances far removed from those in which the legal system finds itself in the real world.

---

[1]   J.S. Mill, *On Liberty and Other Writings*, ed. Stefan Collini (Cambridge University Press, 1989), p. 13.

[2]   Cf. Christopher Bennett, *The Apology Ritual* (Cambridge University Press, 2008), p. 17: '...[Instrumental] approaches justify punishment, not as a response to him or her as an individual, but as something to be imposed on her in order to promote some further overall good.'

[3]   For this objection, see Antony Duff, *Trials and Punishments* (Cambridge University Press, 1986), Ch. 6.

[4]   We may think this on the grounds that consent rebuts the charge of disrespect for autonomy, though Kant himself of course did not think this.

[5]   The denunciation theory, for instance.

[6]   I shall, for brevity, normally omit this extension, though I shall return to it briefly later.
      As is common, I shall take 'interests' to be, roughly, those things that make someone's life go better ('welfare'); cf., e.g. Dwight G. Newman, 'Collective Interests and Collective Rights', *The American Journal of Jurisprudence*, vol. 49 (2004), pp. 127–163, at pp. 129f.

[7]   The idea that punishment can be justified as a form of self-defence has also been defended by Phillip Montague in *Punishment and Societal-Defense* (Rowman and Littlefield, 1995); and Daniel Farrell (see 'Deterrence and the Just Distribution of Harm', *Social Philosophy and Policy*, vol. xii, pp. 220–240; 'On Threats and Punishments', *Social Theory and Practice*, vol. xv (1989), pp. 125–154; and 'A New Paradox of Deterrence', in Jules L. Coleman and Christopher W. Morris (eds.), *Rational Commitment and Social Justice: Essays for Gregory Kavka* (Cambridge University Press, 1998), pp. 22–46). For criticism, see Rodin, *War and Self-Defense*, Ch. 3.

[8]   Judith Jarvis Thomson argues that in such cases one's rights are violated ('Self-Defense', *Philosophy and Public Affairs*, vol. xx (1991), pp. 283–310). Jeff McMahan explains why this is a mistake in 'Self-Defense and the Problem of the Innocent Attacker', *Ethics*, vol. xiv (1994), pp. 252–290 (see pp. 276f.). See also Michael Otsuka, 'Killing the innocent in Self-Defence', *Philosophy and Public Affairs*, vol. 23 (1994), pp. 74–94 (rp. in Michael Otsuka, *Libertarianism without Inequality* (Clarendon Press, 2004), Ch. 4).

[9]   See, for instance, David Rodin, *War and Self-Defense* (Clarendon Press, 2002), Ch. 4; Michael Otsuka, *Libertarianism without Inequality*, Ch. 4; Kimberly Kessler Ferzan, 'Justifying Self-Defense', *Law and Philosophy*, vol. xxiv (2005), pp. 711–749.

10   Cf. McMahan, 'Self-Defense and the Innocent Attacker', p. 287 ('[W]hat most of us believe is that the self-defensive killing of an [innocent attacker] is not wrong but justified, provided that certain conditions are met'). McMahan, however, evinces doubt about whether this view can really be justified, and in a later article he suggests that in some circumstances it is permissible to use force against an innocent threat and in some cases not, but that it is hard to see how to draw the line between these cases (see 'Self-Defense and Culpability', *Law and Philosophy*, vol. xxiv (2005), pp. 751–774, at p. 767)).

11   Actually, it is not quite so clear: perhaps all that could be in one's interest would be *believing* that one had seen this. On this general issue see, for instance, Nicholas Sturgeon, 'Moral Explanations', in David Copp and David Zimmerman (eds.), *Morality, Reason and Truth* (Rowman and Allanheld, 1985); J.J. Thomson, 'Moral Objectivity', in Gilbert Harman and J.J. Thomson, *Moral Relativism and Moral Objectivity* (Blackwell, 1996); Nicholas Sturgeon, 'Thomson Against Moral Explanations', *Philosophy and Phenomenological Research*, vol. 58 (1998), pp. 199–206; J.J. Thomson, 'Reply to Critics', *Philosophy and Phenomenological Research*, vol. 58 (1998), pp. 215–222; and Nicholas Sturgeon, 'Moral Explanations Defended', in James Drier (ed.), *Contemporary Debates in Moral Theory* (Blackwell, 2006).

12   Cf., e.g. Phillip Montague, 'Self-Defense and Choosing Between Lives', *Philosophical Studies*, vol. xl (1981), pp. 207–219; *Punishment as Societal-Defense* (Rowman and Littlefield, 1995); and 'Grading Punishments', *Law and Philosophy*, vol. xxii (2003), pp. 1–19; David Wasserman, 'Justifying Self-Defense', *Philosophy and Public Affairs*, vol. xvi (1987), pp. 356–378; Daniel Farrell, 'Deterrence and the Just Distribution of Harm', *Social Philosophy and Policy*, vol. xii (1995), pp. 220–240; and McMahan, 'Self-Defense and the Innocent Attacker'.

13   However, Jeff McMahan has argued (wrongly, I think) that this fails to be explanatory; see 'Self-Defense and the Problem of the Innocent Attacker', p. 273. He suggests that it is tempting to think that the problem 'reveals... an incoherence in commonsense morality' (p. 290).

14   This is often misstated, as by David Rodin: 'one may only take a harmful measure... if there is no less costly course of action available that would achieve the same result' (*War and Self-Defense*, p. 40). But surely one does not always have to adopt the less costly alternative; if someone is out to kill me, and I can prevent this only by either killing him or going into hiding for the rest of my life, I do not have to adopt the latter alternative even if it is, overall, less costly. One who is defending himself may give more weight to the costs *to himself* than to the more general costs. The requirement of necessity requires only that he not give *unreasonable* weight to the former.

15   Jeff McMahan holds that proportionality must be, in some cases at
     least, proportional to the culpability of the aggressor (see 'Self-Def-
     ense and Culpability', *Law and Philosophy*, vol. xxiv (2005), pp. 751–
     774). But this seems wrong to me. I think that one may use identical
     force against two aggressors who are identical except that, say, one
     is a child and one is an adult, or one is sane and the other insane.
     One might, however, owe compensation to an innocent threat for
     any harm that one did to him. And the law, of course, will treat
     these cases differently, for reasons that I shall explain in a later
     chapter.

16   Sufficiently broadly to include 'deontological constraints' as costs —
     perhaps costs of infinite weight.

17   Jeff McMahan seems to suggest that common sense morality does
     not regard this latter consideration as relevant (at least in cases of a
     lethal threat); see 'Self-Defense and the Innocent Attacker', p. 261.
     This seems wrong even in cases of lethal threat: if someone is malig-
     nantly about to throw a paper dart at me, crazily thinking it will kill
     me, there is presumably some non-zero likelihood of its somehow
     doing that. The extreme unlikelihood of this, however, will surely
     restrain the range of possible responses. But the issue is complex.

18   Not always, however: if the use of force has in any case no chance of
     warding off the threatened harm then it cannot be justified under
     the principles of self-defence. Does it then follow that it is imperm-
     issible to use force or coercion in self-defence if I know that it will
     eventually be unavailing? If, for instance, twenty hoodlums were to
     attack me, would it be impermissible to defend myself if I knew that
     I should eventually succumb to their force? This would not be an
     absurd consequence, for one might think that the humanity of one's
     aggressor always has weight, prohibiting the use of force when this
     will achieve no good. But in the real world, there normally would be
     sufficient chance that my self-defensive actions would have suff-
     icient effect to justify my using force. We could, however, imagine a
     scenario in which one could know that this was not the case: if you
     have launched a torpedo which is certain to sink my boat, I may
     know that any counter-action on my part will be ineffective. May I
     then launch a torpedo at your boat? This would certainly not be *self*-
     defence. It might be an attempt to prevent you from launching
     torpedoes at other boats, and this would probably justify it. But
     without some such justification there would just be nothing to be
     said in favour of the action; certainly, if the action were merely rev-
     enge, or retribution, then this would not justify it. Of course,
     counter-force against certain forms of aggression is so deeply rooted
     in human nature, that, in itself, it is usually beyond reproach even
     when unjustified.

19   It is sometimes suggested that proportionality requires that one may
     inflict no more harm on one's aggressor than is threatened by his

aggression (so that one could kill to save one's life, but not to save oneself from severe bodily injury, for instance). But there is no sensible perspective from which such a general rule would compel acceptance (only the blankest form of act-utilitarianism would demand it, and then only in particular, unusual, circumstances).

20 I assume here that interpersonal comparisons of utility are possible, at least in principle.

21 One might intend the electrifying effect to be merely preventive, of course, and not a threat of retaliation.

22 I am here assuming for the moment that carrying out the threat would be justifiable; we shall return to this issue in due course.

23 So I think that Michael Walzer is wrong to say that 'it is wrong to threaten what it would be wrong to do' (*Arguing about War* (Yale University Press, 2004), p. 48). It depends on whether one will have to do it or not in the event of the threat going unheeded.

24 George P. Fletcher, *A Crime of Self Defense: Bernhard Goetz and the Law on Trial* (The Free Press, 1988), p. 29.

David Rodin has also argued that punishment and self-defence diverge, on the grounds that it is permissible to defend oneself against the criminally insane, but not permissible to punish them (see *War and Self-Defense*, pp. 96f.). The reply is similar to the reply I make to Fletcher: the distinction is not between punishment and self-defence, but between direct self-defence and indirect self-defensive deterrence. I deal with the question of how this applies specifically to the insane later.

25 Between 1977 and 2000, for instance, 12 men were executed in Illinois. In the same time period, 13 death-row inmates were cleared of their murder charges. (In March 2011 the Governor signed a bill abolishing the death penalty in Illinois, citing the imperfections of the penal system.) Between 1973 and March 2010, 138 people in 26 states in the US were released from death row because there was substantial evidence that they were innocent (see http://www.deathpenaltyinfo.org/article.php?did=412&scid=6).

26 Most US states allow, with varying restrictions, the open carrying of firearms.

27 It would depend in part upon the amount of violence that this threat might itself trigger, and in part upon the relative evaluation of sexual autonomy and human life. About that latter consideration a theory of punishment will have, itself, nothing to say. All that can be said is that *if* it is permissible to kill to avoid an otherwise certain rape *then* there will be some conceivable circumstance in which it would be permissible to mount a credible threat of death to deter a potential rapist. (On whether it is ever justifiable to kill to avert rape, see Fiona Leverick, *Killing in Self-Defence* (Oxford University Press, 2006), Ch. 8.)

Chapter Eight

Externalism: Incapacitation and Deterrence

There are traditionally four externalist theories of punishment, or four ways in which punishment is thought to prevent crime: reform, denunciation, incapacitation, and deterrence.[1]

Reform I shall say no more about. The prospect of reforming offenders to any significant degree by punishment is remote.[2] There may be other ways of reforming them, and if so they should be seriously explored; but they have no part in a work on punishment.

The denunciatory effect of punishment is often appealed to, but there is little evidence that *denouncing* crime, as opposed to announcing sanctions against it, actually has any substantial effect in moulding people's attitudes to it, though if it does so that is to be welcomed. Nor is there much evidence to suggest that, *merely by its denunciatory effect*, it contributes significantly to reducing direct or vicarious revenge, though, again, if it does so that is to be welcomed.

By contrast, there is no doubt about the directly preventive, or restraining, effect of some punishments. Of course, most punishments imposed in, e.g. the US and the UK are fines and have virtually no preventive effect.[3] But those who are imprisoned can, for the most part, commit crimes only in prison; whether this is more desirable than their committing them amongst the public at large is another question.

That conceded, it is a complex question how significantly we can affect the level of crime simply by taking offenders out of circulation. In many cases, when an offender is incarcerated someone will simply take his place. That may be because, for instance, there is considerable demand to get into a limited criminal market. Or it may be because crimes are often committed by groups and unless the whole group is incarcerated those who remain at large may recruit new members to replace those who have been imprisoned.[4]

And even if we can make a significant difference to the level of crime by imprisoning offenders there is still the question of whether this represents a reasonable balance of costs and benefits. It is very expensive to keep offenders in prison (and increasingly expensive as they grow older); it is unclear whether those resources might not have more impact if used differently — to improve schooling, for instance, or to boost employment, or to increase the number and quality of the police.

In addition to doubts such as these, however, many have raised more specifically moral objections. There are basically two.

The first rests upon the claim that our ability to predict the future dangerousness of convicted offenders is extremely limited. The result is that, if we wish to have any real impact on the level of crime, we shall have to incarcerate large numbers of people who would not in fact have committed further crimes if left at large; and this may seem unfair, or at least in some way unreasonable.[5] There is surely something right about this objection: costs and benefits should balance appropriately here as elsewhere, and if they do not do so, as is claimed by the objection, then imprisoning offenders because we believe that they will commit further offences is indeed unjustifiable. Whether the costs and the benefits can in fact be made to balance depends in part, of course, upon empirical questions, and we shall not consider them here.

A second objection does not rest upon epistemological claims. It holds that it is intrinsically wrong to 'punish' offenders for offences that they have not yet committed, that it is not indeed really punishment. But if, as I have claimed, the morality of punishment is part of the morality of self-defence, this principled objection surely lapses. With all due weight given to the problems to which pre-emptive action may give rise, any acceptable account of self-defence will allow that it is sometimes permissible: one does not always have to wait until an aggressor has actually launched his attack before one can take forceful counter-measures for sometimes, if one did, counter-measures would no longer be possible. And if the best justification of punishment represents it as a form of self-defence, then it seems likely that it will inherit the permissibility of pre-emptive action. Whether one then wishes to call it punishment or not is perhaps of no importance. All that is important is the recognition that epistemological problems are more troublesome here than they would be in a case in which a particular individual is faced with an immediate and serious threat by another individual. And though these problems do not generate any objection of principle, they do necessitate stringent procedural safeguards.[6]

And legal systems do in fact have all sorts of resources for pre-emptive intervention leading to physical restraint—and resources which few object to. Laws prohibiting possession—possession of handguns, for instance—are typically like this. It is not the mere possession of handguns that worries us; we prohibit their possession in order to head off their use. Again, in the United State, for instance, it is a federal offence to threaten the President. The primary purpose of such a law, as with laws prohibiting possession of handguns, is the ability to remove a threat before it is realized; of course, in law the threatener is imprisoned for the offence that he has *already* committed (the possession, or the threat, that is to say), but this is a legal fiction and hardly obscures the fact that it is, for the most part, his *prospective* offence that mainly concerns us.[7] There is nothing unusual about this. A common justification for laws which prohibit attempts and conspiracies, as opposed to completed acts, is that this enables the police to intervene before an offence (a real offence, so to speak) is committed. Of course, in all of these cases, one is, in legal principle, punished for something that one has already done. But, as I have said, this is, in some degree, a fiction; we do not prohibit conspiracies to carry out actions of which we approve; and we would not bother to prohibit conspiracies to carry out actions of which we disapprove if they could be

guaranteed to be harmless; nor would we prohibit the possession of handguns if we were sure they would never be
fired.

We may say, then, that certain forms of punishment, if
that is what we wish to call it, may be justified by reference
to their incapacitative effect. But, as I remarked earlier, this
leaves untouched the vast majority of punishments. For
them, we shall have to appeal to deterrence.

Deterrence

I have objected to a number of theories on the grounds that
they set a goal for punishment that it has no real prospect of
achieving; could this be true of the deterrence theory too?[8]
That question is, of course, largely an empirical one. But
there is, I believe, a strong presumption that, in normal circumstances, penal systems can have deterrent value, and
sufficient deterrent value to offset their costs.

To see this, we first need to notice that deterrence is a
matter of *degree*. The threat of punishment will normally,
though not always, deter even the most resolute criminal if
there is a policeman at the site of the proposed crime. He
may, of course, merely postpone the crime until the coast is
clear. But, if he does so, it would be a mistake to say that he
had not been deterred. While the policeman was around, he
was indeed deterred from committing the crime *at that time
and place*. He may then commit it at another time and place,
but that is another matter. The deterrent threat worked *to
some degree*.

As we shall see, the fact that someone was deterred in the
presence of a policeman would not show that he had been
deterred by the threat of punishment, for the presence of a
policeman, even in the absence of adequate sanctions for the
offence contemplated, or indeed any sanctions at all, might
be sufficient deterrence; there is little point in trying to commit a crime if a policeman can merely prevent it and send
you on your way. But the idea that the threat of punishment
never had any independent deterrent value would surely be
hard to believe. The threat of punishment works by raising
the probable costs of an offence, and so lowering its expected
utility; and if people were never motivated by that consider-

ation, we should have little or no grasp of their motivational structure.[9]

Deterrent punishment is, of course, merely one social constraint amongst others, in particular internalized moral constraints, self-protection and revenge. Self-protection and revenge work, structurally, in the same way as the law: in some cases, fear of them will wholly deter someone from committing an offence; but when someone is determined to commit the offence, then they will still make it more costly to do so, and thus will still have some deterrent effect. The law adds a *further* deterrent, and one which, in so far as it is effective, reduces the relatively high social costs imposed by the others (though imposing its own). It is not, perhaps, a matter of logic that, if we hold other factors constant, imposing deterrent penalties will actually decrease the amount of crime. But our most basic understanding of human motivation surely suggests that this indeed will be the result.

This reasoning normally applies even in the case of those whose level of rationality does not rise to a very high level. Compare the following, from a UK government white paper:

> There are doubtless some criminals who carefully calculate the possible gains and risks. But much crime is committed on impulse, given the opportunity presented by an open window or unlocked door, and it is committed by offenders who live from moment to moment; their crimes are as impulsive as the rest of their feckless, sad or pathetic lives. It is unrealistic to construct sentencing arrangements on the assumption that most offenders will weigh up the possibilities in advance and base their conduct on rational calculation. Often they do not.[10]

No doubt. Nonetheless, even the most impulsive burglars can normally be relied upon not to indulge their impulses under the noses of the police.

The same is true for crimes which are often said to be 'undeterrable'. I imagine that the demand for murder amongst, say, obsessive serial killers is relatively inelastic — but only relatively. Ted Bundy, for instance, killed many women, but there seems little reason to think that he would not have killed many more had he had a legal *carte blanche* to do so. As I have said, there are other restraints against crime, and these would still have had effect, making it more costly to commit the crimes he was set upon; but there seems no reason to think that the threat of punishment would not have added another.

Of course, as I have said, it does not follow from the fact, if it is one, that the criminal justice system deters crime that it is the threat of punishment alone and directly that has this effect; indeed this is certainly false. People avoid committing offences in order to avoid the inconvenience, financial cost, and shame of being prosecuted, for instance, and these dis-incentives may well remain, in some cases anyway, even if there were no formal system of punishment. Prostitutes' clients, for instance, will often fear public knowledge of their activities considerably more than the relatively light sent-ences that their offence typically attracts, and, in most of the world, this fear would act as a strong disincentive even in the absence of formal punishment. But there is surely a presum-ption that, in general, a significant threat of punishment will add to what other deterrent factors there may be.

One who denies all of this must, it seems to me, bear the burden of proof. The presumption in favour of the view that, ordinarily, people order their affairs roughly in order to maximize their benefits is surely a strong one.[11] Without such a presumption, it would be impossible to understand human affairs at all. But the presumption is of course rebuttable. We know that sometimes people do not behave in this way. But then we expect there to be a story that will explain why they do not do so. The story might be a very commonplace one: people often act in what they can see is a self-destructive way when they are in a rage, for instance, or when they are con-sumed by sexual jealousy. And the story may not be commonplace: evolutionary theorists have sought for an explanation of the fact that, in certain circumstances, people routinely do not seem to try to maximize benefits, and this story, whatever it turns out to be, will almost certainly not be commonplace. But without such a story, we should assume that people act roughly in order to maximize their benefits. And we should, therefore, assume that the threat of punish-ment, given some obvious preconditions about publicity, the likelihood of detection, the level of threat, and so on, will have deterrent value. As I have said, anyone who denies this must carry the burden of proof and show either that the foregoing reasoning is incorrect or that the necessary pre-conditions for deterrence are never met. So far as I know, no one has ever managed to carry that burden.

In principle, this presumption could be defeated by empirical evidence, but such empirical evidence as we have does not do that. It must, of course, be conceded that empirical research in this area presents extraordinary difficulty.[12] For one thing, the appropriate data are hard to get, even just about the level of crime; victimisation surveys are much more useful than police records, but they are far from being perfectly reliable. It is usually easier to know what penalties are stipulated for what offences, but even when we have reliable estimates of the incidence of a certain type of offence and the penalty stipulated for it, it is still hard to relate the two: a penalty set out in a legal code can itself have no deterrent effect; only knowledge of it can have that. So, if it is the *deterrent* effect of punishment we are interested in, what we need to know is not just what penalty is stipulated for a certain offence, but what, in a given population, is actually *believed* to be the penalty, how that belief is related to the actual penalty, and attitudes to it. The likelihood of an offender suffering this penalty is also important—though, again, only as filtered through the mind of potential offenders. Reliable information of this sort is extremely hard to get. And even if, in a particular case, we could get all of this information, it still remains that the level of crime is certainly the result of all sorts of factors, both long term and short term, and including aspects of the criminal justice system other than its sanctions. And it is usually difficult to isolate from these other factors the effects of any particular penalty on the level of crime. Still, with all of these difficulties conceded, I think that we should conclude that the empirical evidence does not defeat the presumption that the threat of punishment does, in general, have some deterrent effect.[13]

This claim is quite consistent with the finding that most people, even career criminals and quite well-educated people, know surprisingly little about precisely what constitutes a particular offence, what penalties are laid down for what offences, and the likelihood of suffering these penalties.[14] But most people know, in a general way, which types of actions are subject to penalties and which are not. For instance, most people could not give a precise legal defin-ition of 'steal' or 'breaking and entering' or 'burglary'; but they know in a general way that it would normally be illegal to break someone's window and make off with their prop-erty, intending to keep it. And they may have little idea of the likelihood of various sorts of burglars being successfully prosecuted; but they know that the likelihood of prosecution normally increases if one commits an offence. We are surely justified in thinking that this general knowledge exercises some deterrent force independent of the other social con-straints.

Now, that the threat of punishment will presumptively carry some deterrent effect is a quite modest claim, because it is consistent with its being the case that no *actual* set of penal institutions has any deterrent effect; but to show that would require showing that the preconditions just mentioned are not met. And to show *that* would require extensive empirical evidence; and, as I have said, such empirical evidence as we have does not do that.

However, on the other hand, no empirical evidence that I know of suggests that the measurable effect of punishment is, for the most part, more than modest.[15] The question, then, is not whether punishment has any deterrent effect, but whether that effect is sufficient to offset its costs. This is a more difficult question. Added to the difficulty of estimating the deterrent effect of penalties is now the difficulty of estim-ating their costs, which are of different types. There are econ-omic costs, for instance, though these are in fact surprisingly hard to estimate (the police, to mention just one example, carry out many activities with only the most remote connec-tion to the criminal law, and it is, in practice, impossible to separate these activities out financially). There are also the costs to innocent people, such as the families of convicted offenders. And some may think that moral costs are incurred – though justifiably – in carrying out some punishments. And some of these costs may raise normative questions that are intractable except by the normal political processes.

However, if it is a default presumption that punishment has *some* deterrent effect, then it seems reasonable to assume that there is, in principle, *some* level of costs that would be proportionate to its benefits. The question is then what a political community must do in the absence of certain knowledge about the balance between costs and benefits. I take it that no more can be required than that it make a reasonable, good-faith estimate of the balance, and try to stay within it. That is what is involved in regarding the exercise of punishment as an exercise of self-defence. So long as a community does this, it will be justified in using punishment.[16] I do not say that many political communities have done this, nor that it is politically easy to do.

---

1   As I remark in Ch. 1, these give rise to a further type of theories which we may call Assurance Theories; but there is no need here to deal with them separately.

2   See, e.g. the US Bureau of Justice report, *Recidivism of Prisoners Released in 1994* (excerpted by Patrick A. Langan and David J. Levin in *Federal Sentence Reporter*, vol. 15 (2002), pp. 58–63).

3   Other punishments, such as revocation of a driving licence, involve partial restraint.

4   For a discussion of the empirical evidence on the effectiveness of imprisonment in reducing crime through restraint, see Franklin E. Zimring and Gordon Hawkins, *Incapacitation* (Oxford University Press, 1995); Stephen D. Levitt, 'Understanding Why Crime Fell in the 1990s: Four Factors that Explain the Decline and Six that Do Not', *Journal of Economic Perspectives*, vol. 18 (2004), pp. 163–190; and, for an attempt to distinguish the effects of deterrence from those of incapacitation, Steven Levitt, 'Why Do Increased Arrest Rates Appear To Reduce Crime: Deterrence, Incapacitation, or Measurement Error?', *Economic Inquiry*, vol. xxxvi (1998), pp. 353–372, finding a significant incapacitation effect for a few types of offence.

5   For this objection, see Andrew von Hirsch, *Doing Justice: The Choice of Punishments* (Hill and Wang, 1976), Ch. 3.

6   On the general issue of the justification of incapacitative sentencing, see Andrew von Hirsch, *Doing Justice*; J. Floud and W. Young, *Dangerousness and Criminal Justice* (Heinemann, 1981); Nigel Walker (ed.), *Dangerous People*.

7   There are, of course, other concerns; such threats can cause costly inconvenience to the President and his protectors.

8   For the claim that punishment does not deter adequately to justify it, see, for instance, Ted Honderich, *Punishment: The Supposed Justifications* (Penguin Books, 1971), pp. 87, 148.

9   This is not to deny that, in special circumstances, people don't pursue expected utility.

10 *Crime, Justice and Protecting the Public: The Government's Proposals for Legislation* (H.M.S.O., 1991), p. 6.

11 Such benefits do not, of course, have to be understood in an egoistic way.
12 For a brief account of the methods used in deterrence research, see Daniel S. Nagin, 'Deterrence and Incapacitation', in Michael S. Tonry (ed.), *The Handbook of Crime and Punishment* (Oxford University Press, 2000), pp. 345–368.
13 The classic econometric work was done by Gary S. Becker in 'Crime and Punishment: An Economic Approach', *The Journal of Political Economy*, vol. lxxvi (1968), pp. 169–217. For a sample of more recent work, see, for instance, Steven Levitt, 'Why Do Increased Arrest Rates Appear To Reduce Crime: Deterrence, Incapacitation, or Measurement Error?'. The general conclusion of the econometrics literature is that 'The probability of punishment seems to be an important deterrent, whereas the evidence regarding the severity of formal punishment is much less conclusive' (B.L. Benson and D.W. Rasmussen, 'Deterring Drunk Driving Fatalities: An Economics of Crime Perspective', *International Review of Law and Economics*, vol. xix (1999), pp. 205–225). There is, of course, considerable controversy amongst economists about the methods used by these researchers. For a more general survey of the effectiveness of punishment, see Nagin, 'Criminal Deterrence Research at the Outset of the Twenty-First Century', *Crime and Justice*, vol. 23 (1998), pp. 1–42; and Nagin, 'Deterrence and Incapacitation' ('I am persuaded that the collective actions of the criminal justice system exert a substantial deterrent effect' – p. 346); Nigel Walker, *Why Punish* (Oxford University Press, 1991), p. 15 ('[No] sensible penologists doubt that penalties operate as deterrents'); and for a sceptical view about 'deterrence-optimizing analysis', though not about the deterrent effect of a system of punishment, see Paul H. Robinson and John M. Darley, 'The Role of Deterrence in the Formulation of Criminal Law Rules: At Its Worst when Doing Its Best', *Georgetown Law Journal*, vol. 91 (2003), pp. 950–1002 ('There seems little doubt that having a criminal justice system that punishes violators... has the general effect of influencing the conduct of potential offenders. This we concede: Having a punishment system does deter').

For a (perhaps) contrary view, see Tracey L. Meares, Neal Katyal and Dan M. Kahan, 'Updating the Study of Punishment', *Stanford Law Review*, vol. 56 (2004), pp. 1171–1210. Though they regard the evidence for the deterrent effect of punishment as 'speculative and inconclusive' (p. 1186), it is not clear that they think it has no deterrent effect (see, e.g. p. 1196). They are clearly correct in saying that the study of deterrence must pay attention to the 'social realities' (p. 1193), though the fact that imprisonment, as we carry it out, actually increases crimes, does not show that it does not also act as a deterrent.

14   See Robinson and Darley, 'The Role of Deterrence in the Formulation of Criminal Law Rules: At Its Worst when Doing Its Best'; and Paul H. Robinson and John M. Darley, 'Does Criminal Law Deter? A Behavioural Science Investigation', *Oxford Journal of Legal Studies*, vol. 24 (2004), pp. 173–205.

15   Note that a modest effect may be sufficient to justify punishment – a point often overlooked by many opponents of the deterrence theory (such as Drumbl, *Atrocity, Punishment, and International Law*, pp. 169ff.). It may, of course, require more than a modest effect to justify the penal systems of, say, the US or the UK.

16   Or excused if it misjudges the balance: the distinction is not important here.

Chapter Nine

The Deterrence Theory: Ends and Means

Ends and Means

The most common version of the deterrence theory of punishment holds that punishment is justified by its achieving two goals. First, we punish the actual offender in order to deter other, potential offenders; this is known as 'general deterrence'. Second, we hope that punishment will make the actual offender more likely to be deterred in the future; this is known as 'specific deterrence'.[1]

The assertion that one of our aims in punishing offenders is to deter other, potential offenders may seem to commit us to the idea that offenders are, in part at least, punished in order to promote the general good, a commitment which may seem to contravene the requirement that we never treat anyone merely as a means. And that punishing offenders in pursuit of general deterrence is to use them merely as a means to promote the general good is perhaps the most common objection to the deterrence theory.[2]

There can be nothing wrong with treating someone as a means, which we do when, say, we take a trip in a taxi. What, if anything, raises a moral qualm is treating someone *merely* as a means, or just as a tool. What using someone 'merely as a means' amounts to in general is not easy to say,[3] but we surely do that when we harm someone without his consent as a means of benefiting others.[4] And that is what we do when we punish an offender in order to deter others. The offender may of course himself benefit from any deterrence achieved; but that is beside the point: we would punish him whether he would benefit in this way or not.

How may the deterrence theorist respond to this charge?

Utilitarians might simply assert that there is nothing wrong with using people in this way, and it is arguable that utilitarianism cannot even make sense of any other way of treating people. But utilitarianism, despite its obvious attractions, does not attract many people.

A second response would be to say that though it may be wrong for individuals to harm others in order to benefit society, it is not wrong for the state to use its citizens in this way.[5] But, again, without the support of some attractive theory, this would seem to be inadequate; and it is hard to think of an attractive theory that would support the assertion.

A third attempt, whilst not denying that it is morally objectionable to treat people in this way, might still try to justify punishing offenders to deter others on the grounds of the likely consequences of refraining from doing so.[6] This strategy is possible unless one takes the implausible view that the ban on using people is an absolute one, not to be contemplated though the Heavens fall. But when we do deliberately harm someone in order to benefit others, then our action, though perhaps justified, is nonetheless morally tainted: apologies and reparation are generally called for.[7] But we surely do not feel that punishment is tainted in this way; we do not feel that we need to apologize to offenders when we punish them, or compensate them for the harm they suffer. The offender may of course himself benefit from any deterrence achieved; but that is beside the point: we would punish him whether he would benefit in this way or not.

A fourth attempt would say that the very essence of an offence is its using one's victim as a tool, and that we therefore have no obligation not to use the offender himself in this way. It is doubtful whether this is true of all offences: when one speeds on a deserted highway, there may be no victims, no one put at risk; and if in fact you injure someone you would not, except in unusual circumstances, be treating them as a means: not caring about others' welfare is not the same as treating them merely as a means. And leaving aside the doubtful claim about the 'essence' of offences, it is surely sufficient to point out that this is simply an appeal to the *Lex Talionis*, and that it is no more plausible here than elsewhere.

A fifth attempt holds that full and free consent to being treated in a certain way blocks the claim that one is merely being used; and since offenders freely choose to offend in the full knowledge that their offences carry a liability to punishment they consent to that liability.[8]

Certainly, if it were correct to say that offenders freely consent to the liability to punishment that would go a long way towards justifying it.[9] But it would surely not be correct to say that. If it were, then offenders could avoid the liability simply by clearly and publicly announcing that they intended to offend and did not accept the liability, just as one could avoid the duty to pay for a taxi-cab ride by making clear to the driver that one had no intention of paying him. But of course we would not take such announcements from offenders as relieving them of their liability; we would treat them in exactly the same way, and for exactly the same reasons, as we would treat those who had omitted to declare that they did not accept the liability. And that is surely enough to show that the talk of consent here is hollow.[10]

There is a sixth way in which we might try to rebut the charge. We might hold that, since offenders anyway deserve to suffer, there can be no objection to making them do so for the general good.[11]

This rebuttal, of course, requires a commensurability between desert and punishment which, if my earlier arguments were correct, is illusory. Offenders, presumably, do not simply deserve to suffer, but deserve to suffer to an extent proportionate to their offences; but this would require that there be some adequate way of determining just how much suffering an offender does deserve. And we have found no such way.

And there are further problems.

First, offenders, let us say, deserve to suffer, and we are therefore justified in making them do so. But, in punishing them in order to deter others, we are doing more than making them suffer: we are also *using them for the general good*; but there was no claim that *this* is what they deserved, and so that element of their punishment remains unjustified.[12]

Second, if our aim in punishing an offender is to deter others, then any moral defectiveness that our action derives from this aim will not be removed merely by the further fact that, as it happens, the offender also deserves to suffer. Imagine that an aggressor intends to shoot you, and you grab an innocent bystander to use as a shield. Most people would certainly condemn this on the grounds that, in putting the bystander at risk, you would be using him as a mere means, using him as a tool in a literal sense. Consider now a second case, the same in all respects except that one seeks out someone who, independently, deserves to be shot — we might imagine a military commander using a deserter as a human shield instead of executing him. This might, in the eyes of some people, seem rather better since, in one sense of 'innocent', an innocent bystander is not killed. Still, if in the first case one unacceptably uses one's victim then it is hard not to think that in the second case one does so too.

Can the deterrence theory, then, rebut the charge that it countenances merely using offenders? In its traditional form, I do not think that it can.[13] But that charge arises from the claim that offenders are punished, in part, in order to deter others, and so it would be avoided by an interpretation of the theory that does not include this claim. I shall refer to this different interpretation as the protective-deterrence theory.

Deterrent Threats and Using the Offender

A Model

Let us start with what is intended to be a simple model of a criminal justice system.

The protective-deterrence theory understands the practice of punishment as part of a system of legitimate self-defence. I assume that individuals are justified in using suitably constrained force in self-defence. Just what those constraints are is, of course, a matter of controversy, and we have looked at the matter briefly already, but they do not preclude deliberately causing harm to one's attacker for one's own good.[14] And the use of self-defensive force against an aggressor cannot be said to use him as a tool.[15]

I also assume that groups may use force in self-defence, and, in particular, that a society or a nation may do so. The most obvious case of such self-defence is presumably that of a nation defending itself against external aggression. But I assume that a group may act forcefully to defend itself against some of its own members. Members of a group may seek to attack or undermine the group as a whole, and the group may, depending on the circumstances, legitimately defend itself against this. But members of the group may threaten other individual members, and I assume that, in the case of certain types of group at least, it would be legitimate for the group as a whole to offer protection against this too. No doubt such group action is in some ways more problematic than individual self-defence; but it is not intrinsically illegitimate.

So much would be widely agreed upon. I earlier suggested that we have the right not only to act directly in self-defence, but also to issue threats of retaliation in order to deter potential aggressors. However, this raises a familiar question: if it is indeed permissible *to threaten* retaliation in order to deter aggression, is it also permissible *to carry out* that retaliation if the threat fails to deter? The justification for *threatening* is that it will prevent aggression (and any harm involved in a self-defensive response). If the threat does not work, however, that justification will not carry over into a justification for *carrying out* the threat, for carrying out the threat will, by hypothesis, do nothing to prevent these harms. Retaliation, then, seems unjustified (at least by the principles of self-defence).

There is a familiar, but unsatisfactory, response to this problem. If I do not carry out the threat then the credibility of future threats will be undermined. Carrying it out, then, does after all serve a self-defensive purpose.[16] But of course the response involves precisely the idea we were trying to avoid, for, in retaliating in order to maintain the credibility of the threat, I am using the offender as a tool.

We can avoid this in the following way. Imagine that in addition to merely issuing the threat I somehow *bound myself*

to carry it out.[17] I mean by this not just that I pledged myself
to carry it out, but that I somehow made it the case that if the
threat were ignored retaliation would be automatic and outside of my control. We could suppose, for instance, that I
constructed a trap surrounding my domain which, once it
was constructed, I could not dismantle, and whose operation
was automatic as soon as anyone crossed my border; I might
then, with the intention of deterring anyone from crossing
the border, announce that I had done this. (This general idea
was, needless to say, a familiar one in the thought of nuclear
strategists.) Perhaps, in such a case, we might have some
reluctance to speak of threats. A threat is a threat *to do* something, and here, once the system is triggered by the aggressor, there is nothing for me actually to do. So it might seem
more natural to say that the announcement of harm to those
who enter my domain is actually a warning rather than a
threat. But we may ignore this nicety. Such an announcement
is made in order to deter, and it works, if it does, in just the
same way that a paradigm threat of retaliation would; so I
shall refer to it as a threat of retaliation. In these circumstances, then, if the threat of retaliation failed, the actual
retaliation would be automatic.

The justification for setting up such a system would be
the same as that envisaged earlier for a simple deterrent
announcement that one would retaliate against an aggressor:
it is generally better to avert aggression rather than to have
to deal with it forcefully should it occur. Whether in fact it
would be justified would depend upon the costs and benefits, suitably broadly construed. If the aggression to be war-
ded off were a substantial one, if the threat could be counted
upon to be wholly effective and did not have significant
costs, and if there were no more attractive way of warding
off the threat, then most people would think that this would
be sufficient justification. After all, if the threat were indeed
wholly effective then there would be no aggression and no
counter-force. In such circumstances, one might not need
even to have armed the system, so to speak; a bluff would be
all that was required. In the real world, of course, a bluff
cannot always be counted on to be effective; and even if it
could there are, as we shall see, other possible reasons why
the threat might have to be genuine. But the genuineness of

the threat would not preclude justification; it would simply invite a more complex weighing of costs and benefits.

Now when an offender is retaliated against by such an automatic system he cannot complain that he is being used. That charge was based on the claim that he was being made to suffer in order to modify the behaviour of others. But, as the system has so far been described, no such aim has been mentioned; it might explicitly have been intended that even Kant's infamous 'last murderer'[18] should be punished, a punishment that, *ex hypothesi*, could not be intended to modify the behaviour of others.

Still, it may be countered, the actual retaliation must play *some* role in the system, and the obvious role might seem to be to maintain the credibility of the threat. But, as I have already remarked, that is not the only reason why the threat might need to be genuine. We could imagine that, for various reasons, a bluff might actually work — sufficiently so at least to maintain the system's effectiveness. In such circumstances, there might still be reasons to arm the system. It may simply be more convenient for some reason. Or, again, a system of bluffs would require dishonesty, and we might object to that. So long as our reason for arming the system is some such consideration, one having nothing to do with its deterrent effectiveness, it cannot be said that offenders are merely being used: it would be in no sense true that they are being punished in an attempt to modify the behaviour of others. The threat is addressed to each individually, and each is punished because he, individually, chose to ignore the threat; the others, and their potential behaviour, are now irrelevant.

There are, of course, other possible problems with such retaliatory systems. One is that they may seem to involve the intention to cause harm at points in time at which it will be anticipated that there will no beneficial effects. But that is only a partial description. What the system certainly requires is that at some time t_1, with the intention of preventing an evil, we set in motion an irreversible process, which, if our intention is not realized, will cause harm at t_2. Now it is certainly impermissible to intend, *tout court*, to cause pointless harm; but it does not follow from this that it is impermissible to intend to prevent harm by setting in motion a train of events which will, if one's intention is not realized, cause harm. If it did, the use of electrified fences would be illegitimate. Whether it is legitimate will depend upon the totality of the circumstances, and in particular whether the agent has observed the Restraining Conditions described in the previous chapter.[19]

A different sort of problem we may refer to as the problem of scatter: unless the system's method of detection was infallible, such a threat would be triggered even by innocent people whom the system mistakenly took to be aggressors.[20] This is not an insuperable objection to such systems, for there are clearly circumstances in which it is permissible to put innocent people at risk as long as this is not our ultimate aim. Indeed, we do this constantly in our own criminal justice systems, requiring only that benefits and risks be appropriately balanced. And if they are, there is, as yet, no objection to such deterrent threats.

One way of making it easier to achieve that balance would be by making the system slightly less automatic, allowing it to be stopped when there is reason to think that an apparent aggressor is in fact innocent. I might do this by dividing the operation into different functions and placing each in the hands of a different person. So one might be authorized to apprehend suspected aggressors, another might be authorized to decide whether they really were aggressors, and another might be authorized to administer retaliation if they were proven to be aggressors. But no one would have authority to act outside of his assigned role. From the point of view of one who sets it up, this system would be substantially similar to the simpler model we envisaged a moment ago. Once he has issued his threat he has nothing further to do in order for an aggressor to be punished; as far as he is concerned, retaliation is now automatic and there is, we are assuming, nothing that he can do to stop it. So, as with the simpler system, no one is punished in order to deter others. In this respect, the systems are no different.

The system is not, of course, automatic as far as those who actually implement the retaliation are concerned; each has actually to decide whether to operate his part of the system.[21] What should we say about them? After all, they may sometimes be involved in what seems like pointless violence:

each is committed to bringing it about that certain, particular offenders are punished even if it is clear that their punishment will have no beneficial consequences. How can they justify this? It may seem that a system that knowingly commits people to pointless violence cannot be a legitimate system, so they cannot say that the legitimacy of their actions derives from the overall legitimacy of the system. And nor, for the same reason, can they say that this is their job, that they have a contract to do it, because a contract that commits one to pointless violence has no legitimacy and so confers no legitimacy on actions carried out under it.

But this is a mistake. It is true that the system commits those who operate it to carrying out particular acts of violence which may be foreseen to have none of the beneficial effects upon whose realisation the justification of the system itself depends. But this by itself cannot make the system illegitimate: there is nothing inherently illegitimate about a system with justifiable aims in which agents are prohibited from taking into account those very aims in their particular deliberations — even when, as they think, they can see that their actions will subvert those aims. If such a system were inherently illegitimate, then this, apart from any other consideration, would condemn our own criminal justice system, in which, for instance, prison warders are not given authority to remit punishment because, in their opinion, punishing a particular offender will achieve none of the benefits supposedly to be gained from the correctional system, and indeed may subvert them. In such cases, we think that a prison warder need offer no more justification for his imprisoning someone than that the justifiable system in which he works gives him no authority to do otherwise.

Everything turns, then, on whether there is good reason to set up the system in this particular way; as we shall see, there is.

I have referred to such a system of automatic retaliation against aggression as a system of punishment. But is it justified to refer to it as a system of *punishment*? As I remarked earlier,[22] punishment is an intentional notion: when an offender is punished, he is punished *for* an offence, not merely as a causal consequence of the offence. When the system is automatic, it may seem that the retaliation is simply a causal consequence of the offence, and that we thereby lose the intentional notion of punishment, the sense that it is 'for' an offence. But that is not so. The nub of the requirement that punishment be *for* an offence is to require that the harm involved in punishment be the *intended* consequence of actions of the offender. And retaliation, whether automatic or not, and whether intended as a method of self-defence or not, precisely does involve intending that harm come about as a consequence of the actions one is retaliating against; that is what makes it retaliation.

Model versus Reality

The system just described does not of course closely model any existing criminal justice system. The question is whether a criminal justice system *could* conform to that model. I argue that it could, and that it would be morally more acceptable if it did.

A criminal statute, we may say, involves a threat, which we can think of as threat of retaliation against anyone who violates the prohibited behaviour. And it is, in the important sense, like the threat in the model we have envisaged: once someone has transgressed, the procedure goes forward fairly automatically.[23]

It is automatic in the sense in which the system just imagined is automatic — a system which, of course, was meant to reflect the separation of powers that, ideally, characterizes modern democracies.[24] The legislature (perhaps in conjunction with some other part of the government) issues threats against anyone who should aggress against the community or one of its members.[25] And the threat is a real one, not because the deterrent effectiveness of the system requires this, but because the legislature in an open, democratic society *has no authority, and little power, to issue false threats to its citizens*. Even if it is justifiable for particular government officials to deceive the public on particular occasions (which, rarely, it may be), we would not give a general authorisation to the government, or to any government agency, to deceive the public. Bluffing is thus precluded. Any threats the government issues must be genuine.[26] Once the threat is made, the legislature does not carry it out, and has virtually no power to do so. That is put into the hands of other bodies. The police, and various regulatory agencies, all branches of the executive, are authorized to detect and apprehend suspected offenders. It is then the judicial system that determines whether they really offended, and what their punishment should be. And a further branch of the executive then carries out the punishment. It would not, then, be misleading to say: we, through the legislature, issue a threat; 'we', however, cannot revoke it in particular cases. From 'our' point of view, punishment is then automatic.

And there is good reason for setting up the system in this way. We think it is in general dangerous to give too much power to the government, and so we separate its powers. But even if we were not convinced about the virtues of a separated government in general, we would surely insist upon it in the case of the criminal justice system. Whatever else might be said, it ought to be generally agreed that the power to sentence and punish should not be in the hands of those who wield political power, or those who are directly answerable to them. This would create scope for corruption and oppression that we should not countenance.[27] So the *point* of the separation of powers is not to make possible a criminal justice system in which no particular punishment need be justified by reference to is deterrent effect upon potential offenders; but that is one of its *results*.

Does it follow from this that no punishment is justified in a criminal justice system not characterized by this separation of powers? If the overriding justification of punishment is, as I have argued, deterrence, then it does, because the justification of deterrent threats lies in their being *threats*, and if a threat does not achieve its aim there is no further justification in self-defence for whoever issued the threat to carry it out, and doing so would then be pointless, unjustifiable violence. The only way to avoid this is by having a system of the sort that I have described. In the ideal case, those who make the threat have no say in whether it is carried out in any particular case; those who carry it out must justify their doing so by reference to the overarching aim of the system, not by reference to any deterrent effect of the particular case with which they are concerned. So at no point is a particular punishment to be justified by its deterrent effect.

But why cannot, say, an absolute dictator set up such a system and appeal to its general deterrent effect in just the way described above: he has set up the system, and he punishes an offender simply because he has offended. The reason is this. In the ideal case I described, the system is justifiably set up at the beginning, in such a way that questions about whether a particular offender should be punished are foreclosed. For the dictator, however, that question has to be raised anew on each particular occasion, and answered unsatisfactorily on each particular occasion. He cannot appeal to the system he has set in place, and its overarching aim, because there *is* no such system: his having said on Monday that offenders will be punished cannot bind his will on Tuesday; on Tuesday—unless he is compulsively attached to honesty—he is faced with a new decision; that is part of what it is to be an absolute dictator. He might, of course, make punishment automatic in some way; but it is hard to see how one could do this in the real world without delegating power to others; but then one is not an absolute dictator. So he is constantly faced with a dilemma: *either* offenders are punished to deter potential offenders, in which case they are being merely used, *or* the violence inflicted in particular punishments is simply pointless violence with no justification.

So an absolute dictator cannot, in normal circumstances, legitimately punish those who disobey his commands.[28] If this seems like a hard bullet to bite we must remember that punishment by the state is, after all, a purely political act, and *no* political act carried out by an absolute dictator can, in normal circumstances, be legitimate.

Of course, we should not under-emphasize the discretion available to the various departments of the criminal justice system.[29] The police, for instance, typically have available to them a number of possible responses to law breaking. They may simply take no further action; or they may issue an informal warning, or issue a formal warning, or refer the case to a mediation scheme (if one is available); or they may decide to prosecute. Prosecutors too exercise discretion, about which cases to prosecute, and how to prosecute them. Even in systems like the German and Austrian, where

prosecution is in principle compulsory when there is sufficient evidence, numerous exceptions have introduced considerable scope for discretion.[30] Again, judges (and juries,
where they have sentencing powers) typically have discretion in sentencing. And the executive often has further
discretion. Some member of the executive, whether the
President of the US in federal cases, or the Governors in state
cases, or the Home Secretary in the UK, will normally have
the power of executive clemency. And in the UK the Home
Secretary still retains some power to determine the length of
some sentences.

Now in so far as this discretion extended to the authority
to take account of the deterrent effects of particular punishment it would, of course, reintroduce the original worry.
And in actual practice, it certainly does so. The police, on
occasion, take into account the deterrent effect of their
decision whether to pursue a particular offence.[31] Judges
frequently take it into account, when deciding on a sentence.[32] Members of the executive, when so empowered, do
so.[33] And private citizens often call for harsh sentences to be
imposed on particular offenders because they think that this
will have a deterrent effect.[34] But we are not bound to all of
this. Discretion in the law is already limited by all sorts of
considerations. Certainly, the police and the various regulatory agencies, for instance, need not investigate every instance of alleged law breaking that comes to their attention;
on the other hand, it is not open to the police simply to
decide not to investigate a murder, or an armed bank robbery, or to the UK Serious Fraud Office to ignore a major financial irregularity. If they are not to investigate an alleged
offence then there should be a good reason for this; it should
be 'in the public interest' for them not to do so. And having
apprehended an offender, they need not proceed to prosecution; the police may, for instance, simply issue a caution.[35]
But the issuing of cautions is, in the UK, governed by guide-
lines set out in a Home Office Circular which requires that a
formal caution should not replace prosecution unless this is
in the public interest.[36]

Similarly, prosecutors are not required to prosecute every
case that the police present them with. They are, on the other
hand, expected to prosecute in cases that meet certain cond-

itions; those conditions, again, refer to matters of public interest. There is, for instance, an evidential standard; prosecutors should not prosecute if there is insufficient evidence to make conviction likely. Such prosecutions would be a waste of public resources, and in many cases unjust to the accused. They may also take into account such things as the seriousness of the offence, and the likely impact of punishment on the offender (who may be very young, very old, or mentally unstable, for instance). But if the standards are met then there is a presumption that they should prosecute.[37]

Nor can executive clemency be given arbitrarily. The United States Constitution gives the President unfettered authority to issue pardons;[38] but he or she may not pardon someone merely because they are friends, or ex-colleagues. We know why the President was granted such a power,[39] and if a President routinely pardoned offenders without good reason, we should object — as indeed did many when Gerald Ford pardoned Richard Nixon, though Ford urged that it was in the national interest to do so.

Discretion, then, is limited by what is in the 'public interest'. We need not now give a full account of what is meant by that phrase, but it need not be, and is not, construed in a narrowly utilitarian way — it already encompasses notions of what is just or fair, for instance. It is not, then, implausible to suggest that it should also encompass the notion of the value of individuals which lays a moral constraint upon merely using them, serving as a regulative ideal for our criminal justice systems.[40] If it did, we could then plausibly say that if, at any stage in a particular case, the question were raised as to whether the law should take its normal course, that question should not be answered by reference to whether doing so would deter others.[41] We could then consistently say that the point of the penal system is to deter, but that we do not punish the offender in order to deter others.

---

[1]   Such a theory can be found in, for instance, Hobbes, *Leviathan*, Ch. 28 (where, as is often the case with Hobbes, he holds that the theory is true by definition); in Locke, *Second Treatise of Civil Government*, §§ 8, 12; and in Bentham, *An Introduction to the Principles of Morals and Legislation*, Ch. XII, § 36, Ch. XIII, § 2, fn. (Bentham thinks that deter-

rence is the primary goal of punishment, though not its only benefit). Almost all modern writers think of the deterrence theory in the same way. See, for instance, Mark A. Drumbl, *Atrocity, Punishment and International Law* (Cambridge University Press, 2007), p. 169; David Boonin, *The Problem of Punishment* (Cambridge University Press, 2009), p. 39; Michael Zimmerman, *The Immorality of Punishment* (Broadview, 2011), p. 42.

2   See, e.g. C.S. Nino, 'A Consensual Theory of Punishment', *Philosophy and Public Affairs*, vol. xii (1983), pp. 289–306, at pp. 291f.; Nicola Lacey, *State Punishment: Political Principles and Community Values* (Routledge, 1988), p. 29; Andrew von Hirsch, *Censure and Sanctions* (Clarendon Press, 1993), p. 42; Deirde Golash, *The Case Against Punishment: Retribution, Crime Prevention and the Law* (New York University Press, 2005), p. 103; Ted Honderich, *Punishment: The Supposed Justifications* (Penguin Books, 1971), pp. 62ff., who does not think much of the objection; Thomas E. Hill, Jr., 'Humanity as an End in Itself', *Ethics*, vol. xci (1980), pp. 84–90 (rp. in his *Dignity and Practical Reason in Kant's Moral Theory* (Cornell University Press, 1992)). Hill offers his own Kantian explanation of why deterrent punishment need not fail to respect the 'dignity of humanity' in 'Making Exceptions without Abandoning the Principle: How a Kantian Might Think about Terrorism', in Ray Frey and Christopher Morris (eds.), *Violence, Terrorism and Justice* (Cambridge University Press, 1991) (rp. in *Dignity and Practical Reason in Kant's Moral Theory*); Antony Duff, *Trials and Punishments* (Cambridge University Press, 1986), and *Punishment, Communication, and Community* (Oxford University Press, 2001), *passim*.

3   For discussion of this Kantian requirement, see Martha Nussbaum, *Sex and Social Justice* (Oxford University Press, 1999), Ch. 8; Derek Parfit, *On What Matters* (Oxford University Press, 2010), vol. 1, pp. 212–232, and vol. 2, pp. 145–147; Susan Wolf, 'Hiking the Range', in Parfit, *On What Matters*, vol. 2, p. 44; Samuel Kerstein, 'Treating Consenting Adults Merely as Means', in Mark Timmons, *Oxford Studies in Normative Ethics, vol. 1* (2011), p. 53 ('there might not be a *univocal* concept of just using another').

4   So Wolf, *op. cit.*

5   This may have been the position that Oliver Wendell Holmes took. See *The Common Law* (Boston, MA, Little, Brown, 1963 (first published 1881)), pp. 37f. But the passage is rather unclear.

6   Cf. Antony Duff, *Trials and Punishments*, pp. 295ff. Kerstein, 'Treating Consenting Adults Merely as Means', p. 52.

7   Cf., e.g. Susan Wolf, 'Hiking the Range', p. 44.

8   For a fuller version of this argument, see C.S. Nino, 'A Consensual Theory of Punishment', *Philosophy and Public Affairs*, vol. xii (1983), pp. 289–306.

9   Whether it would go the whole way is another question. See Larry
     Alexander, 'Consent, Punishment, and Proportionality', *Philosophy
     and Public Affairs*, vol. xv (1986), pp. 178–182, for the issue of whether
     the consent of the offender is sufficient to yield an acceptable prop-
     ortionality constraint.
          We might add that not everyone would agree that if one has freely
     and knowingly consented to some treatment then that treatment
     cannot use one unacceptably.
10   For further criticism see Ted Honderich, *Punishment: The Supposed
     Justification* (Pluto Press, 2006), pp. 48–53; and especially David
     Boonin, *The Problem of Punishment* (Cambridge University Press,
     2008), pp. 156–172.
11   This is perhaps what Kant means in the following passage: the offen-
     der 'must first be found to be deserving of punishment before any
     consideration is given to the utility of his punishment for himself or
     for his fellow citizens' (*The Metaphysical Elements of Justice. Part 1 of
     the Metaphysics of Morals*, p. 331; translated by John Ladd
     (Macmillan, 1965)). However, the passage is (just) consistent with
     the different thought that any utility should be a foreseen but
     unintended consequence.
12   One might argue that offenders increase the general level of public
     apprehension, that they should be made to compensate for this, and
     that imprisonment, for example, can do something towards this end.
     (So David Boonin, *The Problem of Punishment*, Ch. 5.) But this is to
     replace punishment by restitution and Boonin does not believe that
     punishment can be justified.
13   Cf. Tony Honoré, *Responsibility and Fault* (Hart, 1999), p.19. Antony
     Duff, *Trials and Punishments*, and *Punishment, Communication, and
     Community*, *passim*.
14   Some, Aquinas probably, have held that it is not in fact permissible
     deliberately to harm one's attacker in self-defence; any acceptable
     harm must be an unintended though foreseen side effect. But this
     seems wrong: one may need deliberately to harm someone as one's
     means of defending oneself, and this surely need not be unjustified.
     So also Jeff McMahan, 'Self-Defense and the Innocent Attacker',
     Ethics, vol. xiv (1994), pp. 252–290, at p. 272; and David Rodin, *War
     and Self-Defense* (Oxford University Press, 2004), p. 4, fn.
15   So McMahan, 'Self-Defense and the Innocent Attacker', p. 273.
16   For this sort of defence, see Oliver Wendell Holmes, *The Common
     Law*, p. 40: 'The law threatens certain pains if you do certain things,
     intending thereby to give you a new motive for not doing them. If
     you persist in doing them, it has to inflict the pains in order that its
     threats may continue to be believed'; Michael Clark, 'The Sanctions
     of the Criminal Law', *Proceedings of the Aristotelian Society*, vol. xcvii
     (1997), Part 1, pp. 28f.; Montague, *Punishment and Societal-Defense*

(Rowman and Littlefield, 1995), pp. 62–63; and Michael Otsuka, *Libertarianism without Inequality*, Ch. 3.

[17] Warren Quinn also used this idea in a discussion of punishment, though his ingenious argument was different from mine; see 'The Right to Threaten and the Right to Punish', *Philosophy and Public Affairs*, vol. xiv (1985), pp. 327–373. Daniel Farrell has shown that Quinn's argument rests upon a premise which is false; see 'On Threats and Punishments', *Social Theory and Practice*, vol. xv (1989), pp. 125–154; and also 'A New Paradox of Deterrence', in Jules L. Coleman and Christopher W. Morris (eds.), *Rational Commitment and Social Justice: Essays for Gregory Kavka* (Cambridge University Press, 1998), pp. 22–46.

[18] 'Even if a civil society were to be dissolved by the consent of all its members (for instance, if a people inhabiting an island decided to separate and disperse themselves around the world), the last murderer remaining in prison must first be executed, so that everyone will receive what his actions deserve, and so that the bloodguilt thereof will not be fixed on the people because they failed to insist on carrying out the punishment; for if they fail to do so, they may be regarded as accomplices in this public violation of legal justice' (I. Kant, *The Metaphysical Elements of Justice. Part 1 of The Metaphysics of Morals*, translated by John Ladd (Macmillan, 1965), p. 102).

[19] There is an immense and ancient literature to which I cannot here do justice on the logic of the intentions embedded in threats. For a relevant discussion, see Daniel Farrell, 'A New Paradox of Deterrence', pp. 22–46.

[20] For an account of the methods and problems of automatic systems of punishment, see Mark Rieff, *Punishment, Compensation, and Law: A Theory of Enforceability* (Cambridge University Press, 2005), pp. 34ff.

[21] Cf. Deirdre Golash, *The Case Against Punishment*, p. 107; Michael Sprague, 'Who Can Carry Out Protective Deterrence?', *The Philosophical Quarterly*, vol. liv (2004), pp. 443–447; and for a reply, see Anthony Ellis, 'Punishment as Deterrence: Reply to Sprague', *The Philosophical Quarterly*, vol. lv (2004), pp. 98–101.

[22] See p. 15.

[23] Legal systems differ, of course. In some, such as the German and Austrian systems, prosecution of all offences is, in principle, mandatory where there is adequate evidence to sustain a conviction. In others, such as the UK and US systems, there is broad discretion at most levels.

[24] No country fully realizes this ideal. Even in the US, where it is perhaps most pronounced, Supreme Court justices and federal appeals court judges, for instance, are appointed by the President 'by and with the advice and consent' of the Senate; it is no secret that these justices are often appointed, or rejected, partly because of their political views. And in the UK, Parliament is, by tradition, omni-

competent; however, there is, to all intents and purposes, a marked separation between the legislative, executive, and judicial arms as far as crime and punishment are concerned. Even the residual powers of the Home Secretary to determine penal sentences in some cases has been held to contravene Articles 5 and 6 of the European Convention on Human Rights. Speaking of the criminal justice system in the UK, Andrew Ashworth has remarked that '[a]lthough many who speak and write about criminal justice tend to refer to "the criminal justice system", it is widely agreed that it is not a "system" in the sense of a set of co-ordinated decision-makers... [M]any groups working within criminal justice enjoy considerable discretion, and... are relatively autonomous' (*The Criminal Process: An Evaluative Study* (Clarendon Press, 1994), p. 21).

25   This is, of course, vague and oversimplified. Criminal jurisdiction generally extends to crimes committed against anyone within a certain territory, whether 'members of the community' in any real sense or not. And in certain circumstances it may extend further: a court may have jurisdiction over crimes by its nationals against aliens committed on their own territory, for instance, or even against crimes committed by aliens against aliens on their own territory. On the extent of criminal jurisdiction, see Ian Brownlie, *Principles of Public International Law* (Clarendon Press, 5th ed. 1998), pp. 303ff.; Antonio Cassese, *International Criminal Law* (Oxford University Press, 2003), Parts III and IV (cf. 'international bodies have gradually extended, by way of interpretation, the territorial reach of international obligations concerning respect for human rights, incumbent upon states. In this way, such bodies have come to assert a right to pronounce on and, if need be, condemn or stigmatize massive violations committed... outside the territorial jurisdiction traditionally considered as delimiting the State's responsibilities' (p. 11)).

26   Michael Otsuka seems to overlook this. He argues that preserving the credibility of the system is the *only* role to be played by actual punishment, and that automatic systems of retaliation cannot be justified unless one is allowed 'to appeal to the fact that the punishment of the guilty will deter others' (p. 7). 'Suppose that one derives a right to punish an aggressor only from a right of self-protection against that aggressor. It follow that a potential victim of aggression cannot justify punishment on ground of a right of self-protection against a particular aggressor if he knows that punishment that follows an irrevocable threat to punish if harmed makes no more contribution to this protection against that aggressor than a bluff... If such punishment were justified, then it would have to be justified on a ground other than that of his right of self-protection against that aggressor, such as a right to use punishment as a means to deter others...' (pp. 60–61). But this assumes that bluffing is a genuine option, and in the case of punishment by the state, as I argue, it is

not. So Otsuka may be right to say, 'While I believe that deception is morally bad, I do not believe that it is so bad that it ought to be avoided at the cost of the infliction of punishment on an aggressor that does not enhance anyone's protection' (*Libertarianism without Inequality*, p. 61, fn. 12). But this has little bearing on the question of punishment by the government in a democratic polity.

27 Cf. William J. Stuntz, *The Collapse of American Criminal Justice* (Harvard University Press, 2011), p. 68.

28 It is important to remember here that we are speaking of normal circumstances, not circumstances of national emergency, for instance, where an absolute dictator may be needed for a time.

29 For the extent of discretion in the criminal justice system, see Ashworth, *The Criminal Process*, esp. Chs. 5–9; and Ashworth *Sentencing and Criminal Justice* (Cambridge University Press, 4th ed. 2005). For a comparison between some European countries and the US, see Yue Ma, 'Prosecutorial Discretion and Plea Bargaining in the United States, France, Germany and Italy: A Comparative Perspective', *International Criminal Justice Review*, vol. 12 (2002), pp. 22–52.

30 See J. Herrmann, 'The Rule of Compulsory Prosecution and the Scope of Prosecutorial Discretion in Germany', *University of Chicago Law Review*, vol. xvi (1974), pp. 468–505, esp. pp. 475ff.

31 In one famous case in the UK, for instance, defendants were charged with various offences connected with disturbances on the sea front at Ramsgate; when they chose to be tried in the Crown Court rather than in a magistrate's court, the police dropped some of the charges to ensure that the case would be tried in a magistrate's court. It seems that their reason was that the trial would be much quicker, and that this would have a deterrent effect on seaside hooligans in the summer season. The defendants' appeal was turned down. (See *Ramsgate Justices, ex parte Warren et al.* (1981) 72 Cr. App. R. 250.)

32 See Andrew Ashworth, *Sentencing and Criminal Justice* (Cambridge University Press, 4th ed. 2005), *passim*.

In 2011, in the wake of an outburst of riots in various parts of the UK, Judge Elgan Edwards sentenced two men to lengthy prison sentences for trying (unsuccessfully) to incite riots, saying that he hoped it would deter others (*The Guardian*, 17 August 2011; available at http://www.guardian.co.uk/uk/2011/aug/17/england-riots-harsher-sentences-deterrent). The call for deterrent sentences was widespread.

The UK Sentencing Council gives as one of the five aims of punishment: 'the reduction of crime (including its reduction by deterrence). This includes individual deterrence (aimed at preventing the individual offender from committing another crime) and general deterrence (using the sentence imposed on an offender as an example to deter others from committing a similar offence)' (http://sentencingcouncil.judiciary.gov.uk/sentencing/what-sentences-for.htm). And the Criminal Justice Act, 2003, gives as one of the 'purposes of sentencing' 'the reduction of crime (including its reduction by deterrence)'.

33   There are numerous famous examples. In 1996, for instance, the Home Secretary in the UK, Michael Howard, caused a legal storm when he announced that the eight-year sentence given to two ten-year-old children Robert Thompson and Jon Venables, for the murder of James Bulger, a two-year-old, must be increased to a minimum of 15 years; the shorter sentence was, he said, insufficient for 'retribution and deterrence'. (His decision was immediately overruled by the High Court. And in 1999 the European Court of Human Rights ruled that his action breached the boys' human rights, and they were released on licence in 2001.) And in the US in 1996 President Clinton announced that he would not intervene to free Jonathan Pollard, who had spied for the Israelis, on the grounds that this would not serve the interests of deterrence. As Mike McCurry, President Clinton's spokesman, put it, 'The enormity of Mr. Pollard's offences, his lack of remorse, the damage done to our national security, the need for general deterrence and the continuing threat to national security that he posed made the original life sentence imposed by the court warranted.' Almost ten years later, in an interview with Caroline Glick in April 2005, James Woolsey, former director of the CIA, seemed to endorse the emphasis on deterrence, though now with sympathy for Pollard: 'This man would not be my first candidate for clemency, but 20 years is a long time. As a general proposition, one dimension of this is that a substantial penalty has been paid, so that the element of deterrence is dealt with' (see Caroline Glick, 'Pollard's Freedom and Our Freedom', available at http://www.betar.co.uk/articles/betar1114434537.php).

34   Cf., e.g. Jeff Madrick and Frank Portnoy, 'Should Some Bankers be Prosecuted', *New York Review of Books*, vol. lviii, number 17: 'successful prosecutions of individuals as well as their firms would surely have a deterrent effect on Wall Street's deceptive activities' (p. 23).

35   See p. 25 of Andrew Ashworth, *Sentencing and Criminal Justice* (Cambridge University Press, 4th ed. 2005).

36   Cf. Home Office Circular 18/1994.

37   'A prosecution will usually take place unless the prosecutor is sure that there are public interest factors tending against prosecution which outweigh those tending in favour, or unless the prosecutor is satisfied that the public interest may be properly served, in the first instance, by offering the offender the opportunity to have the matter dealt with by an out-of-court disposal' (Crown Prosecution Service, 2010).

38   *The Constitution of the United States of America*, Article II.2 (1).

[39] See William F. Duker, 'The President's Power to Pardon: A Constitutional History', *William and Mary Law Review*, vol. xviii (1977), pp. 475–538.

[40] Cf. Duff, *Trials and Punishments*, p. 195.

[41] 'Exemplary sentences' are now 'widely criticized' (Ashworth, *The Criminal Process*, p. 42). Cf. H.L.A. Hart, *Punishment and Responsibility: Essays in the Philosophy of Law* (Clarendon Press, 1968), p. 24: 'If a certain offence is specially prevalent at a given time and a judge passes heavier sentences than on previous offenders ("as a warning") some sacrifice of justice to the safety of society is involved'.

Chapter Ten

The Deterrence Theory: The Limits of Punishment

The theory of punishment I have outlined tells us that what we think about punishment should derive from what we think about self-defence. There is, however, considerable disagreement about what we should think about the morality of self-defence. That being so, we should expect, what we in fact find, that there is considerable disagreement about what is morally acceptable in punishment. It is quite likely that those disagreements about self-defence cannot be settled by philosophy, that philosophy simply does not have the resources to settle them. But even if it does, we cannot realistically expect any settled consensus about them in the foreseeable future. As I have already said, since punishment by the state is a political act, those differences will have to be settled by the normal political processes.

Still, it is plausible to think that there are some intuitions to which a theory of punishment must conform, intuitions which, if not shared by everyone, are at least recognized to be morally respectable intuitions. There is, for instance, sharp disagreement about whether it is ever permissible to execute offenders as a punishment, but even those who think that it is never permissible to do so should recognize that it is at least morally respectable to think otherwise, that this is a view about which decent people can respectably disagree. By contrast, the idea that we may routinely execute petty thieves is, I take it, not a respectable view: it would reflect badly on someone if they were to think this. So we can demand that where a theory has practical implications, they must fall within the boundary of clearly respectable views, views that fall within the broad community of moral sentiment.[1] These may turn out, in the fullness of time, to be mistaken. But they are all that we have for now.

Punishing the Innocent

A prohibition on deliberately punishing the innocent is perhaps the most obvious constraint on the morality of punishment.[2] It is also a constraint that is often thought to run counter to the deterrence theory, for it may seem that if the aim of punishment is simply to deter potential offenders, then it must be justifiable to punish the innocent whenever this would achieve that aim. One could avoid this result, of course, by importing an independent moral constraint prohibiting the punishment of the innocent. The deterrence theory, understood as I have suggested, does not need to do this; such a prohibition is precisely what we should expect if the principles of punishment are derived from the principles of self-defence. The criminal justice system involves retaliation against those who fail to heed a threat with which they can be legitimately required to comply, and the innocent, those who have committed no offence, have not, save vacuously, failed to do that.

We could set up a crime prevention system in other ways, of course. We could threaten to harm entire groups when only certain members of the group transgress.[3] Or we could issue threats to punish the innocent relatives of potential lawbreakers. But the deterrence theory, as I have understood, can quite consistently object to threats such as these.

One understanding of such threats depends upon a notion of group identity in which a group is held to be responsible for what any of its members do. But this understanding is irrelevant to the present issue, because it implies that the sorts of case just mentioned do not involve the punishment of the innocent.

Alternatively, we may think of such threats as addressed to, say, the relatives of potential offenders with the hope that they will bring pressure to bear upon their relatives in order to avoid harm to themselves. But the deterrence theory can certainly object to this. The principles of self-defence do not routinely allow one to commandeer the aid of third-parties by threatening harm to them if they do not assist. If someone is about to attack me, I cannot routinely threaten harm to one of his innocent relatives if he does not try to persuade the aggressor to desist.

Differently, we may think of such threats as being addressed to potential offenders, with the hope that they will care sufficiently for their relatives that they will refrain from offending in order to avoid harm to them. But again the deterrence theory can object to this. Here, the relatives, perhaps unbeknownst to them, are being held hostage, threatened with harm in order to mould the behaviour of others, and thus being used as tools. This is not normally an acceptable mode of self-defence.[4]

How Much May We Punish?

Everyone agrees that when it is justified to punish someone some proportion must be observed between the seriousness of the offence and the severity of the punishment. We have found reason to think that some theories can attach no suitable sense to this idea, for they have difficulty in explaining what 'proportion' means here. The deterrence theory, properly understood, has no such difficulty; to say that a punishment should be proportional to the seriousness of the offence is to say that, in general, the state may threaten only what it is reasonably necessary to threaten in order to deter such offences.[5]

There will of course be disputes between reasonable people about how serious particular offences are, and what it is 'reasonably necessary' to threaten in order to deter them. And these disputes can have both factual and normative elements. But a theory of punishment should not be expected to settle such disputes. No theory of punishment, by itself, can tell us in concrete terms what is the appropriate punishment for a given offence; the most it can give us is a *formula* from which, with some prior moral or psychological judgments, we can deduce the appropriate punishment. The Simple Desert Theory, for instance, tells us merely that the severity of the punishment should match the moral gravity of the crime, but, even if the theory were internally coherent, it could not itself tell us how morally grave particular offences are, or what punishments match them. Again, the Reform Theory tells us that the point of punishment is to reform offenders, but we do not expect it to tell us how much punishment will be effective in that aim. The deterrence theory I have outlined tells us that a punishment matches an offence when it is reasonably necessary to threaten that punishment in order to deter the offence. Beyond bringing these notions under the umbrella of self-defence, it does not tell us how serious 'serious' is, nor how reasonable 'reasonable' is. At this point, some prior moral judgments will have to be used, judgments that derive from what we think about the morality of self-defence more generally.

What May We Punish?

It should be clear that the theory of deterrence will not legitimate punishment solely on the grounds that the behaviour in question is immoral, behaviour often referred to as 'harmless immorality'; if it is genuinely harmless, then there is no call for self-defence. Perhaps not everyone thinks it impermissible to punish mere immorality as such, but to think so is well within what I called the community of moral sentiment.

Ordinary Offences

If we think of punishment as a form of self-defence, the behaviour that will probably first occur to us as needing to be prohibited will be straightforward acts of aggression such as murder and theft. However, the greater part of most people's intercourse with the law is made up of quite different things — traffic offences and such like — which are hugely neglected by theorists, who concentrate on what have been called 'core' crimes, those crimes that are clearly wrongful independently of legal prohibitions.[6] It may not seem natural to think of our response to such things as traffic violations as falling within the ambit of self-defence. But, on what I earlier argued was a proper understanding of self-defence, it is in fact perfectly natural. The exercise of self-defence includes not merely fending off ongoing attacks, but extends to all attempts to uphold constraints whose point is the protection of individual welfare. So if the regulations are themselves justifiable, then deliberately infringing them is naturally thought of as a form of aggression — not, perhaps, against particular individuals but against the community at large. It is a violation of a constraint which others have a right to uphold in pursuit of individual welfare.

Omissions

Some of the cases just mentioned involve omissions, rather than positive actions. However, all jurisdictions, I should think, punish some harmful omissions. A doctor with certain responsibilities may be punished for not carrying them out; in some jurisdictions ordinary citizens may be punished for failing to render assistance to those in need when the need is very great and the assistance required is not particularly onerous; and probably all jurisdictions require citizens to give certain information to the police, or to courts, and punish them if they fail to do so. Again, it may seem odd to refer to threats of punishment in such cases as self-defence; omissions hardly seem to be acts of aggression. But the oddity is superficial. Like a positive act, an omission can be the violation of a constraint which others have a right to enforce in defence of individual welfare. That is most clearly so when we are thinking of, say, the contractual duties that a doctor has to a patient. But it can plausibly be argued that it is also true in the case of citizens who fail to render reasonable assistance to others to whom they have no special obligation; it is arguable that they have a general obligation to do this, and that we all have a right to enforce this obligation. (It is also arguable that this is false; and indeed jurisdictions differ about this.)

Negligence

A special sort of omission is negligence, the failure to take appropriate care. Again, it may seem odd at first sight to speak of this as a form of aggression. But where there is a reasonable requirement of appropriate care, not taking such care is the violation of a constraint which others have a right to uphold in defence of individual welfare. There is nothing odd in talking about one's taking self-defensive measures against someone's negligence.

Negligence, however, may seem to pose a problem for a theory that assimilates punishment to self-defence. In the law, deliberate misconduct is typically treated more severely than negligence. Mere negligence is usually a tort, not a crime. When it rises to the level of 'gross negligence', or reck-lessness, it may be a crime, but even then it is generally pun-ished less severely than deliberate acts that cause the same harm. With self-defence, however, things seem different, for most people think that we are permitted to protect ourselves just as forcefully against a negligent threat as against a delib-erate one.

Here we must advert again to the difference between direct self-defence and self-defensive deterrence. A particular act of recklessness may pose the same risk as a deliberate threat, and may justify equally forceful action. However, it is rational to be more concerned about the prospect of delib-erate misconduct than the prospect of reckless misconduct, because deliberate misconduct is in general more likely to cause harm than negligent misconduct; we should obviously have more reason to be concerned about someone who posit-ively intends to kill than about someone who simply drives his car recklessly, for, in general, the former will pose a much more serious threat. And, further, it is in general easier to deter negligent behaviour, which requires only more care, than deliberate misconduct, which in general requires aban-doning a positively desired course of action.[7] Other things being equal, these considerations justify a threat of less serious retaliation.

Inchoate Offences

Somewhat more complicated are what are what typically called 'inchoate' offences. These are incipient, or incomplete, offences, such as inciting others to commit an offence, cons-piring to commit an offence, or unsuccessfully attempting to commit an offence. The general justification for such prohib-itions is clear:

> [T]he legal system intends to protect society as far as poss-
> ible. Therefore, in addition to punishing offences already
> perpetrated, it endeavours to prevent the commission of

potential transgressions. It consequently intervenes with its prohibitions at an early stage, before crimes are completed, that is, at the stage of their preparation, so as to forestall the consummation of the harmful consequences of actual crimes.[8]

Even without this general justification it would be natural to prohibit intentional and successful incitement. Such behaviour is properly thought of as part of the aggression (though of course it may be a more or less serious part). But in some legal systems even unsuccessful incitement is an offence; here the general justification just noted is appropriate.

Attempts and *conspiracies*, however, raise slightly more complex issues.

An unsuccessful attempt to commit a crime may itself be a separate crime: one who tries to murder someone but fails may be convicted of attempted murder. This has often been thought to pose a problem for the deterrence theory:

> If we think of the law, as the deterrent theory requires us to think of it, as threatening punishment to those persons who are tempted to commit offences, there can be no need to attach any punishment to the unsuccessful attempt, because those who set about crime intend to succeed and the law's threat has all the deterrent force it can have if it is attached to the crime; no additional effect is given to it if unsuccessful attempts are also punished.[9]

Here we need to distinguish two different sorts of attempt. First, there is the sort of case in which an offender embarks on an offence but later, for whatever reason, gives it up before he has completed it. Second, there is the sort of case in which an offender tries wholeheartedly to commit an offence but fails; perhaps the gun he fires does not go off, or he may fire at a tailor's mannequin thinking it to be a person.

Despite the passage lately quoted from Hart, he thought that the first sort of case posed no problem for the deterrence theory. If we were setting up a system of semi-automatic retaliation, we should not set it up in such a way that the retaliation would be triggered only when the offence was completed. A rational strategy would be to give potential aggressors an incentive not to aggress in the first place, and to give actual aggressors an incentive to desist from their actions even when they had embarked on them. Where

between the mere intention to aggress and successfully aggressing we should put the point at which retaliation would
be triggered is a difficult question. If we set that point very
late, we might encourage potential offenders to embark on
offences, and continue with them, at some cost to others,
knowing that they could later withdraw. If, on the other
hand, we set the point very early — as soon as they had
started planning the act, for instance — then this would
deprive offenders of what might have been an effective
incentive to desist once the act was under way; in addition,
enforcing this would require enormous resources, and considerable general deprivation of liberty. The challenge, then,
is to find the point at which one's self-defensive strategy
would be optimized within the Restraining Considerations
mentioned earlier. And we find, in jurisprudential thought,
just what we should expect, given this aim.[10]

This aim in turn makes intelligible why uncompleted attempts are usually punished less severely than completed attempts.[11] As I have said, given that we want offenders to
desist from their offences even when they have already
embarked upon them, it would be perverse to threaten them
with the full punishment as soon as they embarked on the
offence, for then they would have no incentive to desist as
soon as the likelihood of apprehension were as great as when
the offence were accomplished. A natural thought would be
a sliding scale of retaliation: roughly, and other things being
equal, the further along the course of his action the offender
had progressed, the greater would be the threatened retaliation. For practical purposes, the criminal law simply fixes a
point at which an attempt, as opposed to mere preparations,
really has been made and a point at which the attempt has
been completed; between those two points we punish, but
less severely than for the completed attempt.

Some of these considerations will still be relevant with
the second sort of case, in which an offender tries wholeheartedly to commit the offence but fails: if people are going
to commit offences, then it is wise to give them some incentive to try less hard than they otherwise might, in the hope
that their attempts will sometimes then misfire; we may also
think that, in some cases, the ineptitude of the attempt suggests that it was not a wholehearted attempt, and that it can

therefore be assimilated to the first sort of case; and those who commit particularly inept attempts may be thought to pose no further danger (a consideration relevant to incapacitation, of course, not to deterrence). But such considerations will not carry us far. I think that we shall have to admit that one of the main motivations for treating this class of attempts separately is to be found in the moral sentiment that a successful attempt—simply and in itself—makes one in some way morally more blameworthy than does an unsuccessful attempt; and that sentiment cannot serve as a resource for the theory I have put forward. But here, I think, we may legitimately wonder how far we are required to go to try to make this aspect of the law intelligible. It is widely thought to be problematic.[12] And the moral sentiment on which it is based is by no means universally shared—certainly, its denial does not fall outside the boundary of what I earlier called the broad community of moral sentiment.

Let us turn now to *conspiracies*. It is not, in most jurisdictions, an offence to intend to commit a crime, nor even to plan to do so,[13] nor even to prepare to do so.[14] But if one plans with others to commit a crime—indeed, typically all that is required is that two or more people *agree* to commit a crime[15]—then one may have committed the offence of conspiracy.[16]

If there are reasons for criminalising conspiracies, they are the same reasons as those for criminalising unsuccessful attempts. We wish to deter aggressors before their aggression progresses too far; and we want to have a legal reason to intervene before real harm has been caused. But if an individual who plans an offence cannot be prosecuted merely for that, why is it that if two or more people merely agree to commit an offence they can be prosecuted? Why is this not at least as objectionable as would be prosecuting someone for an attempt who had merely decided to commit the offence, or had merely carried out some preliminary planning? It might be replied that when two people agree to commit an offence, then they have gone further than a single individual who has planned an offence. But this is doubtful, since planning on the part of an individual can usually go a considerable distance before he can be convicted of an attempt.[17] And indeed, given the goal of reducing violence, it seems likely that we should not favour a system in which mere planning, even on the part of two or more people, would trigger retaliation. Conspiracy laws would thus be difficult to justify. But, again, despite their ancient lineage (which goes back at least as far as the *Digests* of Justinian), this is a widely shared view.[18]

Offences of Strict Liability

Another sort of controversial offences are offences of strict liability, offences in which there is no requirement of *mens rea* as to one or more of the elements of the prohibited act: an Act of 1846, for instance, made it an offence in England and Wales to sell adulterated tobacco even if the vendor did not know, and could not reasonably have known, that it was adulterated.

Such prohibitions are often objected to on the grounds that it is unjust, or at least in some way unreasonable, to threaten people with punishment for behaviour that they cannot avoid.[19] The dispute here reflects a difference of opinion about the limits of self-defence that we mentioned in Chapter 7, and which we left unsettled. If we take the view that it is permissible to use force against 'innocent threats', then offences of strict liability will not seem intrinsically problematic. If deterrent threats are our means of self-defence, then all that would be required by the Restraining Conditions is that the threat have a *sufficient* deterrent effect on potential aggressors, and that condition can be satisfied, though of course it need not be, so long as potential aggressors can take some action to make their aggression sufficiently less likely; they do not have to be in complete control of their behaviour. If, for instance, you and I shared an island, it may be permissible to threaten you with retaliation if, even inadvertently and blamelessly, you were to poison my stream. There may be no reasonable course of action you could take that would guarantee that you did not poison the stream. But the threat may nonetheless be permissible, for it may be that only such a blanket threat would impel you to take sufficient care: a more nuanced threat might, for instance, be obviously prohibitively difficult to carry out and so have little credibility.

Such considerations reflect the sort of justification that has typically been given for offences of strict liability. A requirement of *mens rea* would sometimes make it effectively impossible, or just unreasonably difficult, to secure a conviction; abandoning it makes a conviction easier to secure and should therefore impel people to take a higher standard of care than they otherwise would. And the benefit secured by greater likelihood of conviction may outweigh the cost of convicting those who commit offences even when they cannot reasonably avoid doing so. This is, in principle, the right sort of justification. Whether it succeeds depends of course upon empirical calculations, and there is in fact good reason to doubt whether those calculations do in fact justify offences of strict liability except in the most exceptional cases.[20]

All of this, of course, assumes that it is indeed permissible to use harmful force against innocent threats. But if we take the view that it is *not* permissible (except in the most exiguous circumstances) to do this, strict liability will be intrinsically problematic, impermissible except in the most unusual circumstances.

The debate about the intrinsic acceptability of offences of strict liability, then, turns on the resolution of the more general debate about the permissibility of using force against innocent threats, and that debate is hard to resolve. It follows that the debate about the intrinsic acceptability of strict liability offences will also be hard to resolve. But indeed it is.

Excusing Conditions

We have seen why, according to the protective-deterrence theory, we should not punish those who have committed no offence. However, even those who have committed an offence should sometimes not be punished; and if they should be punished, there may be reason to give them less punishment than was threatened. What, then, does the protective-deterrence theory say about those who commit offences but have, to some degree, an excuse?[21]

The law of excuses is complicated and tangled, and I can do no more here than point to a few principles that guide the deterrence theory. But here are six commonly recognized conditions that excuse an offence:[22]

(1) Where it was *necessary* to commit the offence to avoid some much greater evil.

(2) Where there was bodily movement, but no real action ('*automatism*').

(3) Where *mental illness* prevented the offender from knowing what he was doing, or from knowing that it was prohibited.

(4) Where *immaturity* prevented the offender from knowing what he was doing, or from knowing that it was prohibited.

(5) Where the action was the result of an *irresistible impulse*.

(6) Where the offender acted under *severe coercion*.

Can the theory give a satisfactory account of these excusing conditions?

Necessity

The issue of necessity arises in circumstances in which someone is justified in contravening a legitimate norm in order to avoid some much worse alternative, as when, for instance, a mountaineer, in order to save his life, must break into someone else's cabin and steal food.[23] Excusing those who so act poses no special problem for the protective-deterrence theory. Aggression we have characterized as contravention of a norm that others have a right to enforce in pursuit of their own, or others', welfare. In cases of necessity, however, we are speaking of circumstances in which the agent is justified in contravening the norm; others thus have no right to enforce it against him, either in direct self-defence or in punishment.[24]

The remaining five excusing conditions, however, may seem to pose a special problem for the protective-deterrence theory. Most people hold that it is not, in principle, wrong to use harmful force against an innocent aggressor, a lunatic, for instance, bent on killing us. Given that the principles of punishment derive from the principles of self-defence, this might seem to suggest that it should equally not be wrong to punish those who commit offences but do so non-culpably. But the law, typically anyway, in one legal manner or another, excuses them. So it needs to be explained why, if it is permissible to use harmful force against non-culpable aggressors, it is not permissible to punish non-culpable offenders. Do we have here a crucial divergence between punishment and self-defence? No. The crucial difference is not between punishment and self-defence but between direct self-defence and self-defensive threats. As I said earlier, a threat is speech-act, directed at some class of people. There is clearly no point in directing such speech-acts to those who cannot comply with them, and if one cannot comply with a threat, one cannot be said deliberately to ignore it.[25] But punishment, according to the theory I have defended just is harm imposed for deliberately ignoring a threat.

Automatism

The general principle here is perhaps most easily seen in the case of what is known as 'automatism'.

The law typically distinguishes insane automatism from non-insane automatism.[26] The former arises from a 'disease of the mind' (or an 'internal' cause, as it is often put); the latter arises from 'external' causes, such as drug abuse. Where a defence of the latter kind is successful, the defendant is completely exonerated; in cases of the former kind he will be dealt with in whatever way is normal for mentally ill offenders. But common to both kinds is that though there is a bodily movement, there is no genuinely voluntary action. An example would be that of someone, who, asleep and in the throes of a nightmare, strangles his wife. Most people would think that in such a case the wife may use force in self-defence against her husband; the law, on the other hand, would excuse the husband for his attack and he would not be punished. The reason for this difference should now be clear. Though it would be permissible for the wife to use force in self-defence against her husband trying to injure her in the throes of a nightmare, it would not be permissible for the state to mount genuine threats of retaliation to deter him unless there were reasonable precautions that he could take to avoid this behaviour. If there were such precautions, then such threats would be permissible, assuming the Restraining Conditions mentioned earlier were satisfied.

Genuine automatism is quite rare, and English law, at least, is rather piecemeal on the issue, and surely contains anomalies.[27] But the law contains many partial parallels to automatism. Most jurisdictions make it an offence, for instance, to operate a motor vehicle whilst under the influence of alcohol.[28] Well-identified causes of automatism, if there are any, could be dealt with in the same way. One could not legitimately require people to refrain from injuring their wives involuntarily, but one could certainly require that they take reasonable precautions against well-known causes of such events — one might require them to refrain from taking sleeping pills with alcohol, for instance. If someone took whatever precautions were reasonably necessary but still caused harm through an attack of automatism then he could not legitimately be punished, because *he would not have failed to comply with the only requirement that it would have been justifiable to issue*. That is what, in effect, and in the rather piecemeal manner that is common in legal provisions, legal systems typically do.

Insanity

Insanity pleas are more common than pleas of automatism.[29] Insanity is also more complicated than automatism because, in an acceptable sense, actions which are the result of insanity really are, for the most part, genuine actions. Let us take as an example the famous case of Daniel M'Naghten; M'Naghten was insane, and suffered from delusions, in particular that Sir Robert Peel, the Prime Minister, was at the head of a massive conspiracy to kill him. In 1843, he killed Peel's secretary, Edward Drummond, mistaking him for Peel. Now most people would think that Drummond himself would certainly have been justified in defending himself forcefully against M'Naghten;[30] I shall take it, however, that M'Naghten was quite properly excused by the law,[31] and that any adequate theory of punishment must make this intelligible. There is no temptation to say that M'Naghten did not really act, and so we cannot deal with this case in quite the way we dealt with automatism. But the fundamental principle is the same.

It is important to remember that when we issue a deterrent threat it is addressed to each recipient individually. Each is threatened with harm in order to deter him or her individually. But one cannot address a threat to people like M'Naghten in order to deter them, because there is no question of deterrence in their case. Consequently, as long as it were reasonably possible to exempt them, all that one could be doing in including them in the scope of the threat would be subjecting them to a risk of harm in order to help deter *others*. Now, as traditional deterrence theorists have often pointed out, including them in the scope of the threat might actually have this effect, because exempting them may encourage others to think that if they committed offences and were prosecuted they could evade conviction by mounting a defence of insanity. But, the deterrence theory, as I understand it, can object to this because it would be using the insane as tools.

It might be replied that this is not correct. After all, as long as the Restraining Considerations are respected, it is permissible to impose a risk of harm on innocent third parties in the pursuit of self-defence, or so most people believe. That is, after all, what makes permissible in warfare the use of military tactics which pose risks to non-combatants; and indeed it is what justifies our own legal systems, which invariably pose a risk to innocents. Why is subjecting the insane to such a risk any different?

But in the acceptable cases just mentioned, it is crucial that the innocents who may be harmed are not *deliberately* subjected to risk; standard military ethics does not permit the *deliberate* targeting of non-combatants, though it does, given the satisfaction of certain conditions, permit actions which it can be seen will harm them. So too with our legal systems; though we know that innocent people will be punished, we do not *intend* this. But if we refused to excuse insane 'offenders' in order to deter others things would be quite different. We would be deliberately subjecting them to a risk of harm as our means of deterring others, and so this would be using them as tools. Subjecting innocent third parties to a risk of harm as a means of defending ourselves against others is not generally thought to be within the principles of self-defence.[32]

Hence we do not, or should not, include people like M'Naghten within the scope of the warning. That is just to say that they are excused in advance, and this should be set out in statute or settled common law. This does not of course mean that it may not be justifiable to take some defensive action to prevent them from causing further harm. So even if someone like M'Naghten is excused, that will not be the end of the matter. If we think that he poses a continuing danger he may be forcibly detained.[33] This is an act of direct, though pre-emptive, self-defence. It will, we assume, serve a genuine self-defensive purpose, through acceptable means, just as forceful action on the part of Drummond might have. But a threat of punishment would not, and so would not be justified.

But this may now seem to have a troublesome implication. We exclude M'Naghten because we know that the threat of punishment will have no significant effect on his behaviour. But if that is all there is to it, then surely we should have to excuse *all* of those whose behaviour is immune to such threats. And there are many such people, it may be said; they are not insane, they are merely hardened criminals. Of course, with hardened criminals, as with the insane, pre-emptive self-defence in the form of restraint will often be justified.[34] But it seems implausible to suggest that this is the only justification for punishing them.

But in fact the troublesome implication does not follow. First, as I pointed out in an earlier chapter, deterrent effectiveness is a matter of degree, and deterrence does not fail merely because someone eventually commits the offence that it was hoped to deter; it succeeds *to some degree* when it makes committing the offence less desirable, and thus lessens the frequency with which it is committed. Second, deterrability is also a matter of degree—some people are easier to deter than others, and in cases where thought is disordered it may be silly to speak of deterrence at all.

Now the effect of general deterrent threats on people like M'Naghten is, I assume, really negligible.[35] Such threats, then, would almost certainly result in violence towards those to whom they were addressed, with no acceptable benefit, and so would have no adequate self-defensive justification. Such people are thus excused in advance. In the case of 'hardened criminals' we judge differently. They are much more deterrable than people like M'Naghten, a fact which shows itself in the considerably greater effort they will expend in not getting caught. We tend not to think of this as deterrence working, but the result is that the occasions on which even determined criminals can commit their crimes will be greatly circumscribed by a threat of punishment. As I remarked earlier, serial killers would certainly kill many more people if they had *cartes blanches* to do so. So even if 'hardened criminals' continue to offend, and we knew that they would do so, it would still have been justified to address a general deterrent threat to them so long as this could have been predicted to have an adequate effect on their behaviour, adequate in terms of the Restraining Considerations alluded to earlier. Think of a simple, two person case. Though it would not be justifiable for me to threaten you with retaliation in the certain knowledge that it would have no effect whatever on your aggressive behaviour, it could be justifiable to do so if this would have only *some likelihood* of deterring you *to some degree*, because that may sufficiently lower the probability of your aggressing or sufficiently reduce its frequency.

But this may still seem to leave something out. It may seem that the picture so far is that the difference between the insane and the hardened criminal is merely that it is *pointless* to threaten the former with punishment, but not the latter. But this, it may be said, is the wrong picture: the crucial difference is that it is *unfair* to threaten the former with punishment, not that it is merely pointless, because the insane *cannot* direct their behaviour by rational considerations; hardened criminals, on the other hand, *can* do so, even if they choose not to.

Let us assume for a moment, though it oversimplifies both types of case, that it is true that hardened criminals *can* conform their behaviour by rational considerations whereas people like M'Naghten *cannot*. In that case, if one were to address a genuine threat of violence against M'Naghten one would certainly do him a wrong, do something *unjust*, because it is clearly an injustice to 'threaten' people with violence contingent upon behaviour which they cannot avoid. If that is all that the talk about fairness is intended to capture, then the protective-deterrence theory can embrace it.

But perhaps the talk of fairness is supposed to import a *comparative* notion: a system of retaliation aimed at both hardened criminals and the mentally ill would treat people differently, without adequate justification, because the former are threatened with violence that they can avoid, whereas the latter are threatened with violence that they cannot avoid. One may reject this thought on the grounds that, outside of special circumstances, there is no moral requirement that burdens be distributed equally.[36] But governments, in liberal societies, are indeed in special circumstances in this regard, since they must treat their citizens equally in all morally salient respects. So once they have taken the decision to threaten aggressors with violence, they must do so in a manner that respects this requirement, and this means that they must treat hardened criminals and the insane differently. But, as before, there is nothing that prevents the protective-deterrence theory from accepting this.

We have been speaking so far of the most extreme cases of insanity, where deterrent threats are really idle. Needless to say, there are cases intermediate between normality and those extreme cases, where deterrent threats are not idle but have considerably less effect than they do on normal people. (Indeed, there is a spectrum even in the case of people who are in no sense mentally ill: reckless people are harder to deter than cautious people.) I am thinking of such things as kleptomania, in which the patient suffers from a strong temptation to steal things which are of little value. Kleptomaniacs are not entirely immune to deterrent threats, since they confine their thefts, for the most part, to occasions on which the probability of discovery is low; on the other hand, they are less susceptible to such threats than are normal people. To what extent, then, is it justifiable to threaten — and carry out — retaliation for their offences?

As to the first question, we may threaten them with whatever retaliation it is reasonably necessary to threaten. Here we should have to take into account the seriousness of the offence, the likely deterrent effect of the threat, and the costs involved in the retaliation. Since they are harder to deter, would we want to threaten kleptomaniacs with more severe punishment than ordinary thieves, so that a psychiatric diagnosis of kleptomania would increase the sentence for theft?

In principle, we might, just as we sometimes threaten greater punishment for more rather than less tempting forms of theft. In practice, we almost certainly would not. For one thing, it is not clear that such a policy would make much sense from the perspective of self-defence: it would, presumably, tend to lead kleptomaniacs to try to resist the diagnosis of kleptomania when convicted, thus making it less likely that they would get the sort of treatment that might actually help them and their potential victims. But in any case, the policy would strike most people as unduly harsh. After all, to suffer from kleptomania is a misfortune, and it may seem unkind to punish people for it at all. That is not something that the law need ignore:[37] nothing requires that we actually exercise our right to self-defence, either individually or collectively. All that is required is that we not issue threats of pointless violence.[38]

Immaturity

Immaturity is normally thought of as an excusing condition in the law. But it excuses in the same way, and for the same reason, as does mental illness. We thus need say no more about it.

Irresistible Impulse

The idea of irresistible impulse is in fact not easy to understand, and jurisdictions have been resistant to recognising this as an excusing condition.[39] But presumably the idea is that an agent may truly act, though in the grip of a temptation which, in some suitably strong sense, he could not resist. Threats of violence against such acts, if there are indeed such acts, would again be pointless threats of violence and so not justified. Of course, again, it would be reasonable to threaten harm to one who did not take reasonable precautions against getting into such a state.

Coercion

Last, let us turn to the phenomenon of duress, or coercion.[40] And here, again, there may initially seem to be a divergence between the principles of punishment and the principles of self-defence. On the more popular view of what it is permitted to do against a non-culpable threat, the principles of self-defence permit me to use harmful force against someone who is severely coerced into attacking me. (And even those who think that it is not permitted to use harmful force against a non-culpable threat may take the view that coercion does not take away one's culpability, so that those who are coerced into aggressing are nonetheless culpable.) However, in many circumstances, duress is a defence against a criminal charge.[41] Where the duress was such that a 'reasonable person' could not have been expected to resist it, we excuse the defendant. And where it is not a complete defence, it may be urged in mitigation. This may suggest that, at least on the more popular view of self-defence, the principles of self-defence and of punishment do not coincide.

Again, we need to be aware of the distinction between what may be done in direct self-defence and what may be threatened in self-defensive deterrence. Those who aggress under duress may pose as serious a threat as those who aggress willingly (though in general they will not, since they will not wish to perform the action in question). What, then, may we permissibly threaten to do in order to deter such threats? We might issue a warning saying that anyone who aggresses, even if coerced, will be punished, and that no account will be taken of the duress they were under. This approach has been favoured by some legal theorists, for to allow a defence of duress, it has been said, would prove to be 'a charter to terrorists, gang leaders and kidnappers',[42] since it drastically reduces the incentive to resist those who try to coerce one into criminal activity. We should then punish crimes committed under duress just as ordinary crimes (or conceivably even more harshly than ordinary crimes), for this would have the effect of making it harder to coerce. This is not a silly idea. But it would be unlikely to work. Terrorists, gang leaders, and kidnappers have ample means of unpleasant coercion at their disposal, and they are perfectly well able to apply such coercion that a reasonable person – a person of 'normal rectitude and fortitude' – will not in fact resist it, even if not doing so puts them at considerable risk of a criminal prosecution. After all, the risk of punishment will generally be somewhat remote and uncertain, whereas gangsters and terrorists can threaten their victims with immediate and certain harm.

There is, then, little point in addressing threats to those who may commit crimes under severe coercion; it has no significant deterrent value, and any punishment it involves will serve no self-defensive purpose.[43] Our threat, then, is not addressed to the person who is severely coerced; severe coercion is a defence.[44]

However, coercion that is less than severe — when it is such that a normal person could be expected to resist it — is not usually a defence. This makes sense. Coercive pressure that a normal person could resist can normally be countered by deterrent threats, and so such threats need not be preludes to pointless violence. But even in the case of moderate coercion we may still feel some pressure to take it into account when sentencing the offender. Here the offender has no right to be given anything less than the full punishment, for he should have resisted the coercion. But it would strike most people as heartless not to take into account the plight that he found himself in. And here two pressures come into conflict. On the one hand, the legitimate needs of deterrence press towards ignoring the coercion: if the law does in fact take it into account, then this should be known in advance (either through statute or settled legal practice);[45] but this will weaken the deterrent value of the threat. On the other hand, the virtue of compassion dictates some mitigation of sentence. Perhaps a natural response is to balance these two pressures by mitigating the sentence in rough proportion to the severity of the coercion.[46]

If the offender is not a hardened criminal, it may also be natural to think of 'specific deterrence'. We may wish to punish him to some degree in order to stiffen his resolve in the future. After all, he did commit the offence when he should have resisted the coercion, and so some measure of punishment may be required to bring him up to the normal level of deterrability.[47] On the other hand, we may feel that, since his offence was committed under coercion, and we have no reason to think that he would have committed it without this coercion, we have no reason to think that the full measure of punishment is required to make him a more deterrable character.

[1]   Even this weaker demand is problematic because there will in turn be dispute about which moral views are respectable; in addition, it seems at least likely that most people would agree that there will be genuine borderline cases, cases in which one simply does not know whether a view is respectable or not. How one marks boundaries for vague conceptions I put aside until we understand the general notion of vagueness better.

[2]   Cf. F.H. Bradley, *Ethical Studies* (Clarendon Press, 1970), pp. 26f.:

> 'If there is any opinion to which the man of uncultivated morals is attached, it is the belief in the necessary connexion of punishment and guilt. Punishment is punishment only when it is deserved. We pay the penalty because we owe it, and for no other reason; and if punishment is inflicted for any other reason whatever than because it is merited by wrong, it is a gross immorality, a crying injustice, an abominable crime, and not what it pretends to be. We may have regard for whatever considerations we please—our own convenience, the good of society, the benefit of the offender; we are fools, and worse, if we fail to do so. Having once the right to punish, we may modify the punishment according to the useful and the pleasant; but these are external to the matter, they cannot give us a right to punish, and nothing can do that but criminal desert.'

Nicola Lacey refers to this as 'a principle that will be fundamental to the justification of punishment' (*State Punishment*, p. 26).

Ronald Dworkin says, 'Most of us would reject out of hand any conception that seemed to require or permit punishing the innocent' (*Law's Empire* (Harvard University Press, 1986), p. 75).

[3]   Something like this happens in the law of joint enterprise, where a group may be held jointly responsible for a crime committed by one of its members. The main justification for this is that it makes possible guilty verdicts where it is impossible to pin the responsibility on any one member, and thus increases deterrence. But in English law the use of joint enterprise has become increasingly controversial and the Director of Public Prosecutions has been asked to give some guidance as to the threshold at which mere association becomes active participation (see Duncan Campbell, *The Guardian*, 18 January 2012).

Felony-murder statutes in the US are sometimes similar in operation.

[4]   We tend, perhaps, to think it relatively easy to justify the infliction of fairly trivial harm on innocent third parties, whereas we do not think it easy to justify the infliction of relatively trivial punishments on the innocent. This is in part because we do not regard relatively trivial punishments as being trivial by reference to some more important standard, and in part because we are rightly wary of extending dangerous discretion to law enforcement agencies.

5   I leave aside here, for reasons already explained, the issues of restraint and reform.
6   Cf. Douglas Husak, *'Malum Prohibitum* and Retributivism', in R.A. Duff and Stuart Green (eds.), *Defining Crimes: Essays on the Special Part of the Criminal Law* (Oxford University Press, 2005).
7   On the other hand, negligent behaviour may be more difficult to detect, and this might justify enhanced deterrent threats.
8   Antonio Cassese, *International Criminal Law* (Oxford University Press, 2003), p. 190. Cassese here is speaking of legal systems generally which, of course, differ considerably in how they deal with inchoate offences.
9   Hart, *Punishment and Responsibility*, p. 128. (Hart thinks that this is a 'fallacy'.)
10 But for a different approach, see Duff, *Criminal Attempts* (Clarendon Press, 1996).
11 'In law, a person who attempts to commit a crime is generally liable to the same maximum punishment as one who succeeds. But it is the practice of the courts to punish the attempt less severely than the complete offence' (John Smith and Brian Hogan, *Criminal Law* (Butterworth, 9th ed. 1996), p. 5).
12 Cf. 'It may be thought that a rational system would assess punishment by reference to the harm intended or foreseen, or, at least, foreseeable, rather than on the chance of what happens' (Smith and Brian, *Criminal Law*, p. 5). For a defence of the opposite position — unsuccessful, in my view — see Duff's *Criminal Attempts*. (I have criticized Duff's argument in 'Criminal Attempts', *Journal of Applied Philosophy*, vol. xv (1998), pp. 207–212.)
13 But this issue is unsettled in international law — See Cassese, *International Criminal Law*, pp. 192–193.
14 However, in the wake of the bombings in London on 7th July 2005, the UK governments created an offence of committing 'acts preparatory to terrorism' in the Terrorism Act, which received the royal assent on 30th March 2006 (see http://www.opsi.gov.uk/acts/acts2006/ukpga_20060011_en_1).
15 Or sometimes to perform an action which, without the conspiracy, would not itself be a crime; but in English law at least such offences will probably soon disappear. Some US states require that for prosecution at least one of the conspirators should have performed an overt act beyond the mere conspiracy.
16 Civil Law countries traditionally tended to prohibit 'criminal associations' rather than conspiracy as such.
17 In *R v. Robinson* (1915) 2 K.B. 342 11Cr App Rep 124, for instance, a jeweller hid some of his merchandise and tied himself up, intending to claim against his insurance for stolen goods. His plan was uncovered, but since his acts were held to be merely preparatory —

he had not yet tried to obtain the insurance money — his conviction for attempting to obtain money by false pretences was quashed.

[18] Cf. Duff, *Criminal Attempts*, pp. 391f.; Smith and Hogan, *Criminal Law*, pp. 305f.

The issue of 'criminal associations' is perhaps more difficult.

[19] Husak, *Overcriminalization: The Limits of the Criminal Law* (Oxford University Press, 2008), p. 52. Strict liability is less often objected to in cases of fairly minor regulatory offences.

[20] For a general discussion of offences of strict liability, see Smith and Hogan, *Criminal Law*, Ch. 6.

[21] Hart's claim that the deterrence theory of punishment cannot explain excuses such as duress in the law has often been repeated (see H.L.A. Hart, *Punishment and Responsibility*, Ch. 2).

(I do not distinguish here between being found not guilty, being found guilty but excused, and being found guilty but justified.)

[22] Most jurisdictions recognize excusing conditions that do not fit neatly and uncontroversially into any of these categories: diminished responsibility, involuntary intoxication, and provocation, for instance. And others recognize more controversial cases such as the so-called 'Battered Wife Syndrome'. The principles that emerge from the six mentioned in the text are sufficient to deal with these other excuses.

[23] Though most jurisdictions accept the defence of necessity in some circumstances, there is little agreement as to its precise application. The American Model Penal Code recommends that it be accepted when the harm that the defendant sought to avoid by committing an offence was greater than the harm that the law was intended to prevent; but this simple proposal has not found much favour in courts or legislatures.

[24] If contravening the norm harms someone they may, in some circumstances anyway, legitimately seek compensation.

[25] Of course, if one knew that compliance was impossible for the person to whom the speech-act was directed then this would simply not *be* a threat.

[26] For an account of English law on this matter, see Smith and Hogan, *Criminal Law*, pp. 36ff. English law has unfortunately conflated automatism and insanity to some extent.

[27] See Smith and Hogan, *Criminal Law*, pp. 36f.

[28] Recall that automatism requires that there be no voluntary action; so it is typically held not to apply to drunkenness.

[29] They are more common in the UK than in the US, where they are nowadays fairly rare.

The law on insanity in England has been subjected to much criticism since at least the 1970s, but parliament has steadfastly refused to change the law.

30   For the opposite view, see David Rodin, *War and Self-Defense* (Oxford University Press, 2002), pp. 77ff.

31   M'Naghten, defended by a team of four distinguished barristers, was acquitted but committed to Bethlehem Hospital 'to await the Queen's pleasure'. He died there in 1865.

   'The M'Naghten Rules' are still the operative rules in England and Wales. To be found insane under these rules the accused must show that 'at the time of the committing of the act, the party accused was labouring under such a defect of reason, from disease of the mind, as not to know the nature and quality of the act he was doing; or, if he did know it, that he did not know he was doing what was wrong'.

32   Most people think that it is permissible deliberately to harm 'innocent threats' — which is what the insane are — in order to defend ourselves against *them*; that is what we do when we confine them to secure hospitals. But that is quite different from harming the innocent as a means of defending ourselves against *others*. Or so most people think.

33   Of course, there are complications about this, both moral and epistemological; but no one thinks that it is invariably unjustifiable.

34   One might think that this ought not to be called punishment in the case of the mentally ill because this carries with it a stigma of moral wrongdoing. I think that this is false, but it does carry the implication that the offender was deterrable to a fairly high degree. And since, in the case of people like M'Naghten, that would be false, it would indeed be better not to call their treatment punishment.

35   A specific threat issued by a policeman at his elbow might be a different matter (for a time, anyway).

36   Perhaps, in a desert island case, if I threatened violence against some aggressors but, whimsically, not against others, this would not be wrong.

37   Cf. George Fletcher, *Rethinking Criminal Law* (Little, Brown, 1978), p. 808.

38   There are various ways in which it might be appropriate to deal with such things as kleptomania. We might, for instance, refrain from threatening such people with punishment at all, whilst making it known that offenders would be subject to compulsory treatment. The intention would not be deterrence, though the policy might, in addition to legitimising compulsory treatment, have a useful deterrent value that we would consider adequate to the offence. However, the issue requires, I suspect, a better understanding of the psychological phenomena than we at present possess.

39   It is barely recognized at all in English law. However, see *R v. Byrne* (1960). 'Substantial' impairment of self-control is, however, recognized as constituting diminished responsibility (a defence which is itself available only against murder charges) (see *The Homicide Act* of 1957 as amended by *The Coroners and Justice Act* (2009), Part 2, s. 52).

40   For a brief account of the law on duress, See Joshua Dressler, 'Exegesis of the Law of Duress: Justifying the Excuse and Searching for its Proper Limits', *Southern California Law Review*, vol. lxii (1989) (rp. in Michael Louis Corrado (ed.), *Justification and Excuse in the Criminal Law: A Collection of Essays* (Garland, 1994), pp. 379–427); and Smith and Hogan, *Criminal Law*, pp. 231–244. For what is still a useful discussion of the legal issues, see *Lynch v. D.P.P. for Northern Ireland*, [1975], and *Regina v. Howe*, [1987].

41   Typically, that one acted under a serious threat of death or bodily harm is a defence for all crimes except murder.

42   *Lynch v. D.P.P. for Northern Ireland*, [1975] AC p. 653 at p. 432. (*Lynch* ruled that duress could be a defence to murder in the case of a principal in the second degree.)

     Cf. Lord Hailsham in *Howe*, which overruled *Lynch*: 'I have known in my own lifetime of too many acts of heroism by ordinary human beings of no more than ordinary fortitude to regard a law as either "just or humane" which withdraws the protection of the criminal law from the innocent victim and casts the cloak of its protection on the coward and the poltroon in the name of a "concession to human frailty"' (*Regina v. Howe*, [1987] 2 W.L.R. at 579).

43   As with the mentally ill, there may be some temptation to say that it is 'unfair' to demand that people resist severe coercion (see, for instance, Stephen J. Morse, 'Diminished Capacity', in Stephen Shute *et al.* (eds.), *Action and Value in Criminal Law* (Clarendon Press, 1993), pp. 239–278, at p. 252 *et passim*.; George P. Fletcher, 'The Individualization of Excusing Conditions', *Southern California Law Review*, vol. xlvii (1974) (rp. in Corrado (ed.), *Justification and Excuse in the Criminal Law*, pp. 53–94; see pp. 68f.)). The response here is the same as in the case of the mentally ill.

44   The view that coercion should not be a defence against a charge of murder is very ancient, but it is hard to find any logical justification for it; on this, see Smith and Hogan, *Criminal Law*, pp. 234f.

45   However, for the claim that excusing a defendant does not set a precedent that can be relied upon by future defendants, see Fletcher, 'The Individualization of Excusing Conditions' (in Corrado (ed.), *Justification and Excuse in the Criminal Law*, pp. 53–94; see esp. pp. 78ff.).

46   This is certainly not the only defensible response. Cf. the famous pronouncement of Lord Coleridge:

     'It must not be supposed that in refusing to admit temptation to be an excuse for crime it is forgotten how terrible the temptation was; how awful the suffering; how hard in such trials to keep the judgment straight and the conduct pure. We are often compelled to set up standards we cannot reach ourselves, and to lay down rules which we could not ourselves satisfy. But a man has no right to declare temptation to be an excuse, though he might himself have yielded to it, nor allow compassion for the criminal to change or weaken in any manner the legal definition of the crime' (*R. v. Dudley and Stephens*, 14 Q.B.D. 273, 288).

[47] There is, of course, considerable doubt about the effectiveness of 'specific deterrence' in general.

Bibliography

Acton, H.B. (ed.), *The Philosophy of Punishment: A Collection of Papers* (Macmillan, 1969).

Adler, Jacob, *The Urgings of Conscience: A Theory of Punishment* (Temple University Press, 1991).

Alexander, Larry, 'Consent, Punishment, and Proportionality', *Philosophy and Public Affairs*, vol. xv (1986), pp. 178–182.

Aquinas, St Thomas, *Summa Theologica*.

Aristotle, *Nicomachean Ethics*, translated by H. Rackham (Harvard University Press and William Heinemann, 1934).

Arneson, Richard, 'The Principle of Fairness and Free-Rider Problems', *Ethics*, vol. 92 (1982), pp. 616–633.

Ashworth, Andrew, *Sentencing and Criminal Justice* (Cambridge University Press, 4th ed. 2005).

Ashworth, Andrew, *The Criminal Process: An Evaluative Study* (Clarendon Press, 1994).

Augustine, St, *The City of God (De Civitate Dei)* (Penguin Books, 1972).

Augustine, St, *Political Writings* (Hackett, 1994).

Barry, Brian, *Political Argument: A Reissue with a New Introduction* (Harvester Wheatsheaf, 1990 (1st ed. 1965)).

Barton, Charles, K.B., *Getting Even: Revenge as a Form of Justice* (Open Court, 1999).

Beccaria, Cesare, *On Crimes and Punishments and Other Writings*, ed. by Richard Bellamy (Cambridge University Press, 1995 (1st ed. 1764)).

Becker, Gary S., 'Crime and Punishment: An Economic Approach', *The Journal of Political Economy*, vol. lxxvi (1968), pp. 169–217.

Bennett, Christopher, 'The Varieties of Retributive Experience', *The Philosophical Quarterly*, vol. lii (2002), pp. 145–163.

Bennett, Christopher, *The Apology Ritual* (Cambridge University Press, 2008).

Benson, B.L. and Rasmussen, D.W., 'Deterring Drunk Driving Fatalities: An Economics of Crime Perspective', *International Review of Law and Economics*, vol. xix (1999), pp. 205–225.

Bentham, Jeremy, *Introduction to the Principles of Morals and Legislation*, ed. by J.H. Burns and H.L.A. Hart (Methuen, 1970 (1st ed. 1789)).

Bentham, Jeremy, *Panopticon versus New South Wales*, ed. by J. Bowring (Simpkin and Marshall, 1843 (1st ed. 1802)).

Berlin, Isaiah, *Concepts and Categories* (Penguin, 1981).

Boonin, David, *The Problem of Punishment* (Cambridge University Press, 2008).

Bradley, F.H., *Ethical Studies* (Clarendon Press, 1970 (1st ed. 1876)).

Braithwaite, John and Pettit, Philip, *Not Just Deserts* (Clarendon Press, 1990).

Braithwaite, John, *Crime, Shame and Reintegration* (Cambridge University Press, 1989).

Brownlie, Ian, *Principles of Public International Law*, (Clarendon Press, 5th ed. 1998).

Burgh, Richard, 'Do the Guilty Deserve Punishment?', *The Journal of Philosophy*, vol. lxxix (1982), pp. 193–210.

Byrd, B. Sharon, 'Kant's Theory of Punishment: Deterrence in Its Threat, Retribution in Its Execution', *Law and Philosophy*, vol. xliv (1989), pp. 151–200.

Cassese Antonio, *International Criminal Law* (Oxford University Press, 2003).

Clark, Michael, 'The Sanctions of the Criminal Law', *Proceedings of the Aristotelian Society*, vol. xcvii (1997), pp. 25–39.

Cooper, David, 'Hegel's Theory of Punishment', in Z.A. Pelzcynski (ed.), *Hegel's Political Philosophy: Problems and Perspectives*, (Cambridge University Press, 1971).

Copp, David and Zimmerman, David (eds.), *Morality, Reason and Truth* (Rowman and Allanheld, 1985).

Corlett, J. Angelo, 'Making Sense of Retributivism', *Philosophy*, vol. lxxvi (2001), pp. 77–110.

Corrado, Michael Louis (ed.), *Justification and Excuse in the Criminal Law: A Collection of Essays* (Garland, 1994).

Cottingham, J. G., 'Varieties of Retribution', *The Philosophical Quarterly*, vol. xxix (1979), pp. 238–246.

Dancy, Jonathan, *Moral Reasons* (Blackwell, 1993).

Davis, Michael 'Punishment Theory's Golden Half-Century: A Survey of Developments from (about) 1957 to 2007', *The Journal of Ethics*, vol. xiii (2009), pp. 73–100.

Davis, Michael, 'Harm and Retribution', *Philosophy and Public Affairs*, vol. xv (1986), pp. 236–266.

Davis, Michael, 'Nozick's Argument FOR the Legitimacy of the Welfare State', *Ethics*, vol. xcvii (1987), pp. 576–594.

Davis, Michael, 'Revenge, Victim's Rights, and Criminal Justice', *International Journal of Applied Philosophy*, vol. xiv (2000), pp. 119–128.

Davis, Michael, 'Victims' Rights, Revenge, and Retribution', *Australian Journal of Professional and Applied Ethics*, vol. iii (2001), pp. 45–68.

Davis, Michael, *To Make the Punishment Fit the Crime: Essays in the Theory of Criminal Justice* (Westview, 1992).

de Haan, William, *The Politics of Redress: Crime, Punishment and Penal Abolition* (Unwin Hyman, 1990).

Devlin, Patrick, *The Enforcement of Morals* (Oxford University Press, 1965).

Dignan, James, 'Reintegration Through Reparation: A Way Forward for Restorative Justice?', in Antony Duff *et al.* (eds.), *Penal Theory and Practice: Tradition and Innovation in Criminal Justice* (Manchester University Press, 1994).

Dolinko, David, 'Some Thoughts About Retributivism', *Ethics*, vol. ci (1991), pp. 537–559.

Dressler, Joshua, 'Exegesis of the Law of Duress: Justifying the Excuse and Searching for its Proper Limits', *Southern California Law Review*, vol. lxii (1989); rp. in Michael Louis Corrado (ed.), *Justification and Excuse in the Criminal Law*, pp. 379–427.

Drumbl, Mark A., *Atrocity, Punishment and International Law* (Cambridge University Press, 2007).

Duff, Antony and Garland, David (eds.), *A Reader on Punishment* (Oxford University Press, 1994).

Duff, Antony and Green, Stuart (eds.), *Defining Crimes: Essays on the Special Part of the Criminal Law* (Oxford University Press, 2005).

Duff, Antony *et al.* (eds.), *Penal Theory and Practice: Tradition and Innovation in Criminal Justice* (Manchester University Press, 1994).

Duff, Antony, 'Crime, Prohibition, and Punishment', *Journal of Applied Philosophy*, vol. xix (2002), pp. 97–108.

Duff, Antony, 'Penal Communications: Recent Work in the Philosophy of Punishment', *Crime and Justice*, vol. xx (1996), pp. 1–98.

Duff, Antony, 'Retributive Punishment — Ideals and Actualities', *Israel Law Review*, vol. xxv (1991), pp. 422–451.

Duff, Antony, *Criminal Attempts* (Clarendon Press, 1996).

Duff, Antony, *Punishment, Communication, and Community* (Oxford University Press, 2001).

Duff, Antony, *Trials and Punishments* (Cambridge University Press, 1986).

Duker, William F., 'The President's Power to Pardon: A Constitutional History', *William and Mary Law Review*, vol. xviii (1977), pp. 475–538.

Durkehim, Emile, *Moral Education: A Study in the Theory and Application of the Sociology of Education* (The Free Press, 1961; French, 1925).

Dworkin, Ronald, *Law's Empire* (Harvard University Press, 1986).

Dworkin, Ronald, *Taking Rights Seriously* (Duckworth, 1977).

Earley, Pete, *The Hot House: Life Inside Leavenworth Prison* (Bantam Books, 1992).

Ellis, Anthony, 'Criminal Attempts' (A Critical Notice of *Criminal Attempts*, by Antony Duff (Clarendon Press, 1995)), *Journal of Applied Philosophy*, vol. xv (1998), pp. 207–212.

Ellis, Anthony, 'Punishment as Deterrence: Reply to Sprague', *The Philosophical Quarterly*, vol. lv (2004), pp. 98–101.

Farrell, Daniel M., 'Deterrence and the Just Distribution of Harm', *Social Philosophy and Policy*, vol. xii (1995), pp. 220–240.

Farrell, Daniel, 'A New Paradox of Deterrence', in Jules L. Coleman and Christopher W. Morris (eds.), *Rational Commitment and Social Justice: Essays for Gregory Kavka* (Cambridge University Press, 1998), pp. 22–46.

Farrell, Daniel, 'On Threats and Punishments', *Social Theory and Practice*, vol. xv (1989), pp. 125–154.

Feinberg, Joel, 'The Expressive Function of Punishment', *The Monist*, vol. xlix (1965); rp. in Feinberg, *Doing and Deserving* (Princeton University Press, 1970), pp. 95–118.

Feinberg, Joel, *The Moral Limits of the Criminal Law: vol. IV: Harmless Wrongdoing* (Oxford University Press, 1990).

Ferzan, Kimberly Kessler, 'Justifying Self-Defense', *Law and Philosophy*, vol. xxiv (2005), pp. 711–749.

Finnis, John, *Aquinas: Moral, Political, and Legal Theory* (Oxford University Press, 1998).

Finnis, John, *Natural Law and Natural Rights* (Clarendon Press, 1980).

Fletcher, George P., 'The Individualization of Excusing Conditions', *Southern California Law Review*, vol. xlvii (1974);

rp. in Corrado (ed.), *Justification and Excuse in the Criminal Law*, pp. 53–94.

Fletcher, George P., *A Crime of Self Defense: Bernhard Goetz and the Law on Trial* (The Free Press, 1988).

Fletcher, George P., *Rethinking Criminal Law* (Little, Brown, 1978).

Floud, J. and Young, W., *Dangerousness and Criminal Justice* (Heinemann, 1981).

Foot, Philippa, *Natural Goodness* (Clarendon Press, 2001).

Foucault, Michel, *Discipline and Punish: The Birth of the Prison*, translated by Alan Sheridan (Penguin Books, 1979; French, 1975).

Friedman, Lawrence, *Crime and Punishment in American History* (Basic Books, 1993).

Garland, David, *Punishment and Modern Society: A Study in Social Theory* (University of Chicago Press, 1990).

Golash, Deirdre, *The Case Against Punishment: Retribution Crime Prevention and the Law* (New York University Press, 2005).

Goldman, Alan, 'The Paradox of Punishment', *Philosophy and Public Affairs*, vol. ix (1979), pp. 42–58.

Green, T.H., *Lectures on the Principles of Political Obligation, and other writings* (Cambridge University Press, 1986).

Grice, H.P. 'Meaning', *The Philosophical Review*, vol. lxvi (1957), pp. 377–388.

Gross, Hyam, *A Theory of Criminal Justice* (Oxford University Press, 1979).

Grotius, Hugo, *De Jure Belli ac Pacis*, translated by A.C. Campbell (Walter Dunne, 1901 (1st ed. 1625)).

Hampton, Jean, 'An Expressive Theory of Punishment', in Wesley Cragg (ed.), *Retributivism and Its Critics* (Franz Steiner, 1992).

Hampton, Jean, 'The Moral Education Theory of Punishment', *Philosophy and Public Affairs*, vol. xiii (1984), pp. 208–238.

Hanna, Nathan, 'Say What? A Critique of Expressive Retributivism', *Law and Philosophy*, vol. xxvii (2007), pp. 123–150.

Hanna, Nathan, 'The Passions of Punishment', *Pacific Philosophical Quarterly*, vol. xc (2009), pp. 232–250.

Hare, R.M., *The Language of Morals* (Clarendon Press, 1952).

Hart, H.L.A., 'Are There Any Natural Rights?', *Philosophical Review*, vol. lxiv (1955), pp. 175–191.

Hart, H.L.A., *The Concept of Law* (Clarendon Press, 1961).

Hart, H.L.A., *Essays in Jurisprudence and Philosophy* (Clarendon Press, 1983).

Hart, H.L.A., *Law, Liberty and Morality* (Clarendon Press, 1963).

Hart, H.L.A., *Punishment and Responsibility. Essays in the Philosophy of Law* (Clarendon Press, 1968).

Hegel, G.W.F. von, *Philosophy of Right*, translated by T.M. Knox (Clarendon Press, 1952 (1st ed. 1821)).

Herrmann, J. 'The Rule of Compulsory Prosecution and the Scope of Prosecutorial Discretion in Germany', *University of Chicago Law Review*, vol. xvi (1974), pp. 468–505.

Hill, Thomas E., Jr., 'Humanity as an End in Itself', *Ethics*, vol. xci (1980), pp. 84–90; rp. in Thomas E. Hill, Jr., *Dignity and Practical Reason in Kant's Moral Theory* (Cornell University Press, 1992).

Hill, Thomas E., Jr., 'Kant's Anti-Moralistic Strain', *Theoria*, vol. xliv (1978), pp. 131–151; rp. in Thomas E. Hill, Jr., *Dignity and Practical Reason in Kant's Moral Theory* (Cornell University Press, 1992).

Hill, Thomas E., Jr., 'Making Exceptions without Abandoning the Principle: How a Kantian Might Think about Terrorism', in Ray Frey and Christopher Morris (eds.), *Violence, Terrorism and Justice* (Cambridge University Press, 1991); rp. in Thomas E. Hill, Jr., *Dignity and Practical Reason in Kant's Moral Theory* (Cornell University Press, 1992).

HMSO, *Crime, Justice and Protecting the Public: The Government's Proposals for Legislation* (H.M.S.O., 1991).

Hobbes, Thomas, *Leviathan* (Cambridge University Press, 1991 (1st ed. 1561)).

Holmes, Oliver Wendell, *The Common Law* (Boston, MA, Little, Brown, 1963 (first published 1881)).

Honderich, Ted (ed.), *The Oxford Companion to Philosophy* (Oxford University Press, 1995).

Honderich, Ted, *Punishment: The Supposed Justifications* (Penguin Books, 1971 (1st ed. Hutchinson, 1969)).

Honoré, Tony, *Responsibility and Fault* (Hart, 1999).

Howard, John, *The State of the Prisons in England and Wales* (London, 1777).

Husak, Douglas, 'Malum Prohibitum and Retributivism', in R.A. Duff and Stuart Green (eds.), *Defining Crimes: Essays on the Special Part of the Criminal Law* (Oxford University Press, 2005).

Husak, Douglas, *Overcriminalization: The Limits of the Criminal Law* (Oxford University Press, 2008).

Inwood, Michael, *A Hegel Dictionary* (Blackwell, 1992).

Joyce, Richard, *The Evolution of Morality* (MIT Press, 2006).

Kant, I., *The Metaphysical Elements of Justice: Part 1 of the Metaphysics of Morals*, translated by John Ladd (Macmillan, 1965 (1st ed. 1797)).

Kerstein, Samuel, 'Treating Consenting Adults Merely as Means', in Mark Timmons, *Oxford Studies in Normative Ethics*, vol. 1 (2011), pp. 51–74.

Klosko, George, *The Principle of Fairness and Political Obligation* (Rowman and Littlefield, 1992).

Knowles, Dudley, 'Hegel on the Justification of Punishment', in Robert R. Williams (ed.), *Beyond Liberalism and Communitarianism: Studies in Hegel's Philosophy of Right* (SUNY Press, 2001).

Krantz, D.H., Luce, R.D., Suppes, P. and Tversky, A., *Foundations of Measurement, vol. 1: Additive and Polynomial Representations* (Academic Press, 1971).

Lacey, Nicola, *State Punishment: Political Principles and Community Values* (Routledge, 1988).

Langan, Patrick A. and Levin, David J., 'Recidivism of Prisoners Released in 1994', excerpts from the *Federal Sentence Reporter*, vol. 15 (2002), pp. 58–63.

Le Goff, Jacques, *The Birth of Purgatory* (University of Chicago Press, 1984; French, 1981).

Leverick, Fiona, *Killing in Self-Defence* (Oxford University Press, 2006).

Levitt, Stephen D., 'Understanding Why Crime Fell in the 1990s: Four Factors that Explain the Decline and Six that Do Not', *Journal of Economic Perspectives*, vol. 18 (2004), pp. 163–190.

Levitt, Steven D., 'Why Do Increased Arrest Rates Appear To Reduce Crime: Deterrence, Incapacitation, Or Measurement Error?', *Economic Inquiry*, vol. xxxvi (1998), pp. 353–372.

Liew, T.C., *The Soundest Theory of Law* (Marshall Cavendish, 2004).

Locke, John, *Second Treatise of Government* (London, 1690).

Ma, Yue, 'Prosecutorial Discretion and Plea Bargaining in the United States, France Germany and Italy: A Comparative Perspective', *International Criminal Justice Review*, vol. 12 (2002), pp. 22–52.

Mabbott, J.D., 'Punishment', *Mind*, vol. xlviii (1939), pp. 152–167; rp. in H.B. Acton (ed.), *The Philosophy of Punishment* (Macmillan, 1969).

MacCormick, Neil, *Legal Right and Social Democracy: Essays in Legal and Political Philosophy* (Clarendon Press, 1982).

MacKenzie, M.M., *Plato on Punishment* (California University Press, 1981).

Mackie, J.L., 'Retributivism: A Test Case for Ethical Objectivity', in Joel Feinberg and Hyman Gross (eds.), *Philosophy of Law* (Wadsworth, 3rd ed. 1986).

Mackie, J.L., 'Morality and the Retributive Emotions', *Criminal Justice Ethics*, 1982, pp. 3–10.

Mackie, J.L., *Ethics: Inventing Right and Wrong* (Penguin, 1977).

Madrick, Jeff and Portnoy, Frank, 'Should Some Bankers be Prosecuted', *New York Review of Books*, vol. lviii, number 17.

Mason, H.E. (ed.), *Moral Dilemmas and Moral Theory* (Oxford University Press, 1996).

McDermott, Daniel, 'Fair-Play Obligations', *Political Studies*, vol. li (2004), pp. 216–232.

McMahan, Jeff, 'Self-Defense and Culpability', *Law and Philosophy*, vol. xxiv (2005), pp. 751–774.

McMahan, Jeff, 'Self-Defense and the Innocent Attacker', *Ethics*, vol. civ (1994), pp. 252–290.

McTaggart, J.M.E., 'Hegel's Theory of Punishment', *International Journal of Ethics*, vol. vi (1896), pp. 479–502.

Meares, Tracey L., Katyal, Neal and Kahan, Dan M., 'Updating the Study of Punishment', *Stanford Law Review*, vol. 56 (2004), pp. 1171–1210.

Meir Friedman, Lawrence, *Crime and Punishment in American History* (Basic Books, 1993).

Mill, John Stuart, *On Liberty*, in *On Liberty and other writings* (Cambridge University Press, 1989).

Mill, John Stuart, *Utilitarianism* (Bobbs-Merrill, 1957).

Montague, Philip, 'Grading Punishments', *Law and Philosophy*, vol. xxii (2003), pp. 1–19.

Montague, Philip, 'Punishment and Societal Defense', *Criminal Justice Ethics*, vol. ii (1983), pp. 30–36.

Montague, Philip, 'Self-Defense and Choosing Between Lives', *Philosophical Studies*, vol. 40 (1981), pp. 207–219.

Montague, Philip, *Punishment as Societal Defense* (Rowman and Littlefield, 1995).

Moore, G.E., *Principia Ethica* (Cambridge University Press, 1903).

Moore, Michael, 'A Tale of Two Theories', *Criminal Justice Ethics*, vol. xxviii (2009), pp. 27–48.

Moore, Michael, 'Justifying Retributivism', *Israel Law Review*, vol. xxvii (1993), pp. 15–49.

Moore, Michael, 'Moral Reality Revisited', *Michigan Law Review*, vol. 90 (1992), pp. 2424–2533.

Moore, Michael, 'Moral Reality', *Wisconsin Law Review*, vol. 1982, pp. 1061–1156.

Moore, Michael, 'The Moral Worth of Retribution', in Ferdinand Schoeman (ed.), *Responsibility, Character and the Emotions* (Cambridge University Press, 1987).

Moore, Michael, *Placing Blame: A General Theory of the Criminal Law* (Clarendon Press, 1997).

Morris, Herbert, 'Persons and Punishment', *The Monist*, vol. lii (1968), pp. 475–501; rp. in Herbert Morris, *On Guilt and Innocence: Essays in Legal Philosophy and Moral Psychology* (University of California Press, 1976).

Morris, Herbert, 'Guilt and Suffering', *Philosophy East and West*, vol. xxi (1971), pp. 419–434; rp. in *On guilt and Innocence*.

Morris, Herbert, 'The Decline of Guilt', *Ethics*, vol. 99 (1988), pp. 62–76.

Morris, William, *News from Nowhere, or, An epoch of rest: being some chapters from a utopian romance* (Cambridge University Press, 1995 (1st ed. 1890)).

Morse, Stephen J., 'Diminished Capacity', in Stephen Shute *et al.* (eds.), *Action and Value in Criminal Law* (Clarendon Press, 1993).

Murphy, Jeffrie G. and Hampton, Jean, *Forgiveness and Mercy* (Cambridge University Press, 1988).

Murphy, Jeffrie G., 'Does Kant Have a Theory of Punishment?', *Columbia Law Review*, vol. lxxxvii (1987), pp. 509–532.

Murphy, Jeffrie G. and Coleman, Jules L., *Philosophy of Law: An Introduction to Jurisprudence* (Westview, 2nd ed. 1990).

Murphy, Jeffrie G., *Kant: The Philosophy of Right* (Macmillan, 1970).

Murphy, Jeffrie G., *Retribution, Justice, and Therapy* (Reidel, 1979).

Murphy, Jeffrie G., *Retribution Reconsidered: More Essays in the Philosophy of Law* (Reidel, 1992).

Nagin Daniel S., 'Deterrence and Incapacitation', in Michael S. Tonry (ed.), *The Handbook of Crime and Punishment* (Oxford University Press, 2000), pp. 345–368.

Nagin, Daniel S., 'Criminal Deterrence Research at the Outset of the Twenty-First Century', *Crime and Justice*, vol. 23 (1998), pp. 1–42.

Newman, Dwight G., 'Collective Interests and Collective Rights', *The American Journal of Jurisprudence*, vol. 49 (2004), pp. 127–163.

Nietzsche, Friedrich, *On the Genealogy of Morality*, ed. Keith Ansell-Pearson, translated by Carol Diethe (Cambridge University Press, 1994 (1st ed. 1887).

Nino, C.S., 'A Consensual Theory of Punishment', *Philosophy and Public Affairs*, vol. xii (1983), pp. 289–306.

Nozick, Robert, *Philosophical Explorations* (Clarendon Press, 1981).

Nozick, Robert, 'Coercion', in P. Laslett and W.G. Runciman (eds.), *Philosophy, Politics and Society* (Oxford University Press, 1972); rp. in Robert Nozick, *Socratic Puzzles* (Harvard University Press, 1997), pp. 15–44.

Nozick, Robert, *Anarchy, State, and Utopia* (Basic Books, 1974).

Nussbaum, Martha, *Sex and Social Justice* (Oxford University Press, 1999).

Otsuka, Michael, 'Killing the Innocent in Self-Defense', *Philosophy and Public Affairs*, vol. xxiii (1994), pp. 74–94.

Otsuka, Michael, *Libertarianism without Inequality* (Clarendon Press, 2004).

Parfit, Derek, *On What Matters* (Oxford University Press, 2010).

Parfit, Derek, *Reasons and Persons* (Clarendon Press, 1984).

Pelzcynski, Z.A. (ed.), *Hegel's Political Philosophy: Problems and Perspectives* (Cambridge University Press, 1971).

Plantinga, Alvin, *Warrant and Proper Function* (Oxford University Press, 1993).

Plato, *Gorgias*, translated with notes by Terence Irwin (Clarendon Press, 1979).

Plato, *Gorgias: A Revised Text with Introduction and Commentary*, ed. E.R. Dodds (Clarendon Press, 1959).

Plato, *Laws*, translated by A.E. Taylor (Dent, 1934).

Plato, *Protagoras*, translated by C.C.W. Taylor (Clarendon Press, revised ed. 1991).

Plato, *Republic*, translated by Paul Shorey (Loeb Classical Library, 1957).

Plato, *The Last Days of Socrates: Euthyphro, The Apology, Crito, Phaedo*, translated by Hugh Tredennick (Penguin Books, 1954).

Posner, Richard, *The Economics of Justice* (Harvard University Press, 2nd ed. 1983).

Primoratz, Igor, 'Punishment as Language', *Philosophy*, vol. liv (1989), pp. 187–205.

Primoratz, Igor, *Justifying Legal Punishment* (Humanities Press, 1989).

Quinn, Warren, 'The Right to Threaten and the Right to Punish', *Philosophy and Public Affairs*, vol. xv (1985), pp. 327–373.

Rashdall, Hastings, *The Theory of Good and Evil, vol. 1* (Clarendon Press, 1907).

Rawls, J., 'Two Concepts of Rules', *The Philosophical Review*, vol. lxiv (1955), pp. 3–13.

Rawls, J., *A Theory of Justice* (Oxford University Press, 1971).

Reiman, Jeffrey H., 'Justice, Civilization, and the Death Penalty: Answering van den Haag', *Philosophy and Public Affairs*, vol. xiv (1985), pp. 115–148.

Rieff, Mark, *Punishment, Compensation, and Law: A Theory of Enforceability* (Cambridge University Press, 2005).

Roberts, Julian V., *Punishing Persistent Offenders: Exploring Community and Offender Perspectives* (Oxford University Press, 2008).

Robinson, Paul H. and Darley, John M., 'Does Criminal Law Deter? A Behavioural Science Investigation', *Oxford Journal of Legal Studies*, vol. 24 (2004), pp. 173–205.

Robinson, Paul H. and Darley, John M., 'The Role of Deterrence in the Formulation of Criminal Law Rules: At Its Worst when Doing Its Best', *Georgetown Law Journal*, vol. 91 (2003), pp. 950–1002.

Rodin, David, *War and Self-Defense* (Oxford University Press, 2004).

Rotman, Edgardo, *Beyond Punishment: A New View of the Rehabilitation of Offenders* (Greenwood, 1990).

Royal Commission on Capital Punishment, 1949–1953, *Report*, *Cmnd 8932* (H.M.S.O., 1953).

Ryberg, Jesper, *The Ethics of Proportionate Punishment: A Critical Investigation* (Kluwer, 2004).

Sadurski, W., *Giving Desert Its Due* (Reidel, 1985).

Schoeman, Ferdinand (ed.), *Responsibility, Character and the Emotions* (Cambridge University Press, 1987).

Semple, Janet, *Bentham's Prison* (Clarendon Press, 1993).

Sher, George, *Desert* (Princeton University Press, 1987).

Shute, Stephen *et al.* (eds.), *Action and Value in Criminal Law* (Clarendon Press, 1993).

Sidgwick, Henry, *Methods of Ethics* (Macmillan, 1907 (1st ed. 1874)).

Smith, J.C. and Hogan, Brian, *Criminal Law* (Butterworths, 9th ed. 1999).

Sprague, Michael, 'Who Can Carry Out Protective Deterrence?', *The Philosophical Quarterly*, vol. liv (2004), pp. 443–447.

Steinberger, Peter G., 'Hegel on Crime and Punishment', *American Political Science Review*, lxxvii (1983), pp. 858–870.

Stephen, J.F., *A History of the Criminal Law of England, vol. ii* (Macmillan, 1883).

Stephen, J.F., *Liberty, Equality, Fraternity* (Cambridge University Press, 1967 (1st ed. 1873)).

Strawson, Peter, 'Freedom and Resentment', *Proceedings of the British Academy*, vol. xlviii (1962), pp. 1–25.

Stuntz, William J., *The Collapse of American Criminal Justice* (Harvard University Press, 2011).

Sturgeon, Nicholas, 'Thomson Against Moral Explanations', *Philosophy and Phenomenological Research*, vol. 58 (1998), pp. 199–206.

Sturgeon, Nicholas, 'Moral Explanations Defended', in James Drier (ed.), *Contemporary Debates in Moral Theory* (Blackwell, 2006).

Sturgeon, Nicholas, 'Moral Explanations', in David Copp and David Zimmerman (eds.), *Morality, Reason and Truth* (Rowman and Allanheld, 1985).

Tasioulas, John, 'Punishment and Repentance', *Philosophy*, vol. lxxxi (2006), pp. 279–322.

Taylor, Michael, *The Possibility of Cooperation* (Cambridge University Press, 1987).

Ten, C.L., *Crime, Guilt and Punishment* (Clarendon Press, 1987).

Thomson, Judith Jarvis, 'Moral Objectivity', in Gilbert Harman and J.J. Thomson, *Moral Relativism and Moral Objectivity* (Blackwell, 1996).

Thomson, Judith Jarvis, 'Reply to Critics', *Philosophy and Phenomenological Research*, vol. 58 (1998), pp. 215–222.

Thomson, Judith Jarvis, 'Self-Defense', *Philosophy and Public Affairs*, vol. xx (1991), pp. 283–310.

Tonry, Michael S. (ed.), *The Handbook of Crime and Punishment* (Oxford University Press, 1998).

Tonry, Michael S., 'Proportionality, Parsimony, and Interchangeability of Punishments', in Duff *et al.* (eds.), *Penal Theory and Practice: Tradition and Innovation in Criminal Justice*.

UK Home Office, *Crime, Justice and Protecting the Public: The Government's Proposals for Legislation* (H.M.S.O., 1991).

von Hirsch, Andrew, 'Penal Theories', in M. Tonry (ed.), *The Handbook of Crime and Punishment* (Oxford University Press, 1998).

von Hirsch, Andrew, *Censure and Sanctions* (Clarendon Press, 1993).

von Hirsch, Andrew, *Doing Justice: The Choice of Punishments* (report of the Committee for the Study of Incarceration) (Hill and Wang, 1976).

von Hirsch, Andrew, *Past or Future Crimes?* (Rutgers University Press, 1985).

Walker, Nigel (ed.), *Dangerous People* (Blackstone, 1996).

Walker, Nigel, *Why Punish?* (Oxford University Press, 1991).

Walzer, Michael, *Arguing about War* (Yale University Press, 2004).

Warnock, G.J., *Contemporary Moral Philosophy* (Macmillan, 1967).

Wasserman, David, 'Justifying Self-Defense', *Philosophy and Public Affairs*, vol. xvi (1987), pp. 356–378.

Williams, Bernard, 'Moral Responsibility and Political Freedom', *Cambridge Law Journal*, lvi (1997), pp. 96–102; rp. in Williams, *Philosophy as a Humanistic Discipline* (Princeton University Press, 2006).

Williams, Robert R. (ed.), *Beyond Liberalism and Communitarianism: Studies in Hegel's Philosophy of Right* (SUNY Press, 2001).

Wilson, James Q., *Thinking About Crime* (Vintage Books, 1985 (1st ed. 1975)).

Winch, Peter, *Ethics and Action* (Routledge and Kegan Paul, 1972).

Windlesham, Lord, *Responses to Crime, vol. 2: Penal Policy in the Making* (Clarendon Press, 1993).

Wolf, Susan, 'Hiking the Range', in Parfit, *On What Matters , vol. 2.*

Wood, Allen, *Hegel's Ethical Thought* (Cambridge University Press, 1990).

Wootton, Barbara, *Crime and the Criminal Law* (Sweet and Maxwell, 1963).

Wootton, Barbara, *Social Science and Social Pathology* (George Allen and Unwin, 1959).

Zaibert, Leo, *Punishment and Retribution* (Ashgate, 2006).

Zimmerman, Michael, *The Immorality of Punishment* (Broadview Press, 2011).

Zimring, Franklin E. and Hawkins, Gordon, *Incapacitation* (Oxford University Press, 1995).

Index

www.ingramcontent.com/pod-product-compliance
Lightning Source LLC
Chambersburg PA
CBHW020348270326
41926CB00007B/354